The Origins and Development of the European Union 1945–2008

The new edition of this accessible introduction to the history of the European Union (EU) has been fully revised and updated to reflect the significant changes within the EU over the past decade. Revealing the politics beneath the surface, national rivalries and changing positions behind events, meetings and treaty negotiations, the text:

- provides a thematic history of European economic and political integration in its economic, military, monetary and political contexts
- outlines the major schools of thought regarding the causes and motives for European economic integration including the theories of Lipgens, Haas and Milward
- considers the economic and political reasons for establishing supranational organisations
- evaluates the impact of the collapse of communism on the EU, its policy implications and member states' responses
- contains new and updated material on the euro, enlargement of the EU, the constitutional debate, EU economic, monetary and foreign policies and other key recent developments.

Ideal introductory reading for those new to the study of the EU seeking a concise and up-to-date account of the political and economic development of the EU, *The Origins and Development of the European Union* is essential for all students of European politics and European history, and those looking to gain a thorough understanding of contemporary politics.

Dr Martin J. Dedman is currently a visiting Research Scholar at the McBride Center for International Business, Baylor University, Texas and is a former Senior Lecturer at Middlesex University (1970–2007).

The Origins and Development of the European Union 1945–2008

A history of European integration

Martin J. Dedman

2nd edition

Routledge
Taylor & Francis Group

LONDON AND NEW YORK

First edition published 1996
by Routledge
Second edition published 2010
by Routledge
2 Park Square, Milton Park, Abingdon, Oxon, OX14 4RN

Simultaneously published in the USA and Canada
by Routledge
270 Madison Avenue, New York, NY 10016

Routledge is an imprint of the Taylor & Francis Group, an informa business

© 1996, 2010 Martin J. Dedman

Typeset in Times New Roman by
Taylor & Francis Books
Printed and bound in Great Britain by
Antony Rowe, Chippenham, Wiltshire

British Library Cataloguing in Publication Data
A catalogue record for this book is available from the British Library

Library of Congress Cataloging in Publication Data
Dedman, Martin, 1947–
Origins & development of the European Union 1945–2008 : a history or
European integration / Martin J. Dedman. – 2nd ed.
　　p.cm.
　Includes bibliographical references and index.
　ISBN 978-0-415-43560-4 – ISBN 978-0-415-43561-1 – ISBN 978-0-203-
87361-8 1. Euroean federation. 2. European Union. 3. Europe–Politics and
government–1945– I. Title
　JN15.D423 2009
　341.242'209045–dc22

2009003723

ISBN13: 978-0-415-43560-4 (hbk)
ISBN13: 978-0-415-43561-1 (pbk)
ISBN13: 978-0-203-87361-8 (ebk)

ISBN10: 0-415-43560-9 (hbk)
ISBN10: 0-415-43561-7 (pbk)
ISBN10: 0-203-87361-0 (ebk)

To Catherine, Simon, Rachel, Danny and Zoë

Contents

Preface to the second edition

The 1996 edition was heavily weighted towards the origins and early development of European integration in the 1940s and 1950s. This second edition
is intended to remedy the imbalance with much more on developments in the
1970s, 1980s and especially the 1990s onwards, bringing it up-to-date. The
early chapters on the European Defence Community (EDC) (which remain
largely unchanged), for example, involved using Foreign Office files at the
PRO and delving into collections at the Bodleian Library, Oxford, and
Churchill College, Cambridge. EMU in the 1970s (in Chapter 7) was mostly
based on reading *The Economist* and *Financial Times* at the British Newspaper Library, Colindale. The updated and expanded Part II on 'Developments' relied heavily on newspaper articles and press reports invaluable for
establishing the chronology of events, detailed factual information as well as
highlighting conflicting positions and manoeuvrings at EU heads of state
meetings.

This book does not try to deliver an inside account of what transpired
within EU institutions. Richard McAllister's *EC to EU* is an excellent micro-
historical account providing the inside story and analysis using EU official
internal publications. This book and McAllister's do not compete but rather
complement one another. This book uses primary printed press material from
the outside to examine the politics and diplomacy behind treaty negotiations
and other events. Biographies, whistleblowers' exposé accounts, academic
monographs, review and research articles are all used but the main resource
(given the thirty-year rule on government papers) remained press reports.
News of the EC, EU, NATO, geo-politics, Balkan wars, the collapse of
Communism and the Soviet Union extending back to the 1980s forms the
basis of Part II. The EU is not treated in isolation but in the context of
NATO and European affairs.

Press reports and articles from the *Financial Times, Independent, Sunday
Times, Daily Telegraph, Guardian, The Economist* and *Guardian Weekly*
(which proved especially useful as it often contained important extracts from
French, German and Spanish papers) that helped dilute what is admittedly an
Anglo-centric selective viewpoint. These newspapers differ in their focus and
view. The *FT* is liberal and pro- EU; so too generally are the *Independent* and

Guardian, although the latter's economics editor is fairly Eurosceptic (and has never favoured UK entry to the euro); the *Telegraph* is very Eurosceptic and Euro critical, which results in considerable coverage of the EU. All provided useful empirical data about what transpired and carried interviews and articles by key figures at the time in the EU.

References to press reports punctuate much of the text to enable follow-up, and record the date. They might perhaps give an impression of the text being a mere collection of press cuttings but at the risk of that press reports do allow developments to be monitored almost continually during the late 1980s and early 1990s, for example Communism's collapse and the Balkan Wars. Factual details gleaned from newspapers can breathe life into and colour otherwise anodyne content. Newspaper reports are indispensable for accounts of and reactions to politicians' televised broadcasts and interviews, a medium increasingly used and very significantly by, for example, President François Mitterand (see Chapter 8).

Moreover only through the assemblage of news reports over a long period can one trace the ups and downs of, for example, the Franco-German relationship. The Franco-German axis embodied vigour, dynamism and co-leadership when initiating an agreed project in (and with the rhetoric of) 'constructing Europe' (see Chapter 7). At other times rancour, treachery and venomous insult have blighted their pact (see Chapter 9). Journalists' and pundits' pronouncements on the death of the Franco-German relationship have always proved exaggerated though.

Despite several fallings out President Mitterand used dramatic stunts and photo opportunities to publicly demonstrate 'friendship' with Germany and Chancellor Kohl. Helmut Kohl in turn was caught on camera visibly sad and shedding tears at his friend's funeral in Notre Dame, Paris. It is mainly newspaper accounts that reveal such detail, that provide more of a 'feel' and sense of what was going on in the past.

Acknowledgements

I am grateful to my family for their forbearance over many months and to old colleagues John Cole, Harry Hillier, Paul Walker and Nat Levy who read through and checked one or two chapters. I am indebted to Chloe Sideris, who by managing to read my handwriting word processed Chapters 6–9, and also for her electronic skills and essential assistance in fusing the new with existing content.

Abbreviations

BTO	Brussels Treaty Organization
CAP	Common Agricultural Policy
CDU	Christlich Demokratische Union
CEE	Central and Eastern Europe
CEEC	Committee of European Economic Co-operation
CET	Common External Tariff
CFEU	Conseil Français pour l'Europe Uni
CFSP	Common Foreign and Security Policy
CP	Communist Party
CSCE	Conference on Security and Co-operation in Europe
CU	Customs Union
CUSG	Customs Union Study Group
DGB	German Federation of Trades Unions
DM	Deutschmark
Dom-Toms	Departments and Territories of Metropolitan France
DT	*Daily Telegraph*
EBRD	European Bank of Reconstruction and Development
EC	European Community
ECB	European Central Bank
ECSC	European Coal and Steel Community
EDC	European Defence Community
EE	Eastern Europe
EEA	European Economic Area
EEC	European Economic Community
EFTA	European Free Trade Association
EIB	European Investment Bank
EMI	European Monetary Institute
EMS	European Monetary System
EMU	Economic and Monetary Union
EP	European Parliament
EPC	European Political Community
EPU	European Payments Union
ERDF	European Regional Development Fund

ERM	Exchange Rate Mechanism
ERP	European Recovery Programme
ESF	European Social Fund
EU	European Union
FDI	Foreign Direct Investment
FF	French Franc
FRG	Federal Republic of Germany (West Germany)
FT	*Financial Times*
FTA	Free Trade Area
FURI	Federal Union Research Institute
GATT	General Agreement on Tariffs and Trade
GDH	German Dominance Hypothesis
GDP	gross domestic product
GDR	German Democratic Republic (East Germany)
GNP	gross national product
IAEA	International Atomic Energy Authority
IGC	Inter Governmental Conference
JCMS	*Journal of Common Market Studies*
JCWS	*Journal of Cold War Studies*
LRB	*London Review of Books*
MEP	Member of European Parliament
NATO	North Atlantic Treaty Organization
NCB	National Coal Board
NIC	newly industrialized country
NTB	non-tariff barrier
NYRB	*New York Review of Books*
OCA	Optimal Currency Area
OECD	Organisation for Economic Co-operation and Development
OEEC	Organisation for European Economic Co-operation
OPEC	Organization of Petroleum Exporting Countries
PEU	Pan European Union
PRO	Public Record Office
QMV	qualified majority voting
RPF	Rassemblement du Peuple Français
SEA	Single European Act
SEM	Single European Market
SFIO	Section Française de l'Internationale Ouvrière (French Socialist Party)
SGP	Stability and Growth Pact
SM	single market
SPD	Sozialdemocratische Partei Deutschlands
ST	*Sunday Times*
TUC	Trades Union Congress
UEF	Union Européene des Fédéralistes
UEM	United Europe Movement

USD	United States dollar
USE	United States of Europe
VAT	value-added tax
WEU	Western European Union
WMD	weapons of mass destruction
WTO	World Trade Organization
WWII	World War Two

Prologue

Since the EU (1992) came into being in the Treaty on European Union, signed in Maastricht in final metamorphoses from the EC (1986) and the original EEC (1957), the EU has negotiated four more treaties. The Treaties of Amsterdam (1997) and Nice (2001) both of which came into force, made alterations to the rule book and voting procedures in preparation for enlargement from 15 to as many as 30 states (see Chapter 9). The subsequent European Constitution Treaty (2004) and its cloned replacement the Treaty of Lisbon (2007) have both been rejected in referendums (see Chapter 9).

The EU's 27 states and single market of 488 million population (cf. USA's 303 million) still operate quite smoothly under the Nice Treaty's (2001) rules and QMV procedure. The EU represents 8 per cent of the world's population and 40 per cent of the world's trade in goods (double the Americans' share). Sixteen of these 27 EU states also make up the eurozone, sharing a single currency (Slovakia joined the eurozone, January 2009). The euro's tenth birthday was in January 2009.

The fact that after more than 50 years of existence there are still states that want to join (viz. Turkey and Ukraine) is testimony to the EU's attractiveness and success and reveals incidentally the effectiveness of the EU as a 'soft power'.

How did all this start? Why did only six states initially involve themselves in economic integration? What ideas and influences shaped the organisation? Was federation the motive?

This book aims to answer such questions and to strip away the rhetoric surrounding European integration that belies the often more mundane reality of fact. The story of the EEC is a subject that is often quite mistakenly wrapped in all sorts of assumptions regarding its supposed purpose and goal.

Certainly the institutional framework of the 1951 European Coal and Steel Community (ECSC), EEC and EU were part of a continual resolution of Western Europe's fundamental predicament. Since the end of World War II in 1945 Western Europe has faced two big problems – Germany and Russia. How to live safely and securely with them remains the fundamental question facing Europe today. The reason for this is the experience and record of the past. In the case of Germany there have been conflicts in 1864, 1870, 1914–18 and most catastrophically 1939–45. For France, which was invaded three times in 70 years, Germany was always the bigger of the two problems. In 1940 France had to surrender in the same railway carriage in which Germany had signed the Armistice in 1918. It had taken Hitler less than six weeks to humble a historic foe. Germany's victory march through Paris in 1940 followed the identical route to the French victory march of 1918. To end a recurring cycle of vengeance and war was uppermost in French minds. De Gaulle's post-war government in 1944 even signed the short-lived Treaty of Moscow with the USSR, a mutual defence pact which named the potential aggressor as Germany. Between 1944–48 French policy towards Germany was to try and keep it weak and dismembered, on the principle that 'French strength lay in German weakness'.

In 1948 France had to come to terms politically with the reality of an emergent West German state and strong economy. These factors plus the economic necessity of access to German markets and coal supplies produced a volte-face in French policy. A Franco-German alliance has subsequently been the bedrock and motor of European economic integration. It flourished from the Adenauer–de Gaulle era, in 1958–63, up to that of Kohl and Mitterrand in the 1980s.

The objective of safely incorporating a revived German economy into Western Europe, in the absence of any formal peace settlement with the defeated, belligerent former Germany, was solved through economic integration: the creation of common markets originally in coal and steel in 1951 and in industrial goods in 1957. This meant that the recovery of German economic power did not pose a political or military threat to Europe in the 45 years following World War II (whereas Japan's rise to economic superpower status has alarmed its Asian neighbours).

The institutional creations (ECSC, EEC) of European economic integration also formed part of the post-war 'architecture' of what was called 'containment'. This was US President Harry Truman's policy at the start of the 'Cold War' in 1947 of keeping the USSR behind its 1945 frontiers and stopping the further spread of Soviet Communism. From 1947 the US sponsored and encouraged all forms of integration in Europe. Europe was divided by the 'Iron Curtain' into two blocs each within a superpower's sphere of influence – the USSR's in Eastern Europe and the USA's in Western Europe.

Stalin's policy of 'defensive expansionism' turned East and Central European states liberated by the Red Army in World War II into communist states. This westward extension of the 'Soviet Empire' resulted in a chain of 'buffer states'; an insurance against possible future invasion from the West which also violated the wartime agreement made at Yalta in January 1945 when Stalin agreed with Roosevelt and Churchill to the principles of self-determination and free elections for liberated Europe. At the end of the war the two powers which had previously contained the USSR – Germany and Japan – were both defeated. The North Atlantic Treaty Organization (NATO), established in 1949 (a permanent peace-time military alliance operating on the principle of mutual defence – 'an attack on one being an attack on all'), and American atomic weapons deterred the USSR militarily. However, security from Soviet Communism and a resurgent Germany was not simply a military issue: it was also fundamentally economic. Economic growth and higher living standards in Western Europe from the late 1940s through to the 1980s enhanced its security against communist influence. Political stability, particularly democratic stability, depended on a sufficient level of comfort and economic satisfaction. European integration, through a common market, provided a superior framework for facilitating this than Comecon (the Council of Mutual Economic Assistance, established in 1949 as a Soviet reaction to Marshall Aid and the OEEC) and the centrally planned command economies of the Soviet Empire's Eastern Bloc.

The radical changes to the European map following the geopolitical upheavals of 1989–91 upset the balance of power in Europe that had existed since 1945, and marked the end of the post-war era and the old certainties of the Cold War. The fall of the Berlin Wall in November 1989, the peaceful collapse of communist regimes in Eastern Europe (with the exception of Romania), the end of the Warsaw Pact and Comecon and, ultimately, in December 1991 the demise of the USSR itself were events of seismic proportions comparable to the French Revolution two hundred years before in 1789–91 or the Russian Revolution of 1917.

Before 1989–91 the big questions were what Russia's intentions were and what action might they take. After December 1991 the demise of the Soviet Union ended the conventional military threat to Western Europe from the Red Army. The old Cold War certainties had gone by 1991; the same big questions then applied to the remerged Greater Germany. How would it act with its 80 million population and as the world's third largest economy? Contrary to the conjectured fears of worst possible scenarios from President Mitterand, Jacques Delors and prime minister Margaret Thatcher (see Chapter 7), Greater Germany's conduct of affairs was unsurprising. Big Germany became *primus inter pares* in the EU (after the Nice Treaty 2001) with more voting power in the Council of Ministers than Italy, France and the UK due to Germany's far larger population. Germany could not dominate decision making because of qualified majority voting (QMV) rules (see Chapter 9). The architecture and institutional machinery set up in Europe 1949–51 proved quite adequate and sufficiently flexible to accommodate the merger of the two Germanys (facilitated by the Basic Law (article 23) 1949); and with the GDR's automatic absorption, as part of the FRG, into the EC (under the Treaty of Rome (article 227 and Declarations concerning German nationals pp 182–83) 1957). The eventual merged armies of the GDR and FRG were absorbed within NATO following a NATO–Soviet negotiated agreement 1990–91 (see Chapter 7).

Subsequent NATO and EU enlargements have incorporated Poland, Hungary, Czech Republic and eventually the three Baltic states and others into both organisations. Germany felt more secure with Poland in NATO and the EU as it stopped being the 'last country in the West'.

EMU from 1999 meant the end of both the Bundesbank's de facto 'DM Zone' and what UK monetary economists referred to as the 'German Dominance Hypothesis' (GDH) (see Chapter 8).

Russia's invasion and short war with Georgia, August 2008, has revived the 'Russian question' once again (Afghanistan, 1979 was the last time Russia invaded a state). Whereas in 1991 the Russian government, economy and military were in disarray this is no longer the case. The Russian army's operation might be seen as ill judged and indefensible but was considered to be militarily competent by Western military commentators. Although Russia is no longer a superpower it has re-emerged as a regional power in the Caucauses and altered the whole balance of power in that area. This has wider implications not just for the Ukraine and Georgia but concerning future enlargement and possible limits to EU and NATO expansion.

Part I
Origins

1 Definition and theories of European integration, 1945–95

What are the distinguishing characteristics of an integrated organisation as opposed to other international organisations that governments join? Professor Alan Milward and Vibeke Sorensen made the distinction clear between integrated and interdependent organisations (Milward et al., 1993, Chapter 1). International organisations such as the Organisation for Economic Co-operation and Development (OECD), the General Agreement on Tariffs and Trade (GATT) and the North Atlantic Treaty Organization (NATO) operate on the basis of 'interdependence', i.e. a group of national governments co-operate together in certain policy areas and agreements are made based on mutual co-operation. Such organisations do not interfere with the policy-making of their member states, their decisions do not overrule national policies and there is little if any power or sanction to impose policies on member states. This is the most common type of international organisation or basis of agreement.

Integration, however, requires the creation of a 'supranational organisation' such as the European Coal and Steel Community (ECSC) 1951 and the European Economic Community (EEC) 1957. Here the member states transfer some policy decisions to a body of all member states, the decisions of which are binding on all members and have to be followed. So member states within supranational organisations transfer some power (sovereignty) to that organisation. Furthermore, the supranational organisation has the power to impose sanctions on member governments, in cases of non-compliance with policy decisions or breaches of agreements. For example, in the EEC one of the functions of the European Commission is to act as a 'policeman' to ensure compliance and another EEC organ, the European Court of Justice, makes legal judgments (that take precedence over member states' national law) in cases of dispute.

What are the practical benefits of integrated supranational organisations over international interdependent bodies? While acknowledging that the administrative and other costs are higher, Milward et al. (1993) identify three key advantages of European economic integration. In the first place the agreements were 'irreversible' (or at least less easily reversed). The Rome Treaty 1957 establishing the EEC set no time limit, i.e. it is intended to be of an indefinite duration. This is unusual, as treaties normally are for prescribed periods, which can be extended (e.g. the NATO Treaty 1949 was originally for 20 years) or have to be renegotiated (e.g. the original Non-Proliferation Treaty 1963, where states agreed not to acquire nuclear weapons, which expired in 1995). The Rome Treaty also contains no procedures for members to leave the European Economic Community (Greenland left the EEC but this was after achieving independence from Denmark). The significance of these points is that integration provides a much greater guarantee that agreements and policies once made will be adhered to continuously. Such arrangements are therefore secure as there is more certainty that deals struck between nation states will continue and not be broken. (The importance of this is underlined by the instance when Nazi Foreign Minister Joachim von Ribbentrop presented Adolf Hitler on his birthday with a casket containing copies of all the treaties he had broken!)

The second advantage of supranational organisations is their 'exclusiveness' as an integrated body. The six members of the EEC from 1957 onwards could exclude other prospective members unless they accepted their terms, the 'acquis communitaire' concept, i.e. new members have to agree to accept all the 'club' rules. This makes the integrated organisation a strong cohesive force, enhances its bargaining position with outsiders and provides it with the potential to discriminate. Britain in 1955 at first joined but then withdrew from the talks that established the EEC in 1957. Then in 1961 when Britain decided to join after all, it was excluded by de Gaulle (Britain joined 12 years later on its third attempt) and was discriminated against by the Common External Tariff – the EEC's protectionist tariff wall.

The third advantage of an integrated organisation, according to Milward et al., is that they are more 'law abiding'. The Treaty of Paris 1951 and Treaties of Rome 1957 created a new legal system and framework to regulate both the institutions' and members' powers, rights and obligations.

The institutional arrangements for European economic integration in the 1950s were part of the solution to the big question facing Western Europe – how to live safely with Germany and the USSR.

However, whilst this helps explain the integrated organisational form adopted it does not specifically answer why it was that the ECSC 1951 and the EEC 1957 were set up. Why did six governments sign these two treaties? Why did other governments refuse to join? Why, too, does it appear that only economic integration succeeds? (Attempts at non-economic 'integration' have, like the European Defence Community (EDC) of 1950–54, collapsed.)

There are three schools of thought offering explanations for European integration. Most books on the European Community contain a chapter on 'origins' that weaves a story based on the first two types of explanation examined here.

The orthodox explanation for European integration is not historical at all but drawn from political science. The argument is that the increased complexity of both the post-1945 international order and the range and functions of the modern nation state mean that countries are inexorably entwined in a network of functioning international bodies (such as NATO, the United Nations (UN), or GATT), and the scope for independent action by individual states is curtailed by collective decision taking. It is further argued that once integrated organisations are established there is an inevitable tendency for further integration to occur so that the ECSC 1951 led to the EEC 1957 or the Single European Act (SEA) 1986 led to the objective of Economic and Monetary Union (EMU) in the EU Treaty 1992. So, once European integration has started it becomes a self-sustaining process, powered by Brussels Eurocrats, resulting in the piecemeal incremental integration of Europe. This process is expected to result in a Federal United States of Europe. The inevitable result of increasing the scope of an integrated supranational organisation is the eventual demise of the nation state whose functions, responsibilities and sovereignty are transferred to the supranational state (George, 1992; Haas, 1958; Milward et al., 1993).

As we shall see, this orthodox explanation appears less than satisfactory as an interpretation of the facts, namely the limited extent of integration over the past 40 years. The fact is that it has been exclusively economic and that decision-making (and so political power) still lies with national governments acting together within the European Union. The European Commission makes proposals, it does not take decisions. The European Parliament is not a legislature; it has always had the right to be consulted and now has some 'codecision' rights, but has never passed a law in 40 years. Political power in the European Community lies with the member states: decisions are taken collectively by them within the Council of Ministers. It seems highly improbable that the integration process inevitably leads to the disappearance of the nation state and the creation of a federal Europe. Whereas in the 1960s this undoubtedly appeared a plausible outcome and was enshrined in this orthodox explanation, its validity as a theory now looks unconvincing in the light of recent historical analysis of governments' archival records from the 1950s.

The second school of thought attributes European integration to the ideas, growth and influence of European federalist movements particularly from World War II (1939–45) onwards. Professor Walter Lipgens, the main exponent of this view, undertook detailed studies of the numerous movements and organisations advocating European federalism, the nurturing and development of the ideas in various wartime non-communist resistance movements in occupied Europe as well as the intrigue and ideological disputes between the various post-war pressure groups. Lipgens regards Euro-federalism as an inevitable and logical post-war policy based on the ideas and proposals of the resistance movements and the UK's 'Federal Union' 1939–41. Furthermore, he claims that lobbying and publicity by European federalist movements after 1945 resulted in moves to implement Euro-federal ideas, the outcome being the first supranational authority in 1950.

Lipgens' thesis is that a combination of the inherent logic of a federal solution for Europe (as an antidote to the destructive forces of total war, the Holocaust's genocide, totalitarianism, extreme nationalism and human-rights

abuses of the period 1933–45), the public support and promotion of federalism from politicians and intelligentsia, and a rising groundswell of mass
public support for the idea failed to achieve complete fruition only because of
two impediments. What Lipgens referred to as the 'first obstacle' was the
declared antipathy of both the US and USSR between 1943–47 towards the
idea of a federal Europe. However with the beginning of Soviet–American
superpower rivalry in the Cold War from 1947–48, the US became an interested convert and then an enthusiastic advocate of Euro-federal solutions.
Yet, by then a 'second opposing force' was West European governments
themselves (who would have had to approve and implement any federation).
For Lipgens the British, Scandinavian and French governments were 'bastions
of stubborn nationalist traditions' and therefore the federal idea never
achieved a real breakthrough.

Nevertheless, Lipgens argues that between 1945 and 1955 when 'the policies for European Union were taking shape the political pressure groups
advocating union or federation were especially important; one cannot
understand or describe the pre-history of the European movement or its
beginnings without studying the activity of these groups'. The Union Européene de Fédéralistes (UEF) emerged from the Hertenstein meeting in
December 1946 (its membership doubling to 200,000 between 1947–50).
According to Lipgens the UEF by 'increasingly successful lobbying made a
big contribution to the integration effort between 1950–54'. However, the only
instance of successful lobbying by the UEF cited by Lipgens was Article 38 of
the European Defence Community Treaty which assigned to its future parliament the task of framing a European constitution (Lipgens, 1982, pp. 12,
85; 1980, p. 119). The EDC/EPC attempt at integration collapsed – rejected
by the French national assembly in August 1954. The only example Lipgens
provides for successful influence and lobbying by European federalist movements was for an aborted scheme. Lipgens asserts that the European federalist
movements influenced the earlier ECSC 1951 but no supportive evidence is
provided. However, he admits that after the miscarriage of the EDC scheme
the European federalist movements had little or no influence over the subsequent Rome Treaties of 1957 (Lipgens, 1980, p. 137), which remain the
principal instances of European economic integration establishing a common
market in the European Economic Community and a joint programme for
developing atomic energy in Euratom. Also, as Professor Alan Milward
shows, Jean Monnet, 'the father of European integration', appears completely
uninterested and uninvolved with European federalist movements between
1945–48 and is never mentioned by Lipgens in his studies. Furthermore,
Monnet's conversion to the idea of European integration was apparently due
initially to American – not European federalist – influence (Milward, 1992,
p. 335). It was Jean Monnet who was responsible for starting the scheme for
the ECSC.

Lipgens' thesis that the European integration of the 1950s was somehow
the inevitable outcome of the European federalist movements' pressure and

influence is hard to sustain, given the absence of real linkage between the transnational political pressure groups working for a European federation and the actual integrated organisations established by governments in the 1950s. Nevertheless, the European federalist movements remain more than an interesting intellectual and political phenomenon, as the following chapter will show, resulting in the tangible institutional development of the Council of Europe.

Lipgens' focus on the history of European federalist movements as an explanation for what followed appears superficially attractive and plausible but it inevitably ignores all the evidence drawn from national governments' archives that reveal the internal departmental debates over policy options and objectives involved and the basis for decisions taken.

Such documentary evidence, as subsequent chapters show, reveals that the motives and intentions of the six states that signed the Treaty of Paris 1951 and Treaties of Rome 1957 did not (rhetoric aside) include 'federation'.

Nevertheless, it might reasonably be contended that even if the European federalist movements' direct influence over the practice and procedures of European integrated bodies was minimal at least their long publicised prescriptions and prognoses for Europe were relevant. This may be so but their advocacy of a Customs Union (the central mechanism in both the ECSC and EEC) was an old idea: the *Zollverein* centred on Prussia was a Customs Union, incorporating many of the German states as early as 1833, and 1931–32 saw two proposals for Customs Unions between Germany and Austria, and by Belgium and Luxembourg in the Ouchy Convention July 1932.

The third type of explanation of European integration is entirely historical, based on the work of political, diplomatic and economic historians. The '30-year rule' meant that from the early 1980s British government documents covering the establishment of the ECSC and EEC three decades before became available. Through the use of Foreign Office, Board of Trade and Cabinet papers in the Public Record Office, the British government's rather dismal record of decision-making on Europe has been written up by historians such as John Young, Saki Dockrill and others, while economic historians such as Alan Milward and Frances Lynch have tapped into government and economic records in the UK and other European States involved in the integration process.

Alan Milward has produced a thesis firmly based and derived from empirical evidence (drawn from different national archives) to explain the origins and motivations for European integration. In essence the 'Milward thesis' states that European integration only occurs and only works when it is actually needed by nation states, there being no fundamental antagonism between European integration (seen in the ECSC and EEC) and the nation state. This stands in marked contrast to the other two types of explanation, both of which rest on the idea that European integration ultimately results in the demise of the nation state and the creation of a new supranational state or Federal United States of Europe. Milward says that supranational organisations were set up by the nation states for their own specific purposes, not as a step towards the submission and eclipse of the nation state within a federal Europe. The fundamental issue is: where does power lie? Whether in the EEC of the 1960s or European Union of 1990s, power remains with the nation states: all decisions are taken by the member states' governments collectively in the Council of Ministers (either by unanimity or qualified majority voting depending on the issue). The actual extent of surrender, or pooling of national control, to supranational organisations in Brussels decades later are still quite modest and restricted to some, but not all forms of economic activity. The supranational organisation has changed its name from EEC (1958–86) to European Community (1986–91) to European Union since Maastricht, yet it has remained a common or single market primarily concerned with common commercial issues and their related policies. There is, for example, still no such thing as a single common foreign policy for all EU members (although co-ordinated responses are attempted on specific issues). The only policy elements that members have integrated relate to economic or commercial affairs.

Milward argues further that European integration, far from advancing the cause of federation, actually 'rescued the nation state' – the supranational organisations ECSC and EEC were originally created by six states (France, Benelux, Italy and West Germany) because of economic necessity and political security. Euro-federalist ideas and movements, according to Milward's thesis, had nothing at all to do with European integration. He argues that the requirements of economic reconstruction and national rebuilding in Western Europe following World War II, from 1945 onwards, often required international solutions. This was because national governments were not able successfully to pursue their own plans for economic reconstruction in isolation from their neighbours, as they needed access to their West European neighbours' markets and raw materials (e.g. German coking coal). At the same time, in the late 1940s and early 1950s there was no free trade in Western Europe. Tariffs and quota restrictions to protect national markets were the norm.

West European states were mutually dependent economically yet rigged their own markets for national advantage. Also, national reconstruction plans were very similar in aim (increasing steel production figured prominently in French and others' schemes for national economic regeneration from 1946). This accounts for the necessity of commercial agreement between states. The Treaty of Paris 1951 established the ECSC, a common market in coal and steel, which resolved these problems and facilitated the attainment of national economic objectives in an international context.

Milward argues that when national reconstruction plans depended on economic links with West Germany, then integration occurred. An integrated rather than an interdependent organisation was created because of its intrinsic advantages. Milward shows that West German economic revival was crucial in the European economic system – it was the main source of machines and machine tools for its continental neighbours and a big consumer of food and steel. Dutch, French, Belgian and other states all needed to restore secure trading connections with West Germany. Their economic recovery and national reconstruction hinged to a large extent on German economic revival (Milward, 1992, pp. 155–67; 1984, pp. 492–502).

West Germany's political future in Europe was also of central importance. According to Milward, European economic integration took place when rebuilding nation states' economies after 1945 depended on economic links and agreement with Germany and so intersected with the 'big question', i.e. how to fix Germany safely and securely in Western Europe. Then and only then did European integration occur because it was a much more secure, permanent, law-abiding arrangement.

Paradoxically, according to Milward's thesis, far from European integration being a move towards creating a federal union in Western Europe, it was the mechanism by which a Federal Republic of Germany (West Germany) could safely re-emerge as another nation state. The process of European integration was not a first step to subsume Germany or other states in a federation but actually provided the means by which a new German state could be re-established and co-exist, in the absence of any treaty or formal peace settlement, with those Western neighbours it had invaded, defeated and occupied 10–15 years before. West Germany was only freed from external post-war controls over its steel and coal production (ending the international Ruhr Authority's restrictions over coal exports from West Germany) within the confines of the ECSC from 1951. Similarly, within the context of the European Defence Community plan of 1950–54 (the failed integrated scheme to solve the vexed issue of German rearmament) under its Bonn Agreements full sovereignty was restored in foreign affairs and national defence from 1955 to the West German state.

Lipgens attributes European integration to the influence and lobbying of the European federalist movements before 1955 and for some political scientists integration once started is seen as an irreversible and inevitable process of transferring power and sovereignty from the nation state to a supranational state. The Milward thesis regards European integration as a creation of nation states for their own national purposes – the most secure means to achieve national economic policy objectives was by integration. For Milward both the Treaty of Paris 1951 (establishing the ECSC) and the Treaties of Rome 1957 (creating the EEC/Euratom) were primarily commercial treaties; the supranational components were there chiefly because of the German question.

The value of these three schools of thought as interpretations of the driving forces behind integration will be assessed in the following chapters, which trace the development of schemes for European integration from 1945.

2 The impact and significance of the European federalist movements and the Council of Europe (1949)

Movements to unite Europe politically only emerged post-World War I (although the idea originated as far back as the seventeenth century). The horror and carnage of World War I (1914–18) was the motivation behind this wish to end the destructive antagonistic rivalry of European nation states. Count Richard Coudenhove-Kalergi established the Pan-European Union in 1923 as a non-party mass movement for the unification of Europe; another organisation, the Association for European Co-operation, was started in Geneva in 1926 and had committees in Paris, Berlin and London. The inter-war years also saw the early advocacy of a European Customs Union and a recommendation for a single market from 1920 in the face of increasing Japanese and US exports, economic stagnation, economic nationalism and tariff protectionism in Europe. In September 1929 Aristide Briand proposed the creation of a European Federal Union at the Assembly of the League of Nations which was viewed with incomprehension by most other ministers and statesmen, though interestingly not by Winston Churchill, who published articles supporting the idea of a 'United States of Europe' in 1930 and 1938. Churchill believed, however, that Britain was not part of Europe but should support it from outside and that the French and Germans should create it.

However, interest in such movements and proposals had no effect on the realities of European economic and political affairs and such organisations never achieved a mass following but remained a minority preoccupation of certain intellectuals (Lipgens, 1982, pp. 35–42; 1985, pp. 5–7).

The Bolsheviks in Russia were dismissive and contemptuous of federalist schemes for Europe and the Nazis after 1933 banned all pro-European associations as pacifist.

Lipgens argues that the experience of World War II had an overwhelming formative influence on the prospects and nature of European federalist ideas. It changed everything. It increased support for federal ideas as Europe's status diminished compared with that of the super-powers: the US and USSR. Experience of conquest and occupation under Nazi rule and the failure of national governments to provide the minimum of security and independence supposedly weakened public confidence in the nation state and strengthened federalist support.

Lipgens suggests, rather surprisingly, that wartime occupation in Nazi Europe accustomed people to a continental-style unified economy A single centrally controlled economy under the Nazis was in fact more influential than ten years' work of the Pan-European Union as it showed the possibilities for a peacetime single European economy (Lipgens, 1985, pp. 8–9).

A federal state with supranational powers was invariably advocated by non-communist wartime Resistance movements (i.e. a majority of the Resistance) whether French, Dutch or Polish. According to Lipgens, the Resistance hardly ever favoured a return to the pre-war system of nation states in their leaflets and programmes. For example, Philippe Viannay on 'The Future of Germany' in *Défense de la France* (no. 12 (Paris) 20 March 1942) spoke of Germany being integrated into a 'truly European order' and Claude Bourdet (leader of the non-communist Resistance) in *Combat, Organe de Mouvement de Libération National* (no. 55 (Lyons), March 1944), distinguished between the Nazi system and the German people and recognised that the Versailles Treaty was in part to blame for the Nazis' rise to power. He urged that at the end of the war, after the guilty had been punished, Germans should have equal rights with other European nations and Germany join a European federation on equal footing.

Altiero Spinelli, interned on the island of Ventotene by Mussolini in World War II, founded the Movimento Federalista Europeo inside the Italian Resistance and wrote the 'Ventotene Manifesto'. In *The United States of Europe*, he advocated a federal Europe to overcome 'international anarchy'. He argued that this was the true cause of racism and two world wars, for which neither democracies nor communists had the answer, only federalism.

Resistance publications towards the end of the war emphasised that they did not want a new 'Holy Alliance' of 'three great powers' over Europe but wanted instead a supranational European federation with political, military and judicial institutions to maintain peace, freedom and national independence. Liberty and civilisation would only be assured, after the barbarity of World War II, if a Federal Union replaced the existing anarchy of 30 European states (Lipgens, 1985, pp. 674–75; 1986, pp. 213, 214).

The somewhat grandiose sounding International Conference of Resistance Fighters held a clandestine meeting in May 1944 in Geneva (attended by 15 individuals, some of whom were refugees, representing nine nationalities). In their declarations they outlined most comprehensively the arguments for European federalism. Only a European federation would enable the German people to join European life without being a danger to other peoples; it would avoid any recurrence of aggression while recognising that Europe needed the German economy.

A European federation would ensure peace, avoid extreme nationalism, stop 'European civil wars' and allow the exercise of common powers over foreign political security matters and economic planning on a European scale.

A common market was considered by the 1944 Conference to be an economic necessity to avoid the problems associated with the economic crisis of the 1930s, while recognising the interdependence of European national economies. Article V also referred to the integration of 'German chemical and heavy industries into the European industrial organisation so as to prevent their use for German nationalistic ends'. The Conference recognised that Europe could only reassert itself between the two superpowers of the US and USSR if it federated (Lipgens, 1982, pp. 53–55; 1985, pp. 678–82).

Why exactly did European resistance movements come to advocate federalist solutions? Was it perhaps partly because the alternative solution to safe co-existence with a revived Germany was dismemberment of the German state? This was unacceptable to European federalists (though not to the French government of 1945–48), especially as there were two German representatives at the 1944 Conference. There was also a general recognition of the central role of the German economy within Europe's economy. Second, the pre-1939 League of Nations model to prevent war had completely failed and needed replacing in Europe. Third, federalist objectives were adopted as part of post-war planning to help sustain popular revolt *against* Nazi rule and *for* something to replace it.

How far did such federalist ideas penetrate? How influential were they? Lipgens admits that the ideas of the Resistance did not penetrate too far into the mass of the population. Even in the Resistance, federalism was far from being a homogeneous view. Many in the Maquis saw their fight as a purely national struggle (Lipgens, 1982, p. 60; 1985, p. 24). The highest circulation of any Resistance journal was 450,000 for *Défense de la France*, no. 43, January 1944.

Do these ideas, plans and programmes have any significance or are they simply part of the ephemera of intellectual history? The arguments of the Resistance leadership for federalism differed from the interwar period (which was reacting against the slaughter of 1914–18) and stressed a geo-political and economic rationale. The Resistance emphasised the need to regulate the 'nation state system' within a federal framework and so curb national sovereignty through a strong supranational authority to avoid the brutality of totalitarianism and preserve human rights.

There is a continuity in aim and rationale between the Resistance, the post-war European federalist movements and some organisations and institutions that were created between 1947 and 1957. This does not mean that there was a causal connection but merely that the wartime Resistance's agenda for post-war Europe had an enduring logic and relevance.

Britain's experience of the approach and outbreak of war between the Munich Agreement 1938 and the fall of France in June 1940 triggered a brief surge of interest in European federalism in Britain. John Pinder's research revealed 'the remarkable body of literature on plans for federation published between 1939–41 ... it is doubtful, despite the flow of material in the post war years, whether such an impressive amount has appeared in any one country since'. W.B. Curry's *The Case for Federal Union*, a Penguin Special, Autumn 1939, sold 100,000 copies in six months. This text and others developed the theme that the basic cause of war was national sovereignty and that it could be prevented through common federal government managing common affairs. The same argument appeared later in Resistance literature.

Pinder makes the point that the 'literature attained a coherence and force' because it appeared within the framework of two organisations set up in 1939–40: the 'Federal Union' and in 1940 the Federal Union Research Institute (FURI).Federal Union's membership was growing at a rate of 500 a month by December 1939 and between 1939–40 it recruited 10,000 people in 200 branches (Pinder, 1986, pp. 26–28). Although started by three unknown people, it soon attracted distinguished support from, for example, Barbara Wootton, the Labour politician; Lord Lothian, an ex-Liberal minister and Washington ambassador; and Wickham Steed, ex-editor of *The Times*. Federal Union organised big meetings, printed a weekly news sheet and its first conference in March 1940 appointed to its council prominent academics and politicians including William Beveridge, C.E.M. Joad and Ivor Jennings, the constitutional lawyer. The Federal Union Research Institute started work in the summer of 1939 and was formally established in March 1940 to investigate the technicalities of federation under the chairmanship of Beveridge, then Master of University College, Oxford. A brilliant group of experts produced studies on constitutional, economic and other aspects of federation within FURI. Indeed, the Economics Committee anticipated many of the issues that have subsequently arisen in the EEC (a common currency, complete free trade, fixed exchange rates, free labour migration). Ivor Jennings' *A Federation of Western Europe*, 1940, was the first FURI publication and drew up a Federal Constitution. Lionel Robbins' *Economic Causes of War*, 1939, made a powerful case for a European federation, as did Sir William Beveridge's *Peace by Federation?*, Federal Tracts, no. 1 (Federal Union), 1940.

British federalist literature 1939–41 had an enormous influence on continental federalists, particularly in Italy. Alterio Spinelli obtained Federal Union material while imprisoned on the island of Ventotene and it provided most of the ideas he and his small group needed to launch the Italian federal movement. He translated many Federal Union tracts into Italian as well as Lionel Robbins' *Economic Causes of War* and his *Economic Aspects of Federation*. How can this surprising phenomenon of vigorous British interest and activity concerning European federation in 1939–40 be explained?

The outbreak of war was a decisive event: considerable criticism was directed at the doctrine of state sovereignty, which it was thought prevented the League of Nations (established in 1919) from having sufficient powers to stop it. Therefore, following the defeat of Nazi Germany, a European federal structure was advocated. According to Lipgens, 'during the first year of war European federation was a central topic of debate in all sections of British opinion, whatever their (political) allegiance'. Attlee, leader of the Parliamentary Labour Party, said in 1939, 'Europe must federate or perish', and Wilson Harris, editor of the *Spectator*, wrote in March 1940, 'There is no question about the hold the idea of federal union has taken on certain sections of opinion in this country particularly ... youth.'

Pinder, while not doubting the sincerity of advocates of European federalism, thought that an element of expediency was also involved as it was discussed in the wider context of war aims between September 1939 and May 1940. The vision of a better Europe may have inspired public opinion during the 'phoney war', and helped enlist the support of the neutral US, and was even intended perhaps to weaken German support for the war (Lipgens, 1986, pp. 2–4, 23–24).

The concept of federal union was even incorporated, albeit briefly, into British government policy. The offer of complete political union between Britain and France, originally considered in March 1940, became an official government proposal from Churchill's all-party Cabinet on 16 June 1940 to create 'an indissoluble union ... not two nations but one Franco-British Union' with joint organisations for defence, finance, foreign affairs and economic policy. The two populations would acquire a common dual citizenship. However, France collapsed the next day. Reynaud, the French prime minister, argued the case for acceptance in the French Cabinet but it was rejected by 13 votes to 11. He was ousted afterwards and a new government under Petain requested an armistice from the Germans. Churchill's offer of a Franco-British Union was intended to sustain France and its Empire in the war effort.

The fall of France in June 1940 had a formative impact on Britain's military position, her policy options and on public opinion. Discussion of federal ideas as part of war aims tailed off and the flood of publications dried up. Enthusiasm for European federalism never again achieved 1939–40 levels of interest in Britain. The talented team of researchers in the Federal Union Research Institute broke up as they became involved in war service – Beveridge to write reports on full employment and the Welfare State, and Robbins to become Head of Economic Services for the War Cabinet and later to write a report on the expansion of higher education in Britain. As Philip Bell shows, advocates of 'outright European federation' were rare in Britain between 1942–45: 'the general current of opinion had moved on' (Bell, 1986, p. 206).

It moved on because Britain's experience of war diverged from that of occupied Europe's from the summer of 1940, in two fundamental ways. First, from then until summer 1941, a period of over a year, Britain continued the war alone against Nazi Germany's European Empire. This, as Lipgens emphasises, was a formative episode as Britain's national institutions did not collapse and so the sense of national pride and independence was strengthened, unlike most of Europe's. For Britain this amounted to a triumphant vindication of reliance on and belief in national sovereignty. Furthermore, the swift collapse of continental Europe's democracies in 1939–40 served as a deterrent against any closer association with them in future.

Second, once Europe was lost, the US constituted the principal source of military aid and was to take on a special significance. While enthusiasm for

European integration evaporated, the appeal of an Anglo-American Union grew. Once the USSR and US were in the war by the end of 1941, public opinion linked Britain's fate with these two emerging superpowers in 1941–45 (in contrast to the mood of 1939–40 which linked it with Europe). Their combined resources and size made eventual victory certain and also meant that these two powers would largely determine the outcome of any peace settlement (not Britain and France as it had appeared in 1939–40) (Lipgens, 1985, pp. 25–26; 1986, pp. 5–6).

After the war the British public's attention (though not the Foreign Office's, 1945–47) focused on Atlantic and world connections, and Europe was ignored. This was partly as a result of the amount of Anglo-American integration and other pieces of Anglo-American administrative apparatus established in the war, such as the US–UK Combined Chiefs of Staff and the Joint Shipping Board. It was also due to the fact that the British saw themselves as one of the 'Big Three' – the US, USSR and UK instead of one of the big three in Europe. According to Pinder, 'the fall of France, the rise of the USA, alliance with Russia and growing hostility towards Germany combined to turn the thoughts of the British, including many Federal Unionists this way'. Lionel Robbins moved from being a champion of European Union to arguing for an Atlantic Union. Sir William Beveridge, chairman of FURI in 1940, became an advocate for the UK's association with Russia and the US in order to build a world organisation. As Pinder observed, it 'took twenty years for the wheel to come full circle and the UK to seek entry into the EEC and thirty years before it was in' (Pinder, 1986, pp. 25, 32–33).

Others, according to Lipgens, responded in a similar way to Britain. These included the neutral states (Sweden, Switzerland, Ireland, Spain and Portugal), exiles like General Charles de Gaulle and perhaps also the majority of political émigrés (there were over 1 million in Britain during the war), who had fled Europe before its conquest. *All* had a very different experience of the war, not being subjected to the full consequences of national collapse and subsequent rigours of totalitarian Nazi rule. Lipgens said such people 'thought that closer ties with the ruined heartland of the continent was understandably hardly urgent' and they had no reason to draw the same conclusions as those in occupied Europe where federalism at least remained an ideological force. The two groups shared a 'mutual lack of understanding' of the other's thinking after the war, in which their experience determined their position on European federation (Lipgens, 1985, pp. 25–26; 1982, pp. 58–60).

However, it was not primarily Europeans who were to decide the shape and organisational form of the post-war Continent. After 1941 it was the two continental-sized extra-European powers, the US and USSR, whose resources and manpower ensured the military defeat of Nazi Germany and – combined with the UK and the support of its Empire – ended the German occupation of Europe. Accordingly it was the evolving plans of the 'Big Three' that determined the fate of Europe. The Resistance's federalist declarations and proposals counted for nothing.

Initially (1941–42) there were two basic working themes that existed concurrently for Anglo-American post-war architecture to preserve world peace and security (although in many respects they were mutually incompatible). The first was US President Franklin D. Roosevelt's idea of two 'world policemen' in 1941 – the UK and US (by 1942 it had expanded to four 'world policemen' – the UK, US, USSR and China). The second was the idea of three regional or continental unions – including a supranational authority for Europe – upon which a world organisation could be based.

Roosevelt was shocked at the fragility of European democracies which collapsed so rapidly under the 1939–40 Nazi blitzkrieg and was disillusioned with the League of Nations which had singularly failed to preserve peace in Europe. Although not an isolationist, he initially shared their antipathy towards American involvement in any world peace organisation when the war was over, preferring to rely simply on power politics and co-operation with the UK and USSR. Roosevelt never showed any interest in promoting a European federation. Although initially the idea of some form of regional union or close association of European states was a significant component of British and American post-war planning, by the spring of 1943 the US State Department and most post-war planning commissions had broadly agreed to 'support a global peace organisation composed of continental unions'. Three such unions were envisaged among states in Asia, Europe and the Americas.

Winston Churchill, in a broadcast in March 1943, spoke along similar lines, stating that 'under a world institution of the United Nations, and some day all nations, there should come into being a Council of Europe'. The next month, April 1943, Churchill suggested a 'World Council' of the 'Big Three' with representatives of the continental unions. In May in Washington he spoke of 12 states forming a council of the 'United States of Europe'. Cordell Hull, Roosevelt's Secretary of State, basically shared Churchill's interest in a new form of the League of Nations, where small states, grouped into continental unions, would have influence as well as the big powers. Cordell Hull set up a 'Sub-committee on the Problem of European Organization' which met first in June 1943 and considered various plans for some months. The initiative ended with the disbandment of this sub-committee in August 1943; any ideas for regional sub-organisations were ignored henceforth by the US as it focused on the 'world policemen' idea and creating a world organisation.

Why did this American interest in post-war Euro-federalism cease in 1943? First, the USSR under Stalin had always been opposed to any idea of federation or regional association in Europe and in 1943 Roosevelt decided to endorse this. According to Lipgens this was because, after the military feat of winning the battle for Stalingrad in 1943, the USSR carried more political and diplomatic weight in the wartime alliance of the 'Big Three'. The USSR broke off relations with governments in exile favouring federation (such as Poland) and recalled the Soviet Ambassadors from Washington and London.

There were also Anglo-American suspicions and fears that the USSR had considered making a separate peace with Hitler in September 1943. For the US, after Stalingrad, the USSR had shown itself to be the 'indispensable ally' who could not be defeated (the Pentagon and White House had concluded that the US would also not be able to win a future conventional war with the USSR). Therefore Stalin's co-operation became of paramount importance to US policy for defeating Germany and securing peace after World War II.

Roosevelt tried to cultivate and placate Stalin (recognising USSR frontiers as at 22 June 1941, i.e. including annexed territory in Poland and the Baltic States) and eliminating any prospect of European federation. In return, Stalin agreed to Roosevelt's post-war plans for a United Nations Organization. The Resistance, that nursery of Euro-federalism, and organisations like the UK's Federal Union hoped rather airily to replace national sovereignty by uniting Europe in a Federal Union. But they had no influence at all on the two superpowers' policy for post-war Europe which was formally to restore nation states. Stalin had long preferred the restoration of 26 small weak European states that the USSR might then dominate. This process ultimately led to a bipolar division of Europe into two blocs in 1948–49: the Eastern Bloc centred on Moscow and the Western Bloc with its centre in Washington.

The US began to change its policy towards the USSR in 1946–47 as its perception of the USSR's intentions and reliability as a post-war partner who would adhere to agreements was re-evaluated. Soviet rule in 'liberated' Europe was extremely severe. The post-war plight of Poland meant it was saddled with a communist government imposed by Moscow. Stalin had predicted that the end of World War II would be different from other wars as the victors would impose their control over the territories they had liberated. This was at variance with the 'Declaration on Liberated Europe' that Stalin had agreed with Roosevelt and Churchill at the Yalta Conference in February 1945. This incorporated the principles of self-determination and free elections for liberated states.

The growth of East–West tension in 1946–47 shaped the emerging Anglo-American policy of dividing Germany in two, establishing a new state of West Germany (Foschepoth, 1986, pp. 404–5). After the London Conference (of the Council of Foreign Ministers from the four occupying powers) failed on 15 December 1947, this course was more firmly set. A new Bizone Agreement was in force by January 1948. Given that the earlier policy proposals of 'dismemberment' of Germany had been rejected by the US and UK and the concept of a 'united neutral Germany' was dismissed, the only option was a 'divided' Germany. This would ensure that neither superpower could incorporate an undivided big Germany within its own bloc and so upset the whole balance of power in Europe (Foschepoth, 1986, p. 406). The announcement of the Truman Doctrine to Congress on 12 March 1947 (by President Harry S. Truman who succeeded Roosevelt on his death) marked the real beginning of the Cold War between the US and USSR. Truman committed the US to the worldwide containment of communism by means of American aid to counter both communist internal insurgency and external aggression.

This was followed by the connected initiative of the Marshall Plan; the US Secretary of State, George C. Marshall, spoke of this at Harvard University on 5 June 1947. The following year a four-year programme (1948–52) of over $22 billion in American aid to 16 European states started. This was designed to assist economic recovery and lessen any prospect of communism gaining ground within Western European states. Ernest Bevin, the Labour government's Foreign Secretary 1945–51, played a significant role in precipitating this switch in US foreign policy to containment by announcing the end of all British aid to Greece, after 31 March 1947, in its fight against communist insurgents. This action culminated in the Truman Doctrine with the Americans assuming responsibility for Greece and Turkey that Britain could no longer afford. Ernest Bevin is also generally credited with turning the offer of Marshall Aid into a reality in Europe by establishing the Organisation for European Economic Co-operation (OEEC) to administer it (Boyle, 1982, p. 373; Frazier, 1984, p. 715).

The start of Cold War rivalry between the superpowers – the East–West split in Europe and the division of Germany – rekindled American interest in a federal solution to Western Europe's two big problems as it would safely accommodate a revived West Germany and help to contain the USSR. After 1947 the US encouraged any promising moves towards federation or integration in Western Europe that might further the American dream of a 'United States of Europe'.

According to Lipgens, this shift in US policy encouraged the reactivation of old federalist pressure groups and the formation of new organisations advocating European Union. Count Coudenhove-Kalergi revived the Pan-European Union that he had established in 1923, and in November 1946 it sent questionnaires to Western Europe's 4,000 MPs to see if they were in favour of a European federation. Fifty per cent of the Belgians, Swiss, French, Dutch and Italians, 26 per cent of the British and only 15 per cent of the Scandinavians were in favour. He then invited these MPs to participate in establishing the European Parliamentary Union, which held its first Congress at Gstaad in September 1947.

In December 1946, associations working for European federation which had their origins in Resistance movements – like Altiero Spinelli's Movimento Federalista Europeo, 1943 – met in Paris to form the Union Européene de Fédéralistes (UEF). The Swiss 'Europa Union' and the British 'Federal Union' also joined this new transnational pressure group.

The UEF quickly recognised that the East–West split in Europe altered the practical parameters for action. The Hertenstein Programme of 1946 recognised that new geo-political realities meant the limit to any frontier of a future united Europe lay where individual liberty and personal freedom ended, thereby excluding Eastern Europe. The UEF's Montreux Congress 1947 (by then it had 100,000 members in 32 associations), agreed that while not accepting a Europe divided into two blocs as a permanent *fait accompli*, they would nevertheless try to promote federation where a start could be made in Western Europe (Lipgens, 1982, pp. 84, 585).

In addition to the PEU and UEF a rather bewildering variety of pressure groups emerged to campaign on the Euro-federal trail. All-party national organisations formed like the 'groupe parlementaire fédéralistes français' and also transnational party-affiliated pressure groups. Federalists among socialist parties from various countries created their own separate umbrella organisations, such as the 'Mouvement Socialiste pour les Etats-Unis' in 1947. (The Christian-Democrats did the same thing.)

However, arguably the most effective organisations belonged neither to the PEU nor the UEE. The UK's 'United Europe Movement' (UEM), founded by Churchill's son-in-law Duncan Sandys, had Winston Churchill (now out of office) as its president. Churchill's speech at Zurich on 19 September 1946 called for

> a kind of United States of Europe ... [the] first step is to form a Council of Europe ... France and Germany must take the lead together ... Great Britain, the British Commonwealth, mighty America – must be the friends and sponsors of the new Europe.
>
> (Lipgens, 1982, pp. 3, 19–20)

This speech received massive publicity in the press and gave an encouraging boost to the Euro-federalist campaign. A similar body to the UEM was established in France, the 'Conseil Français pour l'Europe Uni'. A joint meeting in Paris in July 1947 led to their first joint action – a Congress at The Hague, 7–10 May 1948. Here 800 MPs, former premiers and foreign secretaries met under the chairmanship and star of the proceedings, Winston Churchill. Lipgens saw this as 'an impressive demonstration of the will to unity which formulated concrete proposals'. These included a common market, a Human Rights Convention, a European Assembly and the transfer of a portion of states' sovereign rights to a Council of Europe.

In October 1948 the Joint International Committee of Movements for European Unity was created. This was established by the British UEM and French CFEU, and other founding organisations joined, including the UEF and transnational party-affiliated pressure groups. It adopted the name 'European Movement' under the Honorary Presidencies of Leon Blum, Winston Churchill, Alcide de Gasperi and Paul-Henri Spaak. Subsequently, following a report produced in January 1949, the Council of Europe was established by the Treaty of Westminster in May 1949 (a month after the NATO Treaty was signed). However, what was quickly agreed by the ten signatory states proved a disappointment to the European Movement's federalists. Its Parliamentary Assembly was a purely consultative body of representative national MPs (appointed by states' parliaments) and invariably those enthusiastic about creating 'Europe'. Its Committee of Ministers was the decision-making body with each foreign minister having both a vote and a veto. This was not the integrated organisation and supranational body that the Congress at The Hague had anticipated the previous year in May 1948. The Committee of Ministers moreover did not make legally binding decisions and member states chose subsequently whether to ratify agreements and conventions passed at the Council of Europe (e.g. the European Convention for the Protection of Human Rights and Fundamental Freedoms came into force in 1953. Britain was the first state to ratify it whereas France only did so in 1974).

Ernest Bevin was reputedly instrumental in ensuring that the Council of Europe did not become an 'embarrassing organisation'. He referred to the European Movement's federalist plans for the Council of Europe as 'Pandora's box full of Trojan horses'. However, there is no evidence that any West European state was prepared idealistically to jump to political federation or union in 1948–49. This would have been a fantastic 'leap in the dark' at a time when the future of Germany had not been fully settled. So the framework of the Council of Europe in 1949 could not provide a complete answer to the German question; there were no Germans present. France was only beginning to reformulate its policy towards Germany from the summer of 1948 and only joined 'Bizonia' in April 1949 (the name for the economic fusion of UK and US occupation zones in Germany since 1947). Moreover, West European governments had many preoccupations in the late 1940s – military and economic security, dollar shortages, economic reconstruction, colonial problems and their position in the world, not just in Europe.

Paul Reynaud, long-standing French MP and ex-premier of France (1940), remarked: 'the Council of Europe consists of two bodies, one of them for Europe, the other against it' – the latter being the Committee of Ministers. Even Paul-Henri Spaak, the Belgian Prime Minister, who was one of the most 'federally' minded statesmen in office, was primarily motivated by the understandable need to enhance Belgium's own military and economic security (Milward, 1992, pp. 320–24).

For many idealistic Euro-federalists in the European Movement it must have seemed in 1948–49 that everything was coming together in Western Europe. They were encouraged in this both by the USSR's threatening behaviour (the Soviet blockade of West Berlin and the Anglo-American airlift to overcome it flying in coal, food and clothing for ten and a half months, finally ending on 12 May 1949) and by the start of Marshall Aid from the US, administered through the OEEC. (From June 1948 $22.4 billion was granted over four years for European reconstruction.) The Americans hoped that the OEEC could be developed into a Customs Union for Western Europe (see next chapter). The NATO Treaty was signed in April 1949, creating a permanent peacetime military alliance (initially planned for 20 years) with national forces assigned to its integrated command structure. It established a North Atlantic Council and an Executive Committee of Foreign Ministers, a Defence Council of War Ministers and a Committee of Chiefs of Staff. It was signed by the original five Brussels Treaty Organisation States – Britain,

France, Belgium, Holland, Luxembourg – and by the US, Canada, Italy, Portugal, Iceland, Denmark and Norway. General Eisenhower became NATO's first supreme commander until he was elected American President in 1952. NATO was very much a consequence of the first big Cold War crisis of the Berlin Blockade 1948–49.

So in 1949 it doubtless appeared for many representatives in the Parliamentary Assembly a highly propitious moment to push for political federation in the Council of Europe, given the formation of NATO and the possibility of a European Customs Union forming, with American encouragement, out of the OEEC. However, this apparent window of opportunity was barred, as was demonstrated during the first session of the Council of Europe in November 1949 in Strasbourg, France (a venue suggested by Ernest Bevin, given its symbolic location on the border of France and Germany and the fact that it had changed hands four times since 1870). According to Lipgens this session had a 'humiliating outcome' as federalists in the Council of Europe tried to modify the Treaty of Westminster. The British and Scandinavians on the Committee of Ministers vetoed all such federalist recommendations from the Parliamentary Assembly. The move to European federation through changing the 1949 Statute of the Council of Europe was blocked.

It was ironic that the only European organisation that can be attributed directly to the European Movement's influence was not an integrated or supranational body. Nevertheless the UEF saw the Council of Europe as the start of 'a real organic co-operation between European States'. It has also been described as 'an important milestone on the road to the closer association of the European community' (Urwin, 1991, p. 39).

However, the Council of Europe and its institutions are quite distinct and separate from those created for the supranational ECSC and EEC. The European Community's European Parliament, Commission, Council of Ministers, European Court of Justice and most confusingly European Council (the biannual heads of state meeting) have nothing whatever to do with the Council of Europe's Parliamentary Assembly, Committee of Ministers, European Commission of Human Rights and European Court of Human Rights. The Council of Europe and the European Community are completely separate bodies formed from very different motivations and for different purposes.

The Council of Europe has produced over 140 European conventions since 1949 notably on human rights, on the prevention of torture, and on the suppression of terrorism. One of the Council of Europe's primary concerns has been the enhancement and protection of human rights in Europe. This was a major objective of Euro-federalists given Nazi atrocities, genocide and the wholesale violation of human rights during 1933–45. Since 1949 the original ten members have grown to 26, with Hungary, Poland and Czechoslovakia joining in 1990–91. Member states must accept the principle of the rule of law and guarantee that everyone under its jurisdiction enjoys their human rights and fundamental freedoms. The Council of Europe is not concerned with economic issues at all.

The only connection between the Council of Europe and the European Community is that the EC's European Parliament holds its plenary sessions at the Council of Europe's Palais de l'Europe in Strasbourg. Also, since May 1986 when EC membership reached 12 states, the EC adopted the Council of Europe's flag as its official emblem. The familiar 12 gold stars on a blue background has been the Council of Europe's flag since 1955; the 12 stars are apparently 'an invariable number symbolising perfection and entirety' (Council of Europe, 1992, p. 15).

Although the Council of Europe is invariably described as a first step or milestone on the road to a closer Europe, in a sense it has been bypassed by the creation of the supranational ECSC and EEC. The evidence suggests that the Council of Europe, despite its disappointing limitations for Euro-federalists, represented not only the highpoint but also a dead-end for organised European federalist movements' influence.

Individual federalists and converts like Jean Monnet (who invented the ECSC's High Authority) and Robert Schuman, the French Foreign Minister, made an immense contribution to European economic integration in the early 1950s. Federalists continued to exercise influence long after this. A group founded by Alterio Spinelli in the European Parliament called 'the crocodile club' was responsible for initiating the parliaments' draft Treaty on European Union in 1982 (Wallace, 1982, p. 67, n. 24). Nevertheless, as an organised idealistic movement that grew in the wartime resistance and was revived in 1946–47, the European federalist movements' pinnacle of achievement was the Council of Europe.

Creating the Council of Europe in 1949 certainly meant that the European Movement focused its attention there in vain attempts to steer it in a more federal direction in 1949–50. The European Parliamentary Union's third and fourth Congresses in 1949 and 1950 were almost wholly devoted to a critique of the Council of Europe's structure and debates (Lipgens, 1980, p. 129). Yet only six months after the Council of Europe's first session in November 1949, the Schuman Plan in May 1950 (leading to the ECSC) and the Pleven Plan in October 1950 (leading to the EDC scheme) were formally proposed by the French government. Despite assertions to the contrary, there are no signs of any notable direct involvement by European federalist movements in either scheme.

So what was the significance of the European federalist movements? They were clearly an interesting phenomenon and subsequent developments in the 1950s demonstrated the opportune relevance and inherent logic of some of their recommendations such as a Customs Union or a common market. Even though their campaign for a European federation failed, the campaign indicated at the very least that there was a more widely recognised need for a new structure and architecture in post-war Europe. However, problems surrounding plans for Europe did not arise with the European federalists' prime activities of formulating and advocating ideal policy options but in actually agreeing and implementing mutually satisfactory arrangements between states. Governments were only motivated to do this (see Chapter 3) by way of solving difficulties affecting specific national economic interests. They were not seduced by Euro-federal idealism but driven, as Milward argued, by the need to find the appropriate international framework both to maintain national economic recovery and to solve the German question. National interest, not Euro-federal idealism, propelled the schemes for economic integration. The ECSC and EEC were the result of lengthy detailed negotiating and bargaining between six West European states.

The European federalist movement is probably accorded too much importance and its role as a force exaggerated in the development of integrated organisations. Even the supposedly influential Hertenstein Conference of September 1946 organised by Dutch and Swiss federalists did not manage to contact the British Federal Union and other groups. These then held their own separate Luxembourg conference in October 1946, to which the Dutch and Swiss were not invited – apparently because their addresses had been lost! (Lipgens, 1982, p. 303). Although the 'Hertenstein programme' was adopted subsequently as the manifesto for most Euro-federal groups, there were only 78 people at this conference and 41 of those were Swiss. Both conferences were concerned as much with world federation as European and received little publicity 'in the ordinary press ... The Hertenstein and Luxembourg conference received, at most, a brief inconspicuous mention' (Lipgens, 1982, p. 317).

It was Winston Churchill's Zurich speech on 19 September 1946 that really energised the campaign for federation in Europe by the publicity it received.

Where does this leave Lipgens' thesis? Lipgens thought that the 'progress of the movement for European Union was comparable with that of Liberal democracy in the 19th century', in so far as over a long period of time the movement began with individuals and writers and extended to national and transnational pressure groups which eventually affected the political elites. Then governments 'increasingly affected by the idea started to put it partially into effect' (Lipgens, 1982, p. vi). This is rather dubious, particularly as governments that were unenthusiastic about political federation in Europe in 1949 were attracted by economic integration in 1950. Nevertheless, Lipgens assumes that the inevitable outcome of economic integration is federal union and therefore whatever gets established is simply a means to that end, not an end in itself. The reality though was that France, Belgium, Holland and Britain still had substantial imperial interests and responsibilities in the late 1940s and 1950s. However, Lipgens surprisingly asserts that 'their sense of being colonial powers prevented these countries in the first decisive years of the European integration movement from understanding what had become inevitable' (Lipgens, 1982, p. 12).

The effectiveness of European federalist movements was probably reduced as a result of the schisms in the movement – experienced in 1949 with the disappointments surrounding the Council of Europe and the setback in 1954 when the EDC collapsed. This was due to ideological disputes (the UEF was 'torn apart over future strategy' in 1954) or to personality clashes among the leadership (the EPU split in 1949 was a result of this). Lipgens mentions that after 1954 the European Movement lost its impetus and ceased to be very active or influential (Lipgens, 1980, p. 137).

How influential were the leaders of European federalist movements before this? Some were prominent, well known and even famous – revered figures like Winston Churchill who was out of government on the opposition benches between 1945 and 1951, and consequently powerless at the time. Many more though were 'hommes d'affairs' who were really 'playing at being influential' (Watt, 1980, p. 109). Moreover, it is conceivable that the European federal movements' campaign might have encouraged or engendered attitudes and organisations opposed to European federation. Certainly in France two big parties, the Gaullist RPF on the right, and the communists on the left, were implacably hostile. In Britain 'ties of kinship with the Commonwealth, were obviously an important counter-influence' (Lipgens, 1982, p. 196).

Lipgens' attempt to attribute the phenomenon of European economic integration of the 1950s to the influence of the European federalist movements' campaign in the 1940s largely ignores the crucial experience of governments' failures in international policy-making in the 1920s and 1930s. The fact is that the late 1940s and 1950s were not the first time that a Franco-German economic rapprochement had been attempted or the problem of access to European raw materials tackled through international organisations. After World War I there was an attempt to maintain wartime allied co-operation in raw materials through a Supreme Economic Council, established in February 1919, which intended to try to ensure an adequate supply of raw materials for the devastated areas. This body was incapacitated by having too limited a remit and inadequate powers and authority to deal with the distribution of raw materials. In August 1919 a European Coal Commission was created to co-ordinate coal production and distribution in Europe but it too lacked sufficient authority (Aldcroft, 1977, pp. 60–61). A Franco-German rapprochement based on a bilateral agreement for coal and steel was developed by the French in the mid-1920s and led to the steel cartel and the short-lived Franco-German Commercial Treaty of August 1927 (McDougall, 1978, pp. 372–4). These and other attempts at international co-operation were wrecked ultimately by the world economic depression of 1929–33. This encouraged protectionism and economic nationalism, i.e. purely national attempts to solve what were international problems (the over-production of world agriculture, surplus capacity in industry, falling prices and export earnings for many countries, and world financial instability), all of which were only solvable through international co-operation.

A basic weakness of the international and European economy in the 1920s and 1930s was the failure to develop international policies which would be adhered to once agreed. The problem was that regulation and enforcement of policy was left almost entirely in national control.

So, as Aldcroft states, 'International efforts to promote reconstruction were woefully inadequate after the First World War, a lesson which was appreciated by the planners responsible for the same tasks after 1945' (Aldcroft, 1977, p. 63). The eventual emergence of schemes for European economic integration, starting significantly with coal and steel, must be seen in the context of the previous post-war experience of failure in the 1920s. Unsuccessful agreements in the 1920s, such as the short-lived Franco-German Commercial Treaty of 1927, demonstrated that something more authoritative, permanent and law-abiding had to be devised for commercial agreements post-1945. The eventual solution of a supranational Customs Union and common market for coal and steel had its origins (as the next chapter shows) in the deliberations of the European Customs Union Study Group 1947–49.

3 Conditions in Europe and American and British policies, 1945–49

Integration or co-operation?

Western Europe's political and economic position and military security looked precarious in 1945–47. Agricultural output in 1946–47 was only 75 per cent of the 1938 level; a UN Commission estimated in 1946 that 100 million Europeans lived on less than 1,500 calories per day (i.e. they were going hungry). In the UK, bread and potatoes were rationed from mid-1946 – not during the war itself – to enable supplies to be sent to the British Military Zone in Germany. In 1947, industrial production in Belgium, Netherlands and France was still 30–40 per cent lower than in 1939. European conditions were made worse in 1946–47 by a wet summer and a severe winter leading to poor harvests and a fuel crisis as snow disrupted coal supplies. There were massive shortages of fuel, food and industrial capital goods (Germany had been eliminated as the main pre-war supplier of the latter); this meant a large trading deficit with the US as the alternative supplier, and a dollar shortage.

Governments were faced with a severe fall in foreign trade (the UK's trade was only 70 per cent of the pre-war level in 1946–47) and were threatened with inflation (prices were driven up by shortages) and the need to increase exports well above pre-war levels. Nevertheless, despite such evidence, Western Europe's economic recovery from this austere state was already remarkably swift, assisted by Marshall Aid, which provided a marked increase in capital goods imports from the US between 1947–52. The recovery was sustained as a long boom through the 1950s and 1960s. Between 1948–50 annual sales of washing machines grew from 94,000 to 311,000 in the UK and from 20,000 to 100,000 in France. By 1950 Western Europe's foreign trade was already 20 per cent above pre-war levels and production was rising every year.

The political situation in post-war Europe was also potentially chaotic. Reinstated national governments (many of which spent 1940–45 in exile in London) were faced with danger from gunmen. The UK had armed communist and non-communist resistance forces in the war. Fifty thousand Sten guns had been dropped and, in wartime, killing military and political opponents was sanctioned, a habit which tended to persist into peacetime as old scores were settled. After liberating each state, the Western Allies tried to disarm the Resistance quickly to avoid the danger of reinstated authorities being overturned by communist or other gunmen in Western Europe, as occurred in Greece in 1944.

The Communist Party also increased its strength in Western Europe after the war (even though only 10 per cent of Resistance forces were communist) because of widespread sympathy for the USSR and its war effort between 1941 and 1944 (it lost between 20 and 40 million civilians and service personnel and killed 3 million German troops). Post-war governments in France, Belgium and Italy included Communist Party ministers up to 1947. Moscow's Cominform in 1947 meant that the USSR exercised control over Western Europe's Communist Parties which duly took Moscow's side in the Cold War. In 1947–48 numerous communist-led strikes in France, Italy and Britain (notably in the docks) were essentially protests against economic hardship and the high cost of living that were exploited by the Communist Parties and the USSR.

Liberation brought exaggerated hopes and expectations. This, combined with the political and economic disruption of the first 18 months of peace, created a dangerous situation. It was in this context that the USA's offer of Marshall Aid was made in 1947. As Ernest Bevin, the British Labour Government's Foreign Minister 1945–51, confessed, this offer seemed 'like a life-line to sinking men'.

The end of the war and the end of the common enemy meant the collapse of the wartime Grand Alliance of the 'Big Three'. The US had not abandoned its 'one world' efforts to reach agreement with the USSR over Germany, Eastern Europe and elsewhere and it reduced its troop strength in Western Europe very rapidly from 3.5 million in June 1945 to 200,000 by June 1947; even at the end of 1945 Britain had 488,000 stationed in Germany compared with 390,000 American troops. This showed that America had not accepted any permanent military commitment to European defence after 1945.

Many aspects of the wartime special relationship with Britain were quickly ended by President Truman in September 1945, including the Anglo-American administrative machinery such as the combined Chiefs of Staff Committee. The atomic partnership was also scrapped, despite being enshrined in the Quebec Agreement of August 1943 and the Hyde Park Memorandum of September 1944. Technical co-operation had ceased by April 1946 and the McMahon Act of August 1946 stopped any further exchanges of nuclear information. This setback meant that from January 1947 Britain started its own atomic weapons programme. As Bevin told the Cabinet Committee authorising it, 'We've got to have this thing over here, whatever it costs ... we've got to have the bloody Union Jack flying on top of it.'

The USA's swift withdrawal from Europe in 1945 took place as the USSR appeared menacing and remained in strength. This meant that Britain (Europe's only undefeated power) bore the main burden of European security against the USSR in the mid-1940s. This accounts for the renewed genuine enthusiasm between 1945 and 1948 for Western European co-operation and unity by the British government. To the Foreign Office, American policy and action over their European commitments in 1945 began to resemble the post-World War I experience. Then the US had reverted to a more isolationist position – like 'the great betrayal' of 1919–20 when it failed to join the League of Nations which it had largely created. The fact that American military assistance could not be relied upon meant that the Foreign Office's aspiration for a 'Western Bloc' was enthusiastically pursued by Bevin. Drawing Western European states together would enhance their mutual security and might also serve to strengthen the UK's world position vis-à-vis the US and the USSR by building up Britain as 'the great European power' (according to Sir Orme Sargent, Permanent Secretary at the Foreign Office, October 1945).

In 1946 Germany was still the principal security problem for the French, who feared a revanchist Germany. Bevin was instrumental in creating an Anglo-French peacetime alliance under the Treaty of Dunkirk on 4 March 1947.

In the absence of a firm permanent American commitment to European defence between 1945 and 1947, Bevin took the lead in creating a 'Western Bloc' for European security. Moreover, in doing this, he hoped to convince the Americans that Europeans were working closely together to defend themselves and that because of the threat from the militarily powerful USSR, the US should become directly involved in European defence. Bevin's objective in 1947–48 was to draw together the Western powers, including the US, into a political, economic and military bloc, with the US becoming directly involved in Western Europe's defence. Bevin played a significant role in precipitating a volte-face in US foreign policy with the Truman Doctrine and the announcement of Marshall Aid by declaring Britain's termination of military aid to Greece and Turkey.

To suggest that Bevin simply played up the Russian threat to get American financial aid is exaggerated. It is also wrong to think that containment was a policy hatched in Washington and imposed on a reluctant Europe in exchange for Dollar Aid. The initiative for containment really came from the UK. Foreign Office papers show the Labour government from 1945 pursuing a policy of firmer resistance towards the USSR than the capitalist US. Frazier (1984) sees it as an inspired stroke of statesmanship: 'Bevin's action in 1947 had to a significant extent been responsible for the Truman Doctrine and the policy of containment' (Frazier, 1984, pp. 725–26). Boyle (1982) argues that the Western response of the Truman Doctrine and Marshall Aid to the Soviet threat was

> neither a policy hatched in Washington and imposed on Europe nor a policy conceived in London which the US was lured into accepting. It was a policy towards which the US had been moving ... with more hesitation and vagaries than are sometimes appreciated. Britain played a role in drawing America towards such a policy.
>
> (Boyle, 1982, p. 389)

The details of containment were discussed and settled between the two states and with Canada and Western Europe.

The American Secretary of State, General George C. Marshall made his Harvard speech on 5 June 1947 in which he proposed a plan for the economic recovery of Europe. Bevin reported to Parliament on 19 June, 'When the Marshall proposals were announced, I grabbed them with both hands' (Kirby, 1977, pp. 96–97). Bevin's enthusiastic response and initiative made the US offer of aid a reality. Washington's aim was to use Dollar Aid as a lever to create a more economically and politically integrated Western Europe (but without clear plans for implementing this). By bringing the 'European Recovery Programme' (ERP) into existence Bevin played the leading role creating the 16-nation Committee of European Economic Co-operation (CEEC) Paris Conference in the summer of 1947, chaired by Sir Oliver Franks, to discuss the Marshall Aid programme. Out of this was created the Organization for European Economic Co-operation (OEEC), a year later in 1948, chaired by Sir Edmund Hall-Patch. Within the OEEC Britain conceived an inter-European payment scheme.

As early as 1946 Bevin had asked the Foreign Office to consider the possibility of an Anglo-French Customs Union that others might join later. During the CEEC discussions the Customs Union idea came to the fore. The British delegation proposed the establishment of a Customs Union Study Group (CUSG) to meet in Brussels, and so away from American pressure in Paris, to consider the whole question of a Western European Customs Union from 1947. In September 1947 at the TUC Conference Bevin envisaged a Customs Union with members retaining their Imperial Preferences.

By February 1948 Bevin and the Foreign Office 'had fully espoused the cause of a West European Customs Union'. On 22 January 1948 Bevin announced to Parliament in his 'Western Union speech' that 'We are thinking now of Western Europe as a unity ... we should do all we can to advance the spirit and machinery of cooperation' (House of Commons Debates, 23 January 1948, vol. 466, col. 397). Bevin and the Foreign Office saw the strong case for a Western European Customs Union lying in its political, military and strategic advantages. A closer association among Western European states was considered essential for security. To Bevin, a Customs Union was not just desirable but a necessary basis for a West European defensive alliance and was given a high foreign policy priority in order to halt 'the flow of the Communist tide'. The Foreign Office motives were purely political, while the UK's economic ministries flatly rejected the idea and so a divide existed between the perceived economic disadvantages and the political advantages.

The Board of Trade feared that the UK steel and chemicals industries would require permanent protection once the limits on the volume of German industrial production were removed. The Treasury was concerned as Britain's reserves were also the Sterling Area's reserves and should not be endangered in any way as this could jeopardise the UK's and the world's recovery. There was a deep suspicion of American policy designs and of their Customs Union idea as a means to attack the position of the City of London and grab its 'invisible business' for New York. However, Bevin was reluctant to abandon the idea of a Customs Union linked to Imperial Preferences (including the Empire and the Commonwealth trade) as a way to independence from the US in January 1948 (Milward, 1984, p. 245).

In the face of opposition from economic ministries in Britain, 'Bevin let the matter drop, overtaken as it was by the spread of alternative defence structures in the Brussels Pact and NATO' (Milward, 1982, pp. 550–51). As Milward says, in retrospect the UK's decision not to participate in the formation of the first proposed West European Customs Union in 1948 was 'a vital moment in British history when a wrong turning was taken ... and everyone involved was aware of being faced with a historical choice of great moment'.

The unanimous opinion of civil servants and those economists consulted was that a Customs Union would 'automatically lead to much closer forms of political union and necessarily to the wholesale harmonisation of economic policies in Europe which in 1945–47 varied enormously'. The UK's political and administrative elite saw the Customs Union idea as a major irreversible shift in policy. So the appeal of the status quo in 1948 seemed extremely comforting. This alternative option also looked more than sound as the UK still had semi-Great Power status with a global military spread, the Sterling Area and worldwide trade connections (Milward, 1982, p. 551; 1984, pp. 236–37). Bevin let the issue drop in the face of economic ministries' objections and because it appeared from available advice that a Customs Union would inevitably restrain the UK's freedom of action in other areas.

Bevin's notion of West European unity was eventually based on co-operation in interdependent organisations rather than unity through integration in supranational organisations. He had a vision of a 'trans-Atlantic Western Union' and this policy started to take shape when Britain, France and the Benelux countries signed the Brussels Treaty of economic, social and cultural collaboration and collective self-defence on 17 March 1948 (the Brussels Pact 1948), thereby creating the 'Western Union'. Bevin was interested in strategic issues here, economic arrangements to him were mainly for ancillary support. Under Article 4, a Western Union Defence Organization was established with Headquarters at Fontainebleau in September 1948 and Field Marshal Montgomery became first chairman of the Chiefs of Staff of the Western Union all of which symbolised Britain's new and strong commitment to the defence of Europe. However, this was a Europe of independent states co-operating together, not a federation.

Once the Brussels Pact was established, Bevin and the Foreign Office let the issue of a Customs Union drop from April 1948, although this was not announced until January 1949 as being official policy and discussions within the CUSG continued.

Bevin constantly pressed for greater US military commitment. The ultimate motive here was that once Britain had sorted out European defence and obtained a US commitment to Europe, it could then get on with its own affairs in the world. In this, Bevin was helped by the USSR's extremely inept foreign policy, such as the stage-managed Prague coup of February 1948, the USSR's pressure on Norway in March 1948 and the start of the blockade of West Berlin in June 1948 all of which served to accelerate American military commitments to Western Europe. US Senate Resolution 239 allowed the US government to become involved in 'collective arrangements for defence' in June 1948 and by July 1948, 60 American B29 atom bombers were operating from East Anglian airfields. The NATO Treaty signed on 4 April 1949 owed much to the work of Bevin and Sir Oliver Franks (the deus ex machina of British government administration in the 1940s and 1950s). For Bevin, the realisation of a vision of a transatlantic Western Union was his crowning foreign policy achievement. The UK's commitment to European defence was now encased in an expanded North Atlantic context more in keeping with Britain's maritime and global traditions.

NATO, in reality, until the outbreak of the Korean War in June 1950, was a 'paper treaty' as members were more concerned with their economic recovery than with rearmament.

The Americans in 1947 expected the UK to take the lead in organising Europe and to bring it to political and economic unity. Bevin accomplished this in his own way through the Brussels Pact. Such co-operation fell short of the vague American objective of a Customs Union and Federation. Bevin seriously considered creating a Customs Union including the British Empire between 1947 and 1948 mainly for strategic purposes. He was motivated to do this and take the lead in Europe given the absence of any permanent American commitment to European defence between 1945 and 1949. The British were criticised for not doing more to create European unity, supposedly denying the Council of Europe in 1949 and also the OEEC supranational authority. British officials saw this accusation as 'a great injustice', given Britain's initiative in establishing the OEEC, Brussels Pact and NATO. As Edwin Playfair, a Treasury official wrote, 'In the OEEC, the easiest alibi … is to put forward a resolution that the moon be dragged out of the sea with nets and say the British blocked it' (Boyle, 1982, p. 383).

As far as Britain was concerned its only acknowledged 'fault' was that it did not immediately and unthinkingly accept the more grandiose schemes for European union, especially some of the 'wilder American bright ideas'.

With the return of Churchill's Conservative government to power in 1951–55, European-minded ministers and MPs ('Tory Strasbourgers') portrayed Bevin and the Labour government as 'anti-European'. This was not in fact the case at all between 1945 and 1949; it was simply that Bevin's prescriptions and designs were ultimately based upon co-operation – interdependent organisations rather than supranational bodies that the US wanted and which the French between 1948–49 were coming to see as essential. The difference between French and British policies on Europe were determined by their different national interests. For France, European interests were their top priority (the German problem dominated attention). For the UK, by 1948–49,

European issues were not the foremost concern. Britain's global economic and military interests took precedence (Young, 1984, pp. x, 180–6) because, by 1949, the US commitment to NATO meant that Europe was more secure from the USSR and that Britain was not the only power shouldering the burden of containing it and organising European defence and co-operation.

Besides, Britain's foreign policy largely followed her economic interests and only 25 per cent of Britain's trade was with Europe in the 1950s which was actually lower than in the 1930s.

In fact, the period 1948–49 – rather like 1940 – was a pivotal moment in British and French history regarding the formulation of their respective European policies. A major rethink in Britain's policy towards Europe was conducted in Whitehall on 5 January 1949 which finally rejected the Customs Union idea, the Foreign Office coming round to the Treasury and Board of Trade's point of view. The US realised from then on that the UK could not be dragooned into economic integration with Europe. This Whitehall meeting decided that within the Atlantic Pact 'we hope to secure a special relationship with the US and Canada ... economic recovery depends not on structural reforms such as federation but on American aid'. The criterion for Britain's continental commitment by October 1949 was 'limited liability' (the same slogan as was used by military planners in the 1930s). What this meant was that Britain was prepared to assist European recovery but at the same time would be careful that such assistance would not weaken Britain so it ceased to be a worthwhile ally to America, should Europe ever collapse. The Treasury and Foreign Office clearly stated that Britain's ties with America and the Commonwealth 'take priority over our relations with Europe' (Reynolds, 1988, p. 235; Young, 1984, pp. 127–31).

The fact that France was politically and economically weak in 1949 whilst the US had renewed its association with Europe through Marshall Aid and NATO meant that an unprecedented peacetime alliance was forming. Dean Acheson, US Secretary of State, described this period of Cold War diplomacy as 'being present at the creation'.

Meanwhile France, having involved itself in the CUSG, saw a Customs Union from the summer of 1948 as the way forward for the reconstruction of Western Europe, especially as a West German state began to re-emerge and German economic recovery commenced during 1947–48 (although more slowly than its neighbours).

According to Milward, 1949 was also a watershed commercially and economically. In 1948 only Britain and Switzerland had higher exports than in 1938. In 1946 Britain's total value of foreign trade was 45 per cent of Western Europe's as a whole and even in 1950 it was still 33 per cent, yet Britain had balance of payments crises and experienced devaluations in 1947 and 1949. In 1949 the long-expected post-war American recession occurred (just as the experience after World War I was a restocking boom, 1919–20, followed by a severe economic collapse in 1920–21). In fact, the US recession was very mild and short-lived. US exports were maintained by the policies of Marshall Aid and rearmament. Nevertheless, the US recession caused a fall in American imports from the rest of the world. The British economy was the main casualty, Britain's dollar earnings were hit and the dollar position of the Sterling Area reserves was damaged by the US recession. Britain's worldwide exports were adversely affected, causing a balance of payments crisis that in turn led to a sterling crisis and a 30 per cent devaluation of sterling against the dollar on 18 September 1949.

Significantly, Western Europe was not adversely affected by the American recession. Western Europe's export boom continued. It was insulated from the US recession of 1948–49 because of the timing of the West German economic recovery which sucked in imports from France, Holland and Belgium and caused export-led growth in Western Europe which continued to dominate the 1950s boom. Britain's exports stagnated relative to Europe's because of its geographical distribution of exports, concentrated in the slow-growing Commonwealth markets. The UK was already excluding itself from the benefits of dynamic West European trade. Although French output stagnated in 1949, her exports increased considerably, according to Milward's research, because of West Germany's growth and this convinced the French that a more liberal trade framework was useful.

Whereas Britain's exports to 'Little Europe' increased by 38 per cent between 1948 and 1950, the exports of these six states to each other increased by 90 per cent (Milward, 1984, pp. 337–39). This showed the weakness of Britain's position for the future, in the 1950s and 1960s. Britain's distribution of exports was ignoring the fastest-growing market of Western Europe and focusing on South Africa and the Commonwealth which were growing more slowly and were more susceptible to volatile fluctuations in the American economy and, in the case of Australia and New Zealand, they introduced import substitution policies to foster their own industries, so curbing British exports.

The 1949 crisis showed the potential health of Western Europe's market and trading system compared with Britain's position. Until 1949 the Labour government, as Milward shows, could have reconstructed Europe its way with a Customs Union including Imperial Preference but they turned away from that to 'limited liability' on Europe and renewing the 'special relationship'.

Milward argues that the movement of foreign trade in Western Europe 1949–50 produced a radical alteration in the scope for political action there. It weakened Britain's position and influence and strengthened that of France. For France in 1947, forming a Customs Union in Europe without Britain was inconceivable and even dangerous. However, with the emergence of the Federal Republic of Germany in May 1948 as both a political entity and a reviving economy – with a boom in German trade in 1949 – a Customs Union was now seen by France and also Holland (even without UK participation) as realistic and essential. Previously, industrial production was strictly controlled by the Western Allies and West Germany was not in the OEEC. West Germany's rapid economic recovery in 1949–50 meant an expanding export market for its neighbours – principally Holland and France. French industrial output in fact stagnated in 1949 – the domestic economy was not expanding – yet French exports to the FRG continued to grow vigorously. For the Dutch and the French, a Customs Union appeared a political and economic necessity in 1948–49.

The British Foreign Office wrongly assumed in 1949 that a Customs Union without Britain was unlikely to emerge, in fact, the reverse was probably true, as it was arguably easier to negotiate and arrange with Britain absent in 1950.

The US in 1949 abandoned any hope that the UK would take the lead in integrating Europe. This gave France her opportunity to create an international framework for European reconstruction that suited French interests and was acceptable to other West European states, rather than reflecting American wishes. The US vision was of a large liberal free-trade unified Europe of the 16 OEEC countries, whereas the emerging French scheme of 1949–50 was of a small, closely regulated market – a 'Little Europe' of six states. As in the 1920s, coal and steel remained the central issue in reconstructing Franco-German economic and political relations – the Customs Union and common market in coal and steel of the Schuman Plan June 1950 was the outcome. The route to this scheme was via discussions in the CUSG between 1947 and 1949 with France seriously considering the Customs Union solution to its 'German problem' from the summer of 1948 – as the FRG began to emerge after the London Conference in July 1948. The three military governments of the Western Zone of Germany handed over the 'Frankfurt Documents' to the Minister – Presidents of 11 West German Lander, calling for a constituent assembly and a parliamentary council. In May 1949 the 'Basic Law' (the FRG'S constitution) was decreed and ratified and on 21 September 1949 the three military governments of the Western Zones – British, American and French – handed over the 'Occupation Statutes' granting West Germany full legal, executive and judicial powers (though not over foreign policy or defence matters until later in 1955). In this way, West Germany's capacity for self-government was created and its sovereignty granted in stages. The first Bundestag elections were held on 14 August 1949, Konrad Adenauer was elected as the first Federal-Chancellor on 20 September 1949 and on 28 October 1949 the FRG was admitted to the OEEC (the exception to the rule that the FRG could not control its own foreign affairs).

September 1948 to September 1949 was a 'turning point', as so much was changing in these 12 months. There were many elements that coincided: the Berlin airlift, the formation of NATO and the American military commitment to Europe, the Cold War and the consequent complete division of Europe into East–West Blocs ('two big dogs chewing on a bone' as US Senator Fulbright described it), the re-emergence of the West German state, the sterling crisis of 1949 and the Whitehall policy rethink in January 1949, a policy which continued with Churchill's government in 1951–55. The West German economic recovery in 1949 focused French attention and converted the Netherlands to a 'French style' regulated Customs Union solution for

Germany The US gave up the idea of the OEEC path to integrating Europe in 1949 and abandoned the idea that the UK was going to lead the way to an integrated Europe. The US saw the UK more as an ally in financial trouble, rather than a trading rival. Moreover, with the UK's global military and economic commitments, Britain was an essential junior partner in the US containment of Soviet communism.

Britain had long enjoyed an ambivalent relationship with both the US and Western Europe. Despite ties of language, culture and people, the UK and US were locked into a *'competitive cooperation'* (Reynolds, 1980, pp. 233–45). When faced with a dangerous common threat (as with Hitler's Germany 1939–45 and Stalin's USSR post-1948) a 'special relationship' developed. This was a deliberate act of policy by the UK from January 1949 and relations became very close as the UK and her Commonwealth were vital to the Cold War containment of the USSR. In fact, the UK was not really treated as a foreign country by the US State Department by the early 1950s. Acheson, US Secretary of State, and UK Ambassador Franks, had weekly, two-hour, wide-ranging conversations.

The UK's foreign relations towards Europe had traditionally followed the 'balance of power' doctrine: namely, the weight of diplomacy was thrown against any new European power bloc (whether Napoleon I, Napoleon III, Tsarist Russia, the Kaiser, Hitler, the USSR, or even arguably the EEC 1956–60 – because of the threat of a Franco-German 'superstate'). However, given the absence of a US military defence commitment to Europe in the immediate post-war years (1945–48), the UK – primarily for strategic reasons – was forced to take the lead in organising collective defence and other co-operative measures to reinforce this (such as exploring the Customs Union idea). So the hiatus of US commitment meant that the UK became more 'European' in its approach during 1945–48. Once the US was committed to European recovery and defence, the UK was able to revert to a policy of 'limited liability' and a more 'semi-detached' position by 1949 – European integration should not be encouraged as the US could leave if it was effective. The British Foreign Office arguably took far too short-term a view – it did not try to look 10–15 years ahead. It lacked vision and long-term objectives and practised 'shop-keeper' or 'mercantile' diplomacy (as opposed to Robert Schuman's bold 'heroic diplomacy'). This meant simply dealing with things as they turned up, not thinking about the future; it meant compromise via negotiation and fair dealing between rivals, not beating them (Schlain et al., 1977, p. 89). The UK was mainly preoccupied by its global military/trade relations, decolonisation and relations with the newly independent states.

What motivated US policy on Europe with Marshall Aid from 1947? Marshall Aid was motivated by America's fear of Europe's impending collapse, economically and then politically. The hard winter of 1947 interrupted British production of steel, coal and manufactured goods. In France agricultural production suffered as wheat was killed by a hard winter followed by spring floods and drought in summer. American reports in 1947 on the state of Europe were extremely pessimistic. The US feared that this would produce a windfall political gain for the USSR's influence (via support for the Communist Party in Europe) and also an economic slump in the US, as its exports to Europe would suffer. The 'Cleveland–Moore–Kindleberger' Memorandum of 12 June 1947 on the ERP emphasised that: 'the heart of the European problem is inadequate production' (Kindleberger, 1987, p. 9). In fact, although conditions were chaotic and economic and political systems weakened post-war, recovery (though only post-1947 in West Germany) was under way from 1945. To Americans, Europe, with its visible austerity, was very poor compared with the US – per capita income was lower in 1946 than in 1938 whereas the USA's had risen by 25 per cent.

Post-war Europe suffered from an acute dollar shortage and the USA's fear in spring 1947 was that European recovery might stop because of a lack of dollars, and given that US industrial capacity had grown so much because of its World War II expansion (as the 'arsenal for democracy') that US output and employment would suffer badly (US industrial labour force grew from 10 million to 17 million in 1940–44). Europe's balance of payments deficit was rising rapidly from \$5.8bn in 1946 to \$7.5bn in 1947 as compared with an approximate balance in 1938. Paradoxically, this was both problematic but also a clear sign of European economic recovery. Germany had traditionally been Western Europe's main supplier of capital goods exports (machinery and vehicles); with the defeat and military occupation of Germany it was eliminated as a supplier. The US remained the only large alternative source of capital goods for Western Europe given that the UK concentrated on trade with the Commonwealth and Sterling Area.

The wide US trade surplus in 1947 – exporting \$16bn goods, importing only \$8bn goods – meant that Europe found it very hard to earn dollars via exports. The US was largely self-sufficient with a high tariff wall and in fact Europe had little to sell to the US and little it needed, while its own demands for American goods were enormous.

However, apart from preventing the possible collapse of Europe, there were two further policy objectives behind Marshall Aid. The US saw it as a means to restore a world economic system that fitted American ideals of multilateral trade (as opposed to bilateral trade – i.e. balancing trade between two states) and full convertibility of currencies (i.e. buying dollars with pounds or francs freely and without limit). This was the international system that completely broke down in 1929–32 and had not been restored by 1947–48. If currencies were freely convertible again, it would facilitate the buying of goods from anywhere. France, Belgium, the Netherlands and Britain were the centres of currency areas that extended into Asia and Africa (because of their colonial territories). Interconvertibility of these European currencies with each other and ultimately with dollars would automatically lead to a freer world trade and exchange system throughout the non-Soviet world. For the US, Britain and the Sterling Area was the vital component to achieving inter-currency convertibility and multilateralism as 50 per cent of the world's trade was conducted with pounds sterling in the late 1940s.

During World War II the UK had created a Sterling Area, a system of strict exchange and import controls and bilateral payments. There were agreements for Imperial and Commonwealth trading preferences (e.g. in 1933 the Australian duty on whiskey was £2.36 per gallon and the preference £0.36). London was the centre for members' sterling balances operating a Sterling Area 'dollar pool' because of the dollar shortages. The UK regarded the Sterling Area as essential to the country's recovery and maintaining sterling's status as a world currency and London as the world's financial centre. The US did not like this as it meant that the UK could buy, using sterling, from those to whom it could sell. The Sterling Area and system of Commonwealth and Imperial preferences meant Britain effectively had its own closed multilateral system. The US Treasury and State Department wanted a multilateral non-discriminatory international economy. From 1941 US and British officials – notably the UK economist John Maynard Keynes and US Harry White tried to find common ground for a joint post-war policy. However, due to the growing imbalance in their respective powers, Britain had to accept the American plan in the Bretton Woods Agreement. Also, the US only agreed to a $3.75bn loan to Britain in 1945 on condition Britain accepted and agreed to the convertibility of pounds and dollars. This would then mean that 75 per cent of world trade was conducted in convertible currency.

Sterling–dollar convertibility would lead to an international trade and payments system of fixed exchange rates (reversing the 1930s scenario) backed up by the International Monetary Fund (IMF) and GATT. At the core of the Bretton Woods US plan was a gold backed dollar as the world's leading currency, with the main institutions – the IMF and the World Bank – located in the US. The clear intention of the US Treasury (and the fear of their UK counterparts) was to shift the locus of economic and financial power to New York away from London.

When convertibility was introduced between sterling and dollars in July 1947, controls had to be reimposed almost immediately in August 1947 (it almost exhausted the $3.75bn credit) as other European states (notably France and Belgium) cashed sterling for dollars and boosted their exports to the UK to earn even more dollars.

The US realised that the sterling crisis and the European dollar shortage were linked. The US Treasury and State Department saw Marshall Aid as a way of fostering European recovery and so fulfilling the Bretton Woods objectives. Milward shows that the 1944 'Bretton Woods system' never had much relevance as a mechanism for European reconstruction – full convertibility was only achieved in 1958 (and the system collapsed in 1971 when the automatic convertibility of dollars to gold ended). Meanwhile, in Western Europe, the European Payments Union was established in 1950 and the ECSC in 1951 (Newton, 1984, pp. 391–93; Milward, 1984, pp. 43–45). It was an illusion that ERP was a step towards the Bretton Woods objectives. The

US had hoped that by closing the dollar gap between America and Europe the Bretton Woods principles would become established (Newton, 1984, pp. 401–7; Milward, 1984, p. 476).

The final but by no means least significant American motive for Marshall Aid or the ERP was that it aimed to use the lure of $22bn of aid 1948–52 to try rather overambitiously to achieve the total political reconstruction of Western Europe, and not simply its recovery. Ernest Bevin and Georges Bidault sent invitations for the ERP Conference in July 1947 to Eastern Europe as well as to the 16 Western European countries. Poland asked the USSR whether they could accept and were told to reject it. Czechoslovakia simply accepted. Jan Masaryk (the Czech Foreign Minister) was summoned to see Stalin in Moscow and ordered to withdraw. A few months later in March 1948 the Czechoslovakian government was overthrown by a communist coup and Masaryk was killed (he was thrown out of a window). These tragic events played a large part in stimulating the US Congress to pass Marshall Aid into law as the Economic Co-operation Act of 1948.

The USSR's satellites could have been allowed to accept Marshall Aid and then have disrupted the whole scheme from within. Why did they not try to do this? C.P. Kindleberger, Chief of the US State Department's German-Austrian Economic Affairs Group, thinks it was the Soviet fear of contamination from exposure to Western ideas and artefacts (Kindleberger, 1983).

The US wanted to see the economic integration of Western Europe into one common economic regional bloc within the lifespan of the ERP and ultimately into a common political area. The US aimed to sweep away the nation-state system and pressure the 16 OEEC states to integrate into a 'free trade Customs Union'. Such a merger would lead to a 'United States of Europe' including part of Germany (Milward, 1984, p. 467). A cohesive integrated European economic bloc, immune from the economic nationalism and protectionism of the 1930s, would safely accommodate a new West German state and its economic recovery. The US vision of an economically integrated Europe of the 16 OEEC states was a liberal, free-trade, all-embracing common market (rather similar to the vision of Euro-federalists). Enormous pressure was exerted by the US on Britain to take the lead in this integration process, and on France and the other states involved. British officials believed they were being harried constantly by the Americans to bring about European unity. Britain felt that US ideas on Europe were hastily devised and rather ill-conceived. Moreover, given that only 25 per cent of the UK's trade was with Europe, Britain's dollar shortage was dependent on the rest of the world (not Europe) getting dollars. Britain and Europe saw the problem as having insufficient dollars to continue recovery. The US saw the problem as one of insufficient production (Milward, 1982, p. 510).

The CEEC, the large conference of Western European participants in the ERP, met in Paris in the summer of 1947 in response to the offer of Marshall Aid. The US hoped that this would be the first stage in a process of integration as the 16 participant states had to draw up a plan for European recovery acceptable to the US Administration and to the US Congress (which eventually approved it by large majorities in March 1948). The US saw the formation of a Customs Union as central to Europe's ability to co-operate and the willingness of Britain particularly to integrate into Western Europe. However, as Milward points out, the CEEC did not lay the foundations of European co-operation, much less integration; rather, it revealed the disagreements between states and the wide gap between Western European and American views.

The fact that the Conference did not produce the results expected in Washington, with a quick early move to integration, meant 'the heaviest diplomatic pressures were brought to bear on the CEEC' and blame was laid at the door of the British and French (Newton, 1984, p. 395; Milward, 1982, p. 514; 1984, p. 467). Milward shows that French policy towards Germany pre-summer 1948 was partition, dismemberment and permanent weakening, whereas the UK–US policy was *Bizone* (the economic fusion of the two zones) in order to foster the gradual controlled economic and political revival of a smaller German state. This basic difference meant that little could really be decided about European integration or even economic co-operation inside the CEEC or OEEC. Nothing could be decided on a permanent European framework for reconstruction (such as the form of a Customs Union), as far as France was concerned until the 'German question' had been answered.

Determined pressure from the US led to the UK suggesting the formation of the CUSG in 1947 through the CEEC. This met in Brussels rather than Paris, away from American interference, and was an attempt by Britain, France et al. to explore possible European designs for a smaller West European Customs Union. It was through this route of CUSG discussions that the shape and form of the first European Community eventually emerged in the Franco-German association of the Schuman Plan. As Milward shows, the CUSG was a much more significant step towards the formation of the European Community than the CEEC, OEEC or EPU.

Such was the diplomatic pressure on Britain in 1948 from the US that the Departmental Under-Secretary of State, Roger Makins, noted in July 1948 that the UK's 'inability to find policies sufficiently spectacular to influence Congress' might mean the UK having to 'take a plunge' and 'rash action in the last resort' of setting up a Customs Union. Other Foreign Office officials considered establishing 'a sham Customs Union' as a sop to American pressure (Boyle, 1982, p. 382).

The CEEC was superseded eventually by the OEEC a year later in 1948 – a standing conference that eventually developed into a bureaucracy of 1,000 people. The US policy was to try to mould the OEEC Council as a prototype Western European Federal Government and a first step to building a United States of Europe. Part of the US strategy was to make the OEEC itself allocate ERP funds. However, although the OEEC was supposed to divide up US aid and so in the process foster an integrated European organisation, according to Milward it only ever produced a 'scramble for dollars' by the member states and was never a real forum for European co-operation, let alone integration (16 countries' interests and views were too diverse).

In 1949 the US wanted the OEEC to have a Director-General with real executive supranational powers (referred to as 'Superman' in UK Foreign Office documents!). The US conspired with Belgium to get Paul-Henri Spaak (the ex-Prime Minister, who was out of office in August 1949) into this post. Although it was Britain that vetoed this move – to the fury of the Americans – the Scandinavians, Dutch and French were just as opposed.

Following this the US abandoned both the attempts to get the OEEC to allocate and distribute ERP funds and any hope that the policy machinery of the OEEC could somehow be transformed via constitutional change into an integrated supranational political organisation for Western Europe (Milward, 1984, p. 206).

The US also finally saw that the UK could not be forced into European integration. However, the US did not abandon its central goal of European integration. It simply pursued a different track towards a European Customs Union by creating a single large market through trade liberalisation in Europe and the abolition of administrative and legal protective barriers to trade between West European states (where tariffs, quotas, quantity restrictions proliferated). Paul Hoffman, the US Administrator of the Marshall Aid Programme, elaborated this in Autumn 1949: 'the substance of such integration would be the formation of a large single market within which quantitative restrictions on the movements of goods, monetary barriers to the flow of payments and, eventually, all tariffs are permanently swept away'.

To sweep away monetary barriers to the flow of payments and foster the US Bretton Woods objective of one trade and payments system for the Western (non-Soviet) world the US promoted the European Payments Union (EPU) Treaty. This was signed on 19 September 1950 (the negotiations were only concluded after the outbreak of the Korean War). The EPU aid did much to encourage and facilitate intra-European trade from 1950 and was the first European organisation which incorporated the FRG. The Americans again hoped that the EPU machinery would provide a functional basis for European integration and lead to monetary union in Europe. In this they were to be disappointed. The US was insistent on full convertibility but the UK's priority was to defend sterling against the threat of convertibility Britain was not keen on the automatic clearing of all multilateral settlements in Europe (when pound–dollar convertibility was tried three years before in July 1947, Belgium's conversion of sterling balances into dollars had caused a run on the pound). The US therefore had to settle in the EPU for a more limited form of multilateralism, having to continue dollar aid to make this possible and face continued discrimination against US goods through the 1950s in Western Europe (Milward, 1984, pp. 326, 333).

The UK was in a strong bargaining position for two reasons. Britain could always threaten to withdraw into the Sterling Area (the 'siege economy' option). This was effectively Britain's own 'multilateral' Imperial trade system based on the pound. Inside dollars were unnecessary. However, this would have divided the world into two payments systems (US hard, UK soft), i.e. the very opposite of the American idea behind the Bretton Woods 'one world' approach. Also, the 1949 sterling crisis and devaluation saw the UK dollar reserves drop to danger level again and made the UK more resistant to the US policy. The US had to give way to the UK inside the EPU.

American Marshall Aid was important for maintaining capital goods imports into Europe, so sustaining European economic recovery by a high rate of capital formation in the late 1940s. Between 1946–53 West Germany got $3.6bn, most of it before the end of 1950. What Marshall Aid did, according to Kindleberger, was to restock warehouse shelves and the component bins of factories. Inventories were well below minimum levels in Germany in 1947 in everything except scrap metal (Kindleberger, 1987, pp. 194–96). Marshall Aid 'restocked all Europe', although Kindleberger thinks the effect of Marshall Aid on the economic recovery was exaggerated by the severe winter of 1947 and good harvest of 1948 (Kindleberger, 1987, pp. 102–3).

The ERP had less success with its other connected objectives of facilitating the US vision for a Bretton Woods system, which was a multilateral trading world with fixed exchange rates and full currency convertibility, and a United States of Europe with 16 states creating a federation with a free-trade, liberal Customs Union at its core. Indeed, as Milward has shown, it was doubtful whether these were compatible objectives, i.e. whether the ERP could have been a step towards a return to Bretton Woods. From 1949 the American administration of ERP and the whole programme was actually under attack in Washington for impeding the solution to a world trade and payments system (Milward, 1984, p. 476).

The combination of $22bn in aid and relentless diplomatic pressure from the US was not enough to impose their own framework for European reconstruction. Why were the Americans unsuccessful in imposing their solution and how were they thwarted? While the EPU in 1950 and the ECSC in 1950–51 were the result of US pressure for integration, to a greater extent they reflected the national interests and wishes of Britain and France. These two states, although unable to ignore US pressure, were capable of blocking American designs for Western Europe to integrate through the OEEC framework even when the US had successfully allied itself with small countries (like Belgium – often seen in London as the tool of US policy in Europe). American policy from 1947 was to create a large all-embracing free-trade common market in Europe. Why did France oppose this?

In the first place it could not satisfy the first requirement of French foreign policy – a solution to the German question. French policy towards Germany until the summer of 1948 was to see it permanently weakened and dismembered, with the Ruhr made an autonomous zone under international control with its resources available for French and Benelux exploitation.

French insistence on this led ultimately to the compromise of an International Ruhr Authority being established in 1948. Anglo-American policy on the other hand was to merge their two German zones economically (*Bizonia*) and gradually revive the German economy. This difference in policy and the fact that no firm decisions had been taken towards the future Germany by the four occupying powers (UK, US, USSR, France) meant that there was no prospect of France agreeing to join any Customs Union without an answer to the German question. Two events compelled France to rethink. The first was currency reform in the Western Zones on 20 June 1948 based on the recommendations of the Colm–Dodge–Goldsmith Report of a 10:1 conversion of Reichmarks to Deutschmarks. This shrank the money supply to a point where they were able to abandon price control, restore the incentive to work, buy goods in the open market and end hoarding and the black market (Kindleberger, 1987, p. 102). The other was the London Conference of July 1948 where the process of reconstructing a West German state commenced.

France then started seriously to envisage a new Franco-German economic association and to explore within the CUSG the possibility of a 'Little Europe' Customs Union, not the 'Big Europe' of 16 states that the US preferred.

The second reason for the lack of US success was that even after this shift in French policy towards Germany the American conception of a Western Europe Customs Union as 'Big Europe' was at variance with the French concept of a 'Little Europe' that was evolving in 1948–50 as a small, closely regulated common market. The French knew that despite the 1946 Monnet Plan their economy was not yet sufficiently competitive and their economic recovery would suffer in a big, liberal free-trade Customs Union. In the French-style dirigiste Common Market there was an attempt to anticipate the consequences and, through negotiation, to control and distribute gains and losses in advance, i.e. actually direct and apportion the economic consequences of a common market before it came into effect. If accurate this process should safeguard members' national interests and so 'guarantee' the success of the Customs Union by ensuring 'fair' trade rather than purely 'free' trade. This was far from the US conception of a liberal free-trade Customs Union, which for the French represented far too great a gamble. France's Schuman Plan of 1950, however, appeared to be a solution both to the German question and for ensuring French modernisation and economic recovery within an integrated organisation.

In the case of EPU, the US was forced to accede to British vested interests and requirements and in the ECSC to those of France (Milward, 1984, p. 333). This was perhaps inescapable as the US had little alternative for reaching their dream or implementing their vision other than by persuading West Europeans to adopt it for themselves. (The USSR in contrast imposed their political and economic vision of central planning and a command economy on Eastern Europe.) European integration in 1947 was considered impossible without France and Britain; in 1949 it was still inconceivable without France.

By then the UK had reverted to 'limited liability', turning its back economically on Europe and focusing on the Sterling Area and Commonwealth. This was ironic given US policy on Europe and the importance of the special relationship to Britain. France then had the chance to create a French-style Little Europe to suit her interests, which in 1948–49 became a more urgent matter with the gradual emergence of a reconstituted West German state.

Nevertheless by 1950, as Milward's meticulous painstaking research demonstrates, the twin pillars of the EPU and ECSC were the start of a reconstructed framework for Western Europe – the new architecture successfully incorporated the newborn West German state with a booming economy (Milward, 1984, p. 367, Table 51; its steel output was 2.72m tonnes 1946, 11.93m tonnes 1950). In this the US was entitled to take much credit because, as Kindleberger argues, without Marshall Aid it would have taken West Germany a long time to refill its empty raw material bins (Kindleberger, 1987, p. 261). The US also encouraged European integration with a clumsy yet vigorous persistence through any available channel and brought a West German state into existence, as a by-product of its Cold War rivalry with the USSR, 1948–49.

The route to the Schuman Plan of 1950 leading to the ECSC in 1951 can be traced back to the advent of Marshall Aid and the CEEC in Paris, July 1947. Britain's CEEC delegation suggested setting up the CUSG in September 1947 based in Brussels. It was within this body's discussions that many ideas embodied in the Schuman Plan were incubating between 1948 and 1950.

When some selected German politicians from the Bizone were first told, in October 1948, of the possibility of creating a Customs Union incorporating West Germany they were 'barely restrained from making an immediate demand for the adoption of a Customs Union at once' (Milward, 1984, p. 250). Such was their desperation to embark on the political rehabilitation of their new country's old reputation with its neighbours.

Part II
Development

4 The Schuman Plan (1950) and the European Coal and Steel Community (1951)

On 9 May 1950 Robert Schuman, the French Foreign Minister 1948–52, made his surprise announcement proposing the pooling of coal and steel production. Following protracted negotiations, the Treaty of Paris was signed by 'the Six' on 19 March 1951, which established the supranational European Coal and Steel Community (ECSC). This created a common market for coal, steel, coke, iron ore and scrap between France, Germany, Belgium, the Netherlands, Luxembourg and Italy. Britain declined to participate in the talks from the outset.

The fact that coal and steel were the first economic sectors to be incorporated into an integrated organisation is acknowledgement of their central importance to nation states' economic and military power. Coal and steel had provided both the military capacity for invasion as well as being a motive for German and French territorial acquisition. Alsace-Lorraine, a French province, and its iron ore deposits changed hands between France and Germany in 1871, 1918, 1940 and 1945. The Saar, a German district rich in coal, was administered by the League of Nations, 1919–35, with its mines controlled by the French to compensate for German damage to French coalmines in the World War I. Following World War II the French again ran the Saarland for its coal between 1945–57. (Plebiscites in 1935 and 1957 resulted in Saarlanders opting to rejoin Germany.) Robert Schuman himself came from the disputed territory of Alsace. He fought in the German army in 1914–18, had German as his first language and only became a French citizen in 1919.

Germany had big reserves of coking coal (used in steel production), whereas France, not being well endowed geologically with coal, depended on German coal supplies. Geology, economics and foreign policy became inevitably and tragically intertwined – it was a significant component of Franco-German relations and rivalry. In January 1923 French and Belgian troops had occupied the coal-producing Ruhr Basin as Germany failed to pay its quota of war reparations (under the terms of the Treaty of Versailles 1919). There was a precedent here as, following defeat in the Franco-Prussian War 1870, France had to pay a five billion franc indemnity in 1871 to Germany whose army remained in France until it was paid. During World War II, under German occupation 75 per cent of French iron ore production and 15 per cent of French coal output was compulsorily exported to Germany. In 1944 this traffic accounted for 85 per cent of all rail movements in France.

At the end of the war in 1945 it was assumed by West European states, occupied by Germany between 1940–44, that their access to German coal and markets would be safeguarded and German steel output heavily restricted. Steel was the major element in states' post-war economic reconstruction (needed for railways, buildings, ships, vehicles, machinery). After the war, Norway and the Netherlands started their own steel industries for the first time. The demand for steel was high and there was a shortage of raw material inputs.

After the war German steel production was restricted by the Allied Coal and Steel Control Boards and military governments, whereas in 1938 German steel output amounted to 38 per cent of Europe's total, by 1949 it was 18 per cent (Milward, 1984, p. 371). The Petersburg Protocols imposed limits on German shipyard capacity, ship size and speed (controls which lasted until 1952) and German steel plants came under the statutory authority of US and UK military governments. The production limit for steel was 7.5m tonnes in 1946. Dismantling of many listed German steel works – Herman Goering works at Salzgitter, Krupps at Essen and Thyssens at Hambourn – continued in French and British zones until 1949. German coal and steel industries were both 'decartelised' (the six biggest steel companies were broken into 24 smaller ones) and 'deconcentrated' – in 1944 33 per cent of coal production in Germany was controlled by steel companies, by 1947 it was 16 per cent (Milward, 1984, pp. 369, 371, 384–86, 411).

In France the Monnet Plan for the Modernization and Re-equipment of the French Economy that started in March 1946 was intended eventually to make the French economy internationally competitive and, following the 'lesson of 1940' to reverse the technological inferiority of the French economy. In 1946 France had 0.5 million machine tools, many of which were 20 years old, whereas Germany had 1.5 million, which were more modern. The success of the Monnet Plan, intended to rectify such relative technological weakness, depended on three conditions being met. The first, according to Frances Lynch, was France getting priority access to the Ruhr's resources of coal and coke, that is, priority over Germany for the Ruhr's coal. The second was that French industry must recover and reconstruct before Germany's economy revived, as German industry had lower production costs (16 per cent lower in the case of steel making). Finally, the Monnet Plan aimed to replace German goods in both Germany and her export markets with French goods (Lynch, 1984, pp. 233, 235, 239).

Therefore, as Lynch shows, the Monnet Plan for the modernisation of the French economy was originally based on 'the traditional view that French political and economic strength lay in German weakness' (Lynch, 1984, p. 242). The best guarantee of French security, peace and avoiding a fourth German invasion was not the reassurance of the protection of France by her allies via guarantees in treaties, but by limiting German capacity for steel production and expanding French steel and heavy industry through access both to German coking coal resources and German markets. French foreign policy towards Germany clearly reflected these French national economic interests enshrined in the Monnet Plan – the permanent dismemberment of the German state, the Ruhr being made an International Zone separate from Germany; and the dismantling, deconcentration and decartelisation of the German steel industry.

The problem for France was that this policy proved unacceptable to the Americans and British: it would mean that the US would have to pay continually to keep German steel-making capacity under-utilised and German labour idle to the detriment of the European Recovery Programme as a whole. While it was US policy in 1945 to limit expenditure on Germany (under directive JCS1067) to the avoidance of 'disease and unrest', this formula was abandoned with the Cold War and Marshall Aid. The Western Zones of Germany received $3.6bn in 1947–50, which along with monetary reform and the Berlin blockade (the coal and steel kept out of West Berlin ironically helped West Germany's revival) fuelled economic expansion. Steel production doubled in a year and coal output rose by 50 per cent, and by 1949 industrial output was at 80 per cent of the 1936 level (Kindleberger, 1987, pp. 34–35,196). German steel production, which had been 'fixed' at the limit of 7.5m tonnes in 1946, was fixed again at 11m in 1947 by the Allied Control Commission, much to the annoyance of Georges Bidault, the French Foreign Minister 1947–48, who argued that with sufficient German coking coal France and the Benelux could produce any increased output.

By the summer of 1948 at the London Conference France had to accommodate herself to two approaching unpalatable developments – the gradual emergence of a new West German State and the revival of its economy. Much of the Conference was devoted to the issue of the exact remit of the International Authority for the Ruhr, which had been set up to placate France, over future allocations of German coking coal and steel production controls. Although the International Authority of the Ruhr from 28 December 1948 divided quantities of Ruhr coke, coal and steel between domestic and export markets with a compulsory allocation to France in accordance with the OEEC programme, in reality it had little real power and no control over German coal and steel production, which remained with UK and US military governments' Coal and Steel Control Boards. It was another rather weak interdependent organisation lacking power and any guarantee of permanence (Milward, 1984, pp. 157, 160). Achieving the conditions required for the Monnet Plan's success looked more remote with this prospect of a revived German state and economy.

This setback to the issue of overriding importance in French foreign policy was potentially dangerous, requiring an urgent solution. It threatened both national security and French national economic recovery through the Monnet Plan. If France opposed the emergence of a West German state, the British and Americans could go ahead anyway in their Bizone and France would appear as an adversary of German democratic revival: undermining French influence over West Germany as a whole and jeopardising any prospect of Franco-German association or co-operation.

French planners had to find a way to guarantee the future of its modernisation and in effect the Schuman Plan subsequently rescued the Monnet Plan, as it guaranteed continued French access to the resources of the Ruhr (Milward, 1984, p. 475; Lynch, 1984, p. 242). The issue of a Customs Union including West Germany was examined in the CUSG from 1948. German economic recovery meant a rising tide of exports from Western Europe to Germany in 1949, cut off from its eastern sources of grain and potatoes (Kindleberger, 1987, p. 39), revealing both the need for and possible advantages of a common market to France and the Netherlands.

Following the 1948 London Conference, Robert Schuman recognised the urgent need for a radical change in French policy towards Germany. The only alternative (to their 1944–48 policy of weakening and dismembering Germany) was a more positive policy of co-operation or association. Dean Acheson, US Secretary of State 1949–53, recognised that only France could integrate Europe (by 1949 it was clear that Britain would not) and he made a personal appeal to Schuman to take the initiative to reconcile West Germany to Western Europe (Milward, 1984, pp. 391–92).

Jean Monnet, who was head of the planning organisation, he was Commissariat Géneral au Plan and eventually High Commissioner of the modernisation and re-equipment plan and played a formative role in the Schuman Plan and invented the concept of a supranational body, the 'High Authority' to run the ECSC. Monnet, who was neither an elected politician nor a French professional civil servant, led the French negotiations with West Germany and the other four states in 1950–51. He said that without the USA there would have been no treaty (Duchêre, 1994).

Jean Monnet subsequently became the first President of the High Authority of the ECSC. Whether he was, as he is invariably seen in retrospect, 'the founding father of Europe', Monnet certainly rescued the modernisation and re-equipment plan and so safeguarded French national economic interests and preserved security, through starting a Franco-German alliance, which has now endured for more than 50 years.

Frances Lynch (1984, p. 242) argues that to disguise the highly political nature of the Schuman Plan the ECSC was created under a smokescreen of idealistic European rhetoric. Statements by Schuman that it was 'the first concrete foundation of European federation' were music to American ears and satisfied the US Congress that Marshall Aid was creating a European framework to contain Germany. Dissimulation concealed this second French attempt to reshape Europe's economic and political environment to suit the needs of the French domestic economy, safeguarding French reconstruction plans by creating a common market in coal and steel, so providing equal access for France to the Ruhr's resources.

What did the ECSC actually do? Schurnan's original announcement on 9 May 1950 proposed that 'the entire French and German production of coal and steel be placed under a joint High Authority within an organization open to the participation of other European nations'. The High Authority was to ensure the supply of coal on equal terms inside a common market. France was keen to end the dual-pricing of coal (with German domestic coal prices lower than for exported coal) and discriminatory freight rates that in 1950 made the price of German coke in Lorraine, France, 46 per cent higher than the Ruhr (Milward, 1984, pp. 378–79), giving German steelmakers a significant cost advantage over France.

The Treaty of Paris 1951 was a complex commercial treaty establishing the ECSC as a regulated market-sharing arrangement under supranational control. It was designed to balance the six states' particular vested interests in coal and steel and to facilitate achievement of national objectives in these two sectors. The common external tariff of the ECSC's Customs Union was fixed lower than that of France but higher than the Benelux and a five-year transition period was allowed before full operation of the agreement.

Italy was allowed nevertheless to retain its fixed tariff to protect its small, high-cost steel industry within the Common Market. Scrap was included in the agreement as this constituted the prime raw material for Italian electric-arc process steel making. Italy also got access to French North African iron ore resources (Milward, 1984, p. 414).

There were complicated arrangements for fixing the price of coal. Prices were set artificially high to allow the restructuring costs of Belgium's declining coal industry to be subsidised mainly from the Netherlands and Germany by $45m between 1953 and 1958 with another $5m as an export subsidy for Belgian coal (Milward, 1984, p. 399; 1992, Chapter 3).

France, negotiating from a strong bargaining position in 1949–51, obtained equal access to the Ruhr's resources within the Common Market and the end of dual-pricing and discriminatory freight rates. France had received $205m for coking plant from the High Authority's investment funds by 1958. In 1952 German steel prices were increased to virtually close the gap between French and German prices prior to the common market in steel coming into operation. Germany also agreed that France would supply the Southern German market with steel for three years (243,000 tonnes in 1952 and 855,000 tonnes in 1954). German car exports from South Germany were manufactured from the output of modern French strip-rolling steel mills (constructed under the Monnet Plan) in the Thionville and Metz area (Milward, 1984, pp. 413–14). Overall German imports of steel doubled between 1953 and 1956 because of the booming German economy and the ECSC agreement.

The ECSC created a single common market from six national markets, in coal, steel, coke and scrap metal, but also safeguarded specific national interests, as in Italy's case, assisted Belgium grappling with its ailing coal sector and facilitated, through international agreement, French national economic objectives. The essential elements of the Monnet Plan were indeed rescued by the Schuman Plan, as Lynch and Milward's research demonstrates, the ECSC providing equal access to Ruhr coal and guaranteed markets for French steel in Germany Moreover, the supranational High Authority meant the collective day-to-day control and regulation of steel and coal markets throughout the Common Market and therefore within West Germany itself. How else might France and Benelux, in the circumstances of 1948–50, have exercised real, certain, durable or better influence over West Germany's coal and steel sectors?

For Monnet, Schuman and Quai d'Orsay officials of the French Foreign Ministry the solution by 1949 of a Franco-German association in an integrated organisation under supranational control was inspired by France's two bad post-war experiences in the 1920s (starting with the failure of the Treaty of Versailles 1919 and the 1927 Treaty) and in 1946–47 (with the Allied Control Council's 'fixed limits' on German steel output being raised regularly). The French were understandably extremely sceptical of the value of treaty guarantees that relied for compliance only on the good faith and consistency of national governments. (France had also broken a 'solemn obligation' contracted with Britain in June 1940 by concluding a separate peace with Germany.) The Treaty of Paris 1951, in contrast, created the first integrated organisation offering the prospects of permanent compliance – with a supranational High Authority policing the Treaty and a Court of Justice to settle disputes. This was Monnet's ingenious solution to the problem of co-existing and conducting business securely with Germany The bold brave political act of Schuman – a massive 'U-turn' in French policy to Germany – created a Franco-German alliance that has endured for 60 years and laid the basis for peace and prosperity in Western Europe since 1950.

Why did West Germany agree to join this alliance on basically French terms? What did West Germany hope to gain from the Treaty of Paris 1951? When the Federal Republic emerged in May 1949 made up of the UK, US and French zones, it was still subject to numerous restrictions and controls. The Occupation Statute prohibited full responsibility for foreign affairs, defence or foreign trade, and ownership and decartelisation of Ruhr industries. The International Authority of the Ruhr 1948 undertook the compulsory allocation of coal between domestic and export markets. Konrad Adenauer, Federal Chancellor 1949–63, had as his main objective the removal of these irksome constraints and to obtain full sovereignty for his fledgling state (in fact West Germany could only start negotiations over the ECSC with the permission of the Allied High Commission in the Federal Republic). Adenauer's strategy for achieving this was full co-operation and close collaboration with the three Western powers. For Adenauer, therefore, political considerations were of upmost importance in negotiating the Treaty of Paris 1951. Adenauer was keen to co-operate with France on equal terms and he insisted on equal terms of entry for the FRG into the ECSC.

In the negotiations France was helped by US pressure on the FRG to accept French terms and by using the International Authority of the Ruhr as a bargaining counter. Professor Walter Hallstein, State Secretary in the Office of the Federal Chancellor 1950, negotiating for the FRG, was told by

Monnet that if West Germany accepted the Schuman Plan France would press for the abolition of the International Authority for the Ruhr.

Indeed when the Treaty of Paris was signed in April 1951 controls on the German steel industry were 'drastically changed' (Milward, 1984, pp. 412, 420), with the end of most of the economic constraints imposed after the Potsdam Conference in 1945.

So the FRG made political gains from the Treaty of Paris by winning recognition as an equal partner having equal status and by the removal of most of the limitations and controls over steel and coal. Whereas for France the prime motive for the ECSC was economic (Monnet and the planners prepared the plan which Schuman and the Ministry of Foreign Affairs then took up), for Germany the motives were political. Accepting the Schuman Plan and signing the Treaty of Paris was the only way to commence their national rehabilitation as an independent sovereign state.

For Adenauer too the stated federalist objective underpinning the scheme (regardless of whether motivated by idealism or dissimilation) was politically useful. He wanted Germans to avoid what he called 'bad thoughts' and come to think of themselves as Europeans.

Although initially much of the German and French steel industry was opposed to a common market and Belgium's coal industry was hostile (Milward, 1984, p. 419), experience soon proved it to be very much in their economic interests.

There was opposition from the SPD in Germany which suspected that the ECSC was not an idealistic internationalist plan but a Catholic, conservative and capitalist plot. (Schuman, Adenauer and de Gasperi, Italy's Prime Minister, were Roman Catholics and Christian Democrats, and had German as their first language.) However, Hans Boekler, President of the DGB and German trade unions generally, did not share the SPD's view. In France, Guy Mollet and the SFIO had reservations: they were disappointed at the British Labour government's absence and considered that Monnet and the French government were wrong to require Britain's prior acceptance of a common High Authority before the talks began. Like the SPD, the SFIO suspected a Catholic plot to keep Protestants out. But Monnet had close links with French trade-union leaders and kept them well informed, ensuring that they were represented on the national delegation and dispelling such fears.

Why did Britain not join the scheme? Britain excluded herself from the talks leading to the ECSC as they were unwilling to sign, prior to the start of negotiations, a communiqué: with the other governments agreeing in advance to the 'pooling of coal and steel production' and accepting the transfer of national control to a High Authority. For Schuman and Monnet the supra-national aspect was vital to French national interests and so non-negotiable. They feared that the UK would work to undermine this essential element of the Plan if it was open for discussion. So Schuman and Monnet made Britain an offer they were sure would be refused. In fact it would have been surprising if the UK had accepted French terms to join the talks as in January 1949 an interdepartmental meeting of the Foreign Office, Board of Trade and Treasury had decided to revert to 'limited liability' with Europe and prioritise the UK's relations with the US and Commonwealth, relegating European links to secondary status.

The Labour government had nationalised coal in 1946 and the National Coal Board's long-term plan was only published in 1950. Neither the government nor the NCB were prepared to relinquish control to a supranational High Authority eventually based in Luxembourg. Herbert Morrison, Acting Prime Minister, is supposed to have said in the Cabinet discussion: 'It's no good, we cannot do it, the Durham miners won't wear it.' Britain's rather condescending, aloof, introverted response towards the Schuman Plan had much to do with the fact that UK production far outstripped Western Europe's. In iron and steel, which the government was preparing to nationalise in 1949–50, UK crude steel output (16m tonnes) was approximately half that of the whole of Western Europe. Europe took only 25 per cent of UK trade, while the Sterling Area took 50 per cent. Only 5 per cent of UK steel exports went to Europe. The instinctive reaction of cautious British officials to the Schuman Plan was not to take any risks with Britain's steel exports. Why complicate current arrangements by joining the scheme? Moreover, unlike France, Britain relied on her Commonwealth and US connections for access to scarce resources and raw materials. The Foreign Office paid much attention to negotiations for more US steel by arranging to 'swap' aluminium and nickel 'loaned' from Canada and minerals from Rhodesia for American steel.

Even so, some officials like Edwin Plowden, Chairman of the Economic Planning Board 1947–53, thought there might be economic advantages in it for Britain and Sir Stafford Cripps, Chancellor of the Exchequer 1947–50, also thought that the UK should join but fell ill and could not argue his case. The Foreign Office opposed the plan. Ernest Bevin was enraged when he first heard of Schuman's announcement in early May 1950, because of the lack of consultation, advance warning and the preconditions attached. On 1 June 1950 the French government gave Britain a 24-hour ultimatum to accept the terms or the talks would proceed without them. Interestingly, when the talks started, without Britain, the objective had altered. Instead of referring to 'pooling coal and steel production' as in the 9 May 1950 announcement, the French working paper on the scheme of 27 June 1950 emphasised the High Authority's role as 'to contribute to a policy of economic expansion, of full employment, and of a rising standard of living for the workers ... it should ensure that the needs of the member countries would be satisfied and exports would be developed without discrimination'. This would be achieved under the best possible economic conditions through the establishment of a broad single market.

This appeared both more moderate and attractive as a communal objective. Nevertheless, the Foreign Office viewed the Schuman process not simply as economic integration but as a move towards the political federation of Europe – Schuman had referred to the 'starting point for a United Europe'.

The Foreign Office wanted to discourage any emergent supranational European federation – fearing the possibility of it becoming either a neutralist third-force between the two superpowers (Young, 1988, ch. 4, p. 109) or creating a Franco-German superstate. The Foreign Office also thought it unlikely that the continentals would agree among themselves – particularly in the absence of British diplomacy. In fact arguably it proved easier without Britain, as it meant one less bargain to strike during the technical negotiations.

In July 1950 Schuman proposed the 'association' idea to Britain as a way of connecting the UK to the ECSC short of full membership. Subsequently Bevin, Morrison and then Eden after 1951 pursued the same policy of 'close association short of full membership' with both the ECSC and the Pleven Plan's EDC. Eden's Plan was to use the existing Council of Europe's institutions for the ECSC and the EDC. However, Bonn and Rome in particular suspected that Britain wanted to act as a brake on the process of integration. Monnet, too, was fearful of British sabotage. Young shows that as a result by September 1952 the Eden Plan was dead. Eden and the UK then adopted a benevolent attitude towards the ECSC (Young, 1988, ch. 4, pp. 110, 113–15, 118) and proceeded to formulate the terms of the UK's association. Paradoxically an internal Foreign Office 'Schuman Plan Committee' report proposed in 1953 that the UK should actually join a common market in steel as the competition would be good for the industry and also recognised that the 'Schuman Community could create a unit of great economic power with which the UK must come to terms'. Peter Thorneycroft, President of the Board of Trade, was also willing to consider UK entry into a common market for steel. The Commonwealth, when consulted on their reaction to a closer UK–ECSC link, did not object at all. Canada and New Zealand supported it and Australia and South Africa accepted British assurances that Commonwealth interests would be safeguarded (Young, 1988, ch. 4, pp. 123–4). The real opposition came from the steel, coal and engineering industries and trade unions in 1953–54 and also from the Treasury. Rab Butler, Chancellor of the Exchequer 1951–55, was very hostile to the idea of closer links with the ECSC. Eden also did not want to do anything to encourage European integration (which ruled out joining a common market) yet at the same time had to avoid appearing to sabotage the process (which would have enraged the Americans). This only left a rather limited form of 'association' as a policy option.

Moreover, if in 1953–54 the UK had decided to join a common market in steel, in spite of opposition from industry and elsewhere, it would have been much harder to argue the case for Britain keeping out of the EDC. A closer UK–ECSC link would have encouraged 'the Six' and the Americans to increase the pressure on Britain to join the scheme for a European army The UK's long delayed association agreement with the ECSC was only formalised in December 1954 after the EDC scheme had been dead and buried for four months.

1954 was the third but not the last missed opportunity by Britain to join an integrated Europe. In retrospect this policy choice can be seen as a costly failure as the Common Market proved to be a more successful commercial venture than the UK's Commonwealth links.

However, unlike France in 1950, the UK's vested economic interests and national recovery were not dependent on commercial links with Germany and, unlike France, the UK did not see the main threat to its national security as a resurgent West Germany The French-integrated solution of a Franco-German association under a supranational High Authority when presented as the first move towards a United Europe was guaranteed to appeal to Americans and repel the British.

How did the ECSC operate? The parliaments of the six states surrendered sovereignty over coal and steel to the supranational High Authority which assumed full executive power over these sectors. The Authority consisted of nine members in office for six years; eight were designated by the governments of 'the Six' acting together and the ninth was elected by the original eight members. The High Authority members, president, and auditor of accounts, were appointed jointly by the participant governments – none of them were simply nominees of individual states.

Negotiations between July 1950 and March 1951 reduced the derogation of national sovereignty involved. At the insistence of the Netherlands and Belgium, a Council of Ministers modified the powers of the High Authority. The High Authority could issue 'decisions' which were binding, 'recommendations' which were binding in objective but not in the means to obtain them and 'opinions' which had no binding force. The High Authority was assisted by a rather ineffectual consultative committee of between 30 and 51 producers, workers, consumers and dealers. On certain specific issues the High Authority was obliged to consult this committee but was free to ignore its advice. The High Authority was responsible to a Parliamentary Assembly, which at its short annual session to consider the Authority's report, could cause the Authority to resign en masse by passing a vote of censure by a two-thirds majority. As Schuman said. 'for the first time, an international assembly would be more than a consultative organ; the parliaments themselves, having surrendered a fraction of their sovereignty, would regain that sovereignty, through its common exercise'. A Court of Justice was established to settle national disputes and hear industrial appeals.

In August 1952, after ratification by the six parliaments, the ECSC started to function and in 1953 the Common Market commenced operations. Between 1952 and 1962 iron ore production increased from 62m to 92m tonnes, new patterns of trade developed and there was a greater harmonisation of working conditions. Early opposition to the scheme by industrialists, most notably in France but also in Belgium and the Ruhr, soon dissipated as did exaggerated fears of the competitive strength of other producers. The ECSC operated successfully for 20 years apart from technical difficulties and a crisis in 1958 when coal surpluses, unsold stocks and cheap US coal caused problems. The High Authority proposed to fix production quotas but governments rejected this idea and started to take unilateral action to safeguard their own coal and steel interests.

This 1958 crisis in the ECSC coincided with the start of the EEC and Euratom that marked a decline in political influence of the ECSC, whose institutions were eventually absorbed by these new communities in 1967. However, overall, the ECSC successfully functioned through the 1950s and 1960s when demand and production were expanding, guaranteeing equal French access both to Ruhr coal and German markets.

The political impact of the ECSC was also significant. The institutions operated well and rules on competition were agreed easily, to the surprise and relief of the nine-man High Authority. Europeans from states which had spent years at war with each other proved quite capable of working and co-operating together, obeying common rules and paying a common tax. A group of influential ministers, civil servants, journalists, trade unionists and industrialists from the six states worked together on a daily basis. Monnet, as first President of the ECSC, formed a tight cohesive cadre of enthusiastic evangelical 'Eurocrats' at the Luxembourg headquarters. The Parliamentary Assembly served almost as a graduate school for European integration to many of the leading politicians of 'the Six' – people like Erich Ollenhauer, who succeeded Schumacher after his death in 1952, as leader of the SPD in West Germany. Such developments were to have an effect on future initiatives in 'Little Europe' after 1954.

Meanwhile, in June 1950, only four weeks after Schuman announced his plan, the Korean War started. Events in the Far East were to affect the whole process of European integration over the next four years.

5 German rearmament, the European Defence Community and the demise of the European army, 1950–54

The European Defence Community never came into existence, so why bother to consider it? There are two reasons for doing so. The EDC and the ECSC plans were in fact closely linked. The team that drafted the ECSC scheme also devised the EDC. In the summer of 1950 the prospect of German rearmament in NATO offered an alternative route than the ECSC for Germany to regain full control over its industry. The EDC was intended to stop this and so protect the ECSC until signed and in force.

The EDC scheme of civil and military integration was contrived to protect economic integration in the ECSC, a device for delaying West Germany's rearmament and its complete control of national and foreign affairs.

The issue of rearming the West Germans first arose in 1949 when the USSR exploded its first atomic device. This was much sooner than the US expected, and was partly as a result of Soviet spies at the Los Alamos research laboratories and KGB scientists interviewing the theoretical physicist Niels Bohr in Denmark after the war. Some consideration was given then, by the US, to the question of West German rearmament and strengthening ground defence. There was, however, no urgency despite Soviet conventional military superiority – the Russians had 22 divisions out of 175 in Eastern Europe as a whole, compared with two each for the US and UK in West Germany out of a total of 14 NATO divisions (Kirby, 1977, p. 100; Dockrill, 1991, p. 10). The American nuclear umbrella over Europe was still a credible deterrent – the US had an effective monopoly of atomic weapons, as the USSR had no delivery system until 1955, when a long-range Tupolev bomber came into service. The US was also developing 'the super' fusion H-bomb from 1950, testing a device in 1952 and the weapon in 1954. Yet it was clearly recognised that once US nuclear superiority started to fade in the mid-to-late 1950s, so the deterrent effect of American nuclear retaliation to a Soviet invasion of Western Europe would also decline. Then the US would be keen to improve conventional forces, including a West German contribution by the late 1950s.

West German rearmament only became an issue in 1950 because of the Korean War. This war made German rearmament a predominant theme of US policy in Western Europe. On 25 June 1950 the North Korean army equipped with Russian-built tanks and supported by Soviet Yak fighters crossed the 38th Parallel into South Korea, sweeping aside lightly armed South Korean troops. News of this Soviet-backed communist invasion of South Korea caused a wave of panic in West Berlin and Dr Konrad Adenauer wanted immediate reinforcements to be sent (Dockrill, 1991, p. 22). Why? What relevance did Korea have? The fear was that the Elbe could become another '38th Parallel', the worst possible scenario being a Soviet–East German invasion of West Germany. Although, unlike South Korea, the presence of American, British and French forces in West Berlin and West Germany made this less probable as it would trigger a Soviet–American conflict, it remained a possibility, especially as the East Germans already had a 60,000-strong paramilitary 'people's police' organised into 'alert units'.

Stalin was testing President Truman's resolve to contain communism behind its 1945 frontiers and the strength of its commitment to allies. If the US had not taken the initiative for a United Nations resistance to North Korea and sent US forces, then it would have appeared weak and timid compared with the USSR and undermined NATO, only created the year before in 1949, as West Europeans would feel they too would be abandoned in a crisis. American intelligence sources had warned Washington of an impending invasion yet it became the 'Pearl Harbor' of the Cold War because the intelligence was discounted (as in December 1941) for not fitting the Pentagon's preconceived notion that Stalin would only launch an invasion when he wanted to start World War III. Accordingly the Pentagon had no plans for sending troops to South Korea, no plans for a 'flexible response' in a 'limited war', only plans for dropping atom bombs. American soldiers were rushed to South Korea from bases in the US and Japan.

Stalin meant Korea to undermine NATO and the US position in Europe by diverting US attention and troops away from Europe to Asia. In fact it had the opposite effect. The Korean War globalised Truman's containment policy and militarised containment in Europe. In June 1950 the Americans wanted a stronger local defence of Western Europe to deter the USSR, including a West German contribution organised in a NATO integrated force under centralised command with a supreme commander. Seventy-five per cent of US military aid went to Europe even after the Korean War started. In 1950 there were only 14 runways from which jets could operate in Western Europe and only 800 jets to put on them: by 1954 there were 120 runways and 4,000 jets. American military aid helped re-equip the French air force and the RAF via 'off shore sales' (as opposed to 'legitimate off shore sales'). Some of the jet aircraft built in British and French factories were bought with US military aid and given to the air forces. These planes, paid for with dollars, were exports of a sort. Clement Attlee had announced a £3.6bn rearmament programme for 1951–54. By 1952 UK arms production exceeded all her European NATO partners combined – a fact that predisposed the US to give UK additional financial aid in 1952.

At the September 1950 NATO Council meeting in New York, Ernest Bevin had agreed both to Britain's contribution under revised NATO force goals rising to four divisions, and also with the American demand for the immediate creation of German formations under NATO command (Dockrill, 1989, p. 151). For the Americans, after June 1950, a German military contribution was indispensable to fill the big manpower gap at the centre of Western Europe's defence line. The Soviet threat made some restoration of West Germany's capacity for self-defence an urgent matter. Adenauer was keen to co-operate but at this time stopped short of a national German army and general staff. Adenauer in fact wanted a militarised police force of 150,000 men. Moreover, he wanted to anchor the FRG firmly in the Western camp, end occupation controls and regain full sovereignty. The US plan, backed by Britain, for German rearmament in NATO opened an intriguing possibility of an alternative and perhaps preferable route to these goals than via France's Schuman Plan. The German Social Democrats (SPD) were against any West German rearmament, wanting to see Germany reunified.

Robert Schuman when confronted at the New York NATO Summit in September 1950 with the prospect of a rapid reappearance of an independent German army flew into a rage full of anti-German invective. He argued in what was described as a lively and traumatic meeting that the whole issue of German rearmament should be postponed until the ECSC was in place. For Truman, the issue of adding West German manpower to Western Europe's defence was non-negotiable; it was clear according to Truman that 'without Germany the defence of Europe was a rearguard action on the shore of the Atlantic Ocean, with Germany there could be a defence in depth, powerful enough to offer effective resistance to aggression from the East … '. Moreover, this was essential and realistic given the heavy US military involvement in Korea, Britain's global military responsibilities and France fighting a colonial war in Indo-China.

The French government instructed Schuman not to yield. They resented the Americans trying to impose their own swift solution to the German problem through rearmament. Yet France was in too weak a position to prevent any determined American rearmament of Germany; they could only hope to complicate and delay the process.

Monnet, like Schuman, was also alarmed that this US scheme for German rearmament on a national basis in NATO would wreck the ECSC plan. Monnet wrote to Schuman in New York saying the only alternative was 'to integrate Germany into Europe by means of a broader Schuman Plan, taking the necessary decisions within a European framework' (Fursdon, 1980, pp. 84–85). German rearmament, only five years after the war, was a distasteful and alarming prospect for most Europeans, Russians and many Germans. For France it also jeopardised the Schuman Plan. If West Germany regained full sovereignty through a defence contribution to NATO they would be under American control and also be less motivated to proceed with the Schuman Plan on the agreed French terms.

Only a month before, on 11 August, Winston Churchill in the Council of Europe at Strasbourg had called for 'the immediate creation of a unified European army subject to proper democratic control and acting in full co-operation with the US and Canada'. Although Churchill envisaged a European army with a European Minister of Defence of 36 divisions (15 French, 6 British, 6 American, 5 West German, 3 Benelux), 17 per cent of the force would have been American (Dockrill, 1991, p. 24). The European Assembly enthusiastically endorsed Churchill's proposal, voting 85 to 5 in favour.

Churchill's idea inspired and the vote encouraged Monnet's Plan as did Adenauer's refusal to accept a German national army whilst welcoming the idea of an integrated force. The threat from a reconstructed German army, in any form, guaranteed French opposition to American plans. Monnet, chairman of the Schuman Plan team, after consulting Schuman and Pleven (the French Prime Minister), used the same team that was working on the Schuman Plan's continuing coal and steel conference, to devise a scheme for a European army. He deliberately excluded any military expertise, as the priority was to devise a political solution acceptable to France. By 14 October the essential elements of the 'Pleven Plan' were in place and following redrafting both the French Cabinet and the National Assembly had accepted the Pleven Plan by 24 October 1950 (Fursdon, 1980, pp. 86–88).

What did the original Pleven Plan propose? It aimed to create a European army with a European Defence Community, copying the institutional form of the ECSC. It was to be created once the ECSC Treaty had been signed. The EDC was to be linked to a European Political Community (EPC) that would exercise democratic control over the EDC. The EDC would have common forces, a common uniform and a single Ministry of Defence. However, Monnet and Pleven envisaged an EDC that was only ostensibly supranational as the 100,000-strong European army, including West Germans, was to contain a 50,000-strong French contingent. So the EDC was intended to be half French with the West German contingent controlled by French cadres. All participating states, except for West Germany, would retain national control over their forces not placed in the EDC. As Dockrill shows, French counter-proposals to American demands to rearm Germany in October 1950 were designed to deny them the opportunity for independent action and so from becoming a military threat again. Under the guise of supranationality, a *fusion complète* of military forces, France aimed to attain military superiority over West German forces organized into battalions of 1,000 men in the European army under French generals as the best insurance against any resurgence of German militarism and excessive American interference in European affairs. The Pleven Plan intended the European army to be dominated by France – under French command with a French Minister of Defence (Fursdon, 1980, pp. 89–90; Dockrill, 1989, pp. 153–54; 1991, p. 42).

The EDC appeared to the Dutch and British Foreign Ministers as a means of French national aggrandisement and a platform for French political hegemony. Four days after the French National Assembly had approved it, the

French counter-proposal for solving the vexed question of German rearmament was presented at the Defence Committee meeting of Western powers to consider how to incorporate German forces in European defence. The French initiative was generally welcomed as a positive alternative strategy based on Churchill's Strasbourg proposal in August. France was thus able to avoid complete isolation with her NATO partners on the issue, and also retain essential US support for France in its Schuman Plan negotiations with Germany. Dr Adenauer did not like the inherent discrimination against German forces in the French proposals nor the fact that achieving progress with the Pleven Plan was linked up and conditional upon the success of the Schuman Plan negotiations (the Treaty of Paris was signed in April 1951).

These two distinct solutions to German rearmament were debated inside NATO from the start of 1951. The Petersburg Conference in Bonn considered the 'Spofford Proposals' for German forces to be wholly integrated under the NATO command. This was the quick American military solution preferred by everyone except France. The Paris Conference considered the Pleven Plan that offered the possibility of a long-term political solution to the German problem through 'political unity in a community'. The Dutch (like the US and UK) remained as observers not participants at the Paris Conference as Dirk Stikker, the Dutch Foreign Minister, simply did not believe that the French were serious about the EDC or really prepared to relinquish any sovereignty over the French Army (Fursdon, 1980, pp. 91, 99, 105–9).

Dr Adenauer pursued a successful trade-off policy at these conferences. He wanted equality of treatment for the West Germans, and the price of German military co-operation with the West was West Germany's political independence. Negotiations on a new contractual relationship between the three Western occupying powers and West Germany started in Bonn in May 1951. The West Germans insisted on having a Ministry of Defence, divisional formations and in return they were prepared to provide a ground force of 100,000 men by the end of 1951 (Dockrill, 1991, pp. 59–62). Moreover, the two-track NATO debate meant that concessions won by the FRG at the Petersburg Conference from January 1951 became prerequisites at the informal exploratory talks of the European Army Conference in Paris, February–June 1951. Here the West Germans insisted on the 'Bonn requirements' of equality and political independence.

West Germany was in a strong negotiating position at the Paris Conference (through the Bonn talks on new contractual agreements) and France was forced to make some very big concessions to retain German involvement at the European Army Conference including acceptance of a *fusion complète* (all forces being in EDC from the start) meaning the French army would cease to exist. If the West Germans had left these talks they were doomed and the NATO solution, a new West German army and a politically independent West Germany, could follow.

The US had originally agreed to a Pleven Plan conference in Paris in late 1950 in return for the immediate remilitarisation of Germany on an interim basis. However, German demands for equality, talks on a new contractual agreement with Germany and the ongoing Paris Conference meant no swift rearmament on an interim basis. The Americans then began to look more favourably at the French scheme as a long-term solution to German rearmament.

Monnet lobbied hard with US officials visiting or based in Europe. He was well connected with the US political establishment, particularly the State Department in Washington, and Europe. John McCloy, the US High Commissioner in West Germany and David Bruce, US Ambassador in Paris, were both good friends of Monnet and also convinced Euro-federalists. Over lunch in the Waldorf-Astoria in Paris, Monnet converted Eisenhower to the French Plan. Monnet told Eisenhower, NATO's commander, that 'to rush into raising a few German divisions on a national basis, at the cost of reviving enmity between our peoples would be catastrophic for the very security of Europe it was intended to ensure', whereas the French approach was a community approach encouraging a common European interest in defence and a will to resist. Eisenhower's views, as NATO's Supreme Commander, were transformed: 'what Monnet's proposing is to organize relations between people and I'm all for it'. Eisenhower threw his weight behind the Paris Conference and staunchly defended the European army idea (that he once considered 'crazy and impractical') before the Senate Sub-committee on Foreign Relations in July 1951. Konrad Adenauer seeing the way US policy was moving also put his support behind the Paris Conference. Dean Acheson, US Secretary of State, was eventually persuaded by these developments and by David Bruce to switch American policy from the Petersburg NATO solution to going 'all out for' the EDC alternative at the Paris Conference. President Truman formally agreed to this on 30 July 1951. After protracted negotiations the vast Treaty of Paris of 27 May 1952 establishing the EDC was signed, having 132 articles and 12 protocols. A protocol to the NATO Treaty on reciprocal guarantees with EDC was signed. The Allied–German Contractual Agreement was signed in Bonn the previous day, 26 May 1952, to grant the Federal Republic 'full power over its domestic and foreign affairs' once the EDC came into effect. However, the real problem of getting parliamentary ratification in the six states, especially France, was only now beginning (Fursdon, 1980, pp. 117–21, 151; Dockrill, 1991, pp. 68–72).

What was Britain's attitude towards a European army? Britain always preferred a NATO solution to German rearmament. Anthony Eden, the Conservative Foreign Secretary from October 1951 to 1955, continued with the policy established by Ernest Bevin. Bevin indicated at the Labour Party Conference in September 1950 that he had no time for a European army. His response to the Pleven Plan on 29 November 1950 made clear that it was not the 'policy of His Majesty's Government to contribute United Kingdom forces to a European Army ... Europe is not enough, it is not big enough' (House of Commons Debates, 29 November 1950, vol. 481, col. 1175). Bevin for a time advocated an 'Atlantic Confederate Force' under the NATO

Supreme Commander to counter the Pleven Plan for a European army. The Cabinet, suspecting that the US Congress would never agree to this, preferred the American idea of a NATO integrated force. At a NATO meeting in Washington in September 1951, Herbert Morrison, who took over when Bevin fell ill, announced that although the UK could not merge its forces in a European army, Britain fully supported the idea and wished to be closely associated with it (Dockrill, 1991, p. 49; Dedman and Fleay, 1992, p. 12).

Hopes were raised in Europe, only to be swiftly dashed, of a change in British government policy from October 1951. Winston Churchill became Conservative Prime Minister and Anthony Eden the Foreign Secretary. The Conservative Party included a group of 'Tory Strasbourgers' and the Cabinet contained several European-minded Ministers such as Duncan Sandys, David Patrick Maxwell-Fyfe and Harold Macmillan, who, partly inspired by Churchill's Zurich and Strasbourg speeches in 1946 and 1950, wanted to see a more decisive British lead in Europe. In November 1951, in what has been described as the 'betrayal of Strasbourg' or 'the Rome coup', Maxwell-Fyfe, the Home Secretary hand-picked by Eden, went to read a Cabinet-approved statement at the Council of Europe Assembly. This was a cautious though not discouraging statement concerning the UK and a European army and denied that there was any 'closing of the door' by Britain. That same evening, 28 November 1951, Eden, at a NATO meeting in Rome, slammed the door shut. He stated bluntly and categorically that the UK would not join a European army. When news of this reached Strasbourg, Paul-Henri Spaak, President of the European Assembly, resigned immediately. Maxwell-Fyfe was on the brink of resigning and was subsequently castigated and vilified in the British press for exceeding his brief. Although the statements arguably differed more in tone than substance, in reality Maxwell-Fyfe was not to blame. Eden had spoken the day before to General Eisenhower, who instead of urging the UK to join the EDC told him it would be a mistake. Eden explained to Churchill that Britain should support the EDC but offering to enter it at this stage of the negotiations 'would further complicate the budgetary and other technical arrangements and would delay rather than hasten a final solution'. Churchill replied on 29 November that Eden's position 'combined the disadvantages of two courses: neither keeping out of it nor having a say' (Young, 1985, pp. 928–29; Dockrill, 1991, pp. 85–88; Dedman and Fleay, 1992, p. 13).

This public divergence of view within the government did not help Britain's standing on the Continent. Churchill had an emotional attachment to both the US (he was half-American) and to Europe. He was an enthusiastic exponent of European schemes and although consistently careful to say that Britain was 'with Europe not of it', he was prone to spirited visionary prose on the matter. Eden, as Churchill's named successor, shared none of these characteristics. To the chagrin of Tory-Strasbourgers with their vague ideas of Britain playing its part in Europe, Eden (who was described as 'in every sense a NATO man' by Anthony Nutting of the Foreign Office) was having none of it.

On 6 December in the House of Commons, Churchill confirmed Bevin's rejection of the EDC and Eden's line in saying that once formed 'a European Army containing a German contribution ... will stand alongside the British and US armies in a common defensive front' (House of Commons Debates, 6 December 1951, vol. 494, col. 2591). Following a meeting with Pleven, Schuman and Eisenhower in Paris on 18 December, the Bevin–Morrison–Eden policy was reaffirmed in the announcement that Britain 'would associate [herself] as closely as possible with the EDC in all stages of its political and military developments'.

Why did British policy adhere so consistently to a NATO solution, with German rearmament in an Atlantic and not a European context between 1950–55? Britain was afraid that once the EDC was established the US, satisfied that Europe was capable of self-defence, would be able to withdraw its forces from Western Europe and Germany. Britain's policy, even before the 1949 NATO Agreement came into effect, was based on getting and keeping a permanent US military presence in Europe. The UK would not consequently support or encourage anything that might weaken this essential US commitment. The American policy was the converse of Britain's in Western Europe. They wanted to deter the USSR and contain any resurgence of German militarism without the need for permanently stationing US forces there. The EDC seemed their best solution. Once support for the EDC became US policy from July 1951 the UK could not reject it outright and had to support it from outside (closest possible association) and avoid any accusation of sabotage or responsibility if or when the EDC scheme failed (Dockrill, 1989, pp. 158, 161–4; Mager, 1992, p. 127). Britain's refusal to join made the EDC's failure more likely, as France felt uncomfortable in a *fusion complète* of its armed forces with those of West Germany without the reassuring counterpoise of British membership to any resurgence of German strength. The need to avoid responsibility for any EDC collapse prompted Britain to breathe some life into its policy of 'closest possible association' through a declaration maintaining British troops in Europe; signing a treaty with the EDC promising UK support if attacked; and close collaboration in training and joint exercises (Dockrill, 1989, p. 153; Young, 1988, ch. 3, p. 90; Mager, 1992, p. 127).

Avoiding blame for any EDC failure was important to Britain given the particularly close special relationship that existed in the Truman–Acheson era (and the risk that alienating the US Congress might prejudice votes on US military aid to Britain); it was ironic that the UK and US's aspirations for the EDC were diametrically opposed.

Britain was determined to avoid being in any pact which included Italy and West Germany but not the US as it would be far harder to deal with any resurgent militarism with only rather weak European partners (Dockrill, 1989, p. 161; 1991, p. 2).

Britain's consistent policy towards the EDC had been to wait for the Pleven Plan originally and then the EDC Treaty to die (meanwhile keeping quiet about its NATO alternative) and then after its collapse to push for the UK's preferred NATO solution. The UK's response to the whole Pleven Plan/EDC scheme episode between 1951–55 was a cautious, patient waiting game (Young, 1988, ch. 3, p. 102; Dockrill, 1989, p. 167). The Foreign Office was determined to avoid the complex unwanted commitment that membership of a supranational EDC would bring. It would have constrained Britain's political and military independence while encouraging the development of a European federation. British Foreign Office observers at the EDC talks were mainly concerned to see if the EDC countries negotiated a better deal for military aid with the US than Britain already had – it soon became clear that they did not. Once the EDC was operable, rather like Marshall Aid and the OEEC, US military aid was to be 'pooled' and apportioned by the supranational EDC, a prospect that worried the Dutch a good deal. There was concern too in the British Foreign Office that when the FRG joined the EDC the £80m p.a. that Germany paid the UK to keep troops in Germany might cease. The immediate prospect for the Foreign Office, anxious about the balance of payments, was that the EDC could cost Britain £80m p.a. even though she was not a member.

For the French it was much more than a matter of money. France was opposed in principle to rearming Germany. The Pleven Plan and EDC were not attractive prospects, simply a lesser evil than a new Wehrmacht in NATO. France was torn between its need to integrate any German military forces into an EDC and its reluctance to integrate its own army. To most Frenchmen it seemed absurd to give arms to Germans when they did not appear to want them. (The West German Social Democrat Party resisted the issue of rearmament all the way to the FRG's Supreme Court.) It also appeared to represent the abandonment of a traditional ally, Britain, for too close an association with the ex-enemy. Hence the opposition slogans of 'No Europe without Britain', and 'The European Army destroys the French Army and rebuilds the German Army'.

Political opposition to the EDC in France was wide-ranging. The left wing of the Socialist Party was hostile to the rearmament of Germany. Nationalists were opposed to the dissolution of the French army and communists were opposed to the whole Atlantic policy. This opposition was a formidable alliance of left and right, including the communists and Gaullists. General de Gaulle, out of office, said at an RPF conference:

> The European Army plan would be either the end of the French Army or just a smoke screen which would permit the resurrection of the German Army without the least guarantee of its use. It would be a fatal blow to the French Army. We alone would be surrendering our army. To whom? To Europe? But it does not exist. We would be giving it to General Eisenhower. For centuries our value and prestige have been merged with those of the French Army. We therefore must not and cannot give up an army of our own.

These were views that were widely shared in France. The US hoped for speedy ratification of the EDC Treaty after May 1952 but Schuman felt that there was no majority in the National Assembly to vote it into law. Over the next two years three more French governments claimed to support the EDC but failed to ratify it. Other states postponed doing so too because of French delays.

Why was the Pleven Plan acceptable to the French National Assembly but the EDC Treaty, 18 months later, thought not to be? The Pleven Plan was widely recognised in October 1950 as a device to stop, not create, something. It was intended to prevent instant German rearmament and to protect the basic bargain that lay behind the Schuman Plan. The Milan journal *Relazioni Internazionali* (December 1950) recognised this, questioning whether the Pleven Plan represented 'truly supranational motives or the mere tactical desire to control German rearmament'. (The EDC Treaty, unlike the Pleven Plan, was not a sketchy scheme hastily devised in less than a month.) If the EDC was ratified, a European army, including German soldiers, would come into existence and members' national armies would cease to exist. Moreover, German forces could then be stationed throughout the community, for example in France or Holland.

The EDC Treaty differed substantially from what was originally envisaged in the Pleven Plan. The Pleven Plan intended the European Army to be half French, the US Spofford Plan envisaged the German contribution to NATO forces to be one fifth, and under the EDC Treaty 1952 the European army was to be one-third German (Dockrill, 1991, p. 55). The West Germans insisted on the principle of absolute equality in the European army and so, unlike the Pleven Plan, France came to agree to a *fusion complète* with all members' forces integrated into the EDC from the start. Moreover, the Pleven Plan was from the outset inherently flawed in a crucial respect, in envisaging German *groupements* being no bigger than a brigade or regimental combat teams. The French objected to there being German divisions, and even to the use of the word. This, however, was eventually acknowledged to be impractical militarily and logistically (*groupements* were ultimately intended to be small divisions of 13,000 men). It meant there would have to be a German War Office to organise these German divisions, which also meant it would be possible to re-form a German General Staff. The whole point and purpose of the Pleven Plan was to avoid this (Dockrill, 1991, pp. 48–49, 71, 89).

The Pleven Plan envisaged a French General being in overall command of a European army but instead, under the EDC, a Board of Commissioners, including German members, was to run it. Article 15 set the quorum at five of the nine commissioners, voting on a majority basis (Fursdon, 1980, p. 155; Dockrill, 1991, p. 42).

Articles 9–16 of the EDC Treaty which dealt with the withdrawal of troops from the EDC for use elsewhere, placed unwelcome constraints on French colonial rule and national sovereignty However, it was Article 43 that worried the French the most. This stated that member states' votes in the EDC

Council were weighted by the size of their national contribution to the EDC. More soldiers meant more votes. Whilst unanimity applied to key matters, on a day-to-day basis Article 43 applied. Assuming the Treaty was ratified by January 1952, France was to have 14 *groupements*, Italy and Germany 12 each, and Benelux six in place by July 1954 (Fursdon, 1980, pp. 158, 199; Dockrill, 1991, p. 89).

The problem was that the demand on French military manpower, due to its colonial war in Indo-China, meant that in February 1952 France decided to reduce her number of *groupements* in the EDC from 14 to ten. It chose to do this rather than to send conscripts to fight in Indo-China or to extend conscription to two years (as in the UK) and as promised to NATO in 1950 (Dockrill, 1991, p. 107).

This meant France, with ten *groupements*, would have fewer votes under Article 43 compared with Rome and Bonn who had 12 each. Given Germany's undoubted military expertise (1939–45) and the restoration of their economic strength from 1950, this meant that West Germany would dominate the EDC. Moreover a Board of Commissioners, not a French General, would run it and, unlike France, West Germany was not distracted or weakened by problems of decolonisation.

This was entirely the wrong result, the very reverse of the Pleven Plan and almost wholly unacceptable and unsellable politically in France. The Dutch too, who had been reluctant participants at the start, were concerned originally that the ECSC plus the EDC would be a platform for French hegemony in Western Europe. By 1952 both France and all three Benelux States were worried that a supranational EDC would not stop the resumption of German dominance.

Such misgivings resulted in delays to parliamentary ratification of the EDC Treaty and to increased pressure on the UK to participate or to provide binding guarantees to the EDC. In an effort to reassure EDC signatories the ECSC Assembly agreed on 10 September 1952 to devise plans for the EPC to cover the ECSC and EDC, as allowed for under Article 38 of the EDC Treaty. Alcide de Gasperi, Italy's Prime Minister, had inserted this clause because of his federalist beliefs and to allay the fears of the small states of domination by the big ones. By March 1953 the draft plan allowed for a bicameral parliament, a senate representing the six states and a popularly elected assembly to provide for political control over both the EDC and ECSC. Eden's alternative idea, which would not have had to wait for EDC ratification, was to adapt the existing machinery of the Council of Europe for the ECSC and eventually the EDC too. This would permit close UK political 'association' with both bodies and allow the six members to vote on defence, coal and steel issues with non-members as participant observers. Eden's initiative of a fast track to a political authority was rejected by 'Little Europe' in favour of the Article 38 route. Monnet, too, saw this Eden Plan as a threat to the ECSC's independence (Fursdon, 1980, pp. 213–14).

In January 1953 the US government changed: Eisenhower became the first Republican President for 20 years, with John Foster Dulles as his Secretary of State. They were determined to speed up progress with EDC ratification. The French were blamed for delays and prevarication, and the UK for lack of vigour and a lukewarm diplomacy in pushing for the EDC. In January 1953 Dulles threatened 'a little rethinking on Europe' to hasten developments. Between March and June 1953 this became the threat of the US reverting to a 'peripheral strategy' (a US withdrawal from Western Europe except for bases in Spain, UK and Iceland). These threats were directed at France particularly because of mounting US impatience with delays in ratification.

However, the actual prospects for EDC ratification deteriorated when Stalin died on 5 March 1953, and the USSR seemed less menacing as Malenkov, his successor, appeared more moderate. The Korean War, which started the saga of West German rearmament, ended in an armistice signed on 27 July 1953. In May 1953 Churchill called for a summit conference with Malenkov to end the Cold War. This strengthened opponents of German rearmament providing an excellent excuse for delaying ratification. Malenkov's 'peace offensive' aimed to undermine the process of West European military integration and German rearmament by Soviet proposals for a 'neutralised' united Germany (Young, 1986, pp. 889–95; Fish, 1986, pp. 33–34).

By December 1953 American exasperation with French delays to ratification and annoyance with Churchill's proposal for four-power talks with the Russians before the EDC was in place meant renewed pressure from the Americans. Eden was warned by Dulles in December 1953 of an 'agonising reappraisal' of US defence commitments if the EDC failed. Dulles threatened to swing over to 'hemispheric defence', abandoning Europe and putting Asia first. Eden told Dulles that the French were 'impervious to cajolery or the prospect of dire alternatives', and urged the NATO solution for German rearmament should the EDC fail.

Eden, unlike the French, did not dismiss this threat as a complete bluff. On 12 December 1953 he wrote to the Minister of Defence urging him to consider the possibility of putting a UK unit into the EDC as he was 'convinced we were at a turning point in the whole relationship of the US to Europe and we must have recourse to all our imagination and ingenuity to help the EDC through'. Eden faced a dilemma. If the EDC passed it might facilitate US withdrawal from Europe (once West German troops were in place). Dulles now threatened withdrawal if the EDC failed.

Why were the French impervious to such US threats? France was much more concerned with the German question than the Russian threat and could only gain by delay. If France had attempted to ratify the Treaty in the National Assembly, and by some miracle it passed, a European army would have been created, with West Germany rearmed and the French army disbanded. If the EDC failed in the Chamber the Anglo-Americans could then have rearmed Germany via the NATO solution. Only through delaying ratification did France gain by effectively freezing the whole issue of German rearmament and the restoration of full sovereignty to West Germany.

The French were immune to Dulles' bullying for three other reasons. France was logistically crucial to the US and NATO defence strategy for Western Europe. US bases in France and French troops in NATO made France a vital ally for America. Second, the vagaries of the French party political and parliamentary systems, under the constitution of the Fourth Republic 1946–58, meant that foreign governments had to deal with eight French coalition governments during the lifetime of the European army scheme 1950–54, and seven different Prime Ministers, although only three different Foreign Ministers (Williams, 1954, p. 440, Appendix 3).

Finally, France was engaged in a colonial war in Indo-China against the Vietminh, struggling for national liberation with Chinese communist support. For Eisenhower and Dulles France was at the frontline containing the spread of communism in Indo-China. By 1954 the US was funding 80 per cent of the cost of France's colonial war: some $800m on supporting France in Indo-China, amounting to a third of the total US military aid budget. France was desperate to extricate itself from Indo-China and the US was very concerned that France might simply throw in the towel and abandon the struggle. This would have been a major setback for US foreign policy and influence in Asia. Eisenhower in his memoirs complained that the French were always 'tying the fate of the EDC to our willingness to do things in Indo-China as the French government desired'. The military situation in Indo-China was deteriorating rapidly from February 1954, and the US sent 400 US Air Force mechanics and light bombers to support French forces there. Dulles at the Berlin Conference (of the UK, US, USSR and French Foreign Ministers) in January–February 1954, had very reluctantly agreed to support Laniel's (the French Prime Minister) and Bidault's urgent request for a conference on Indo-China to end the war. This was agreed with Molotov, the Soviet Foreign Minister, at Berlin and scheduled for Geneva in April. Dulles gave way on this because he believed Laniel would swiftly ratify the EDC Treaty, and felt betrayed when this did not happen.

Between January and April 1954 four states ratified the EDC Treaty; only France and Italy had not done so (Dockrill, 1991, p. 139). For Dulles, Soviet intransigence at the Berlin Conference made the EDC indispensable but events there, in Indo-China and in France, reduced the prospects of attainment.

Molotov, at the Berlin Conference, had contrived to publicise a clause in the Bonn Contractual Agreements, stating that any future unified Germany would be free to withdraw from the EDC as it was not bound by the obligations of the FRG. French opponents of the EDC fastened on this fact, further reducing chances of ratification.

For France, preoccupied both with ending its Indo-China crisis and the fate of besieged French defenders at Dien Bien Phu, it meant there was little prospect of ratification until the outcome of both the conference and the battle were known. Paradoxically, the European army plan that was born in Korea was to die in Indo-China. Anthony Eden said 'the fate of the EDC was in part dependent on a solution in Indo-China' (Eden, 1960, p. 84).

Ratification in France was delayed further by the Foreign Affairs Committee of the National Assembly examining the Treaty until April, and by Laniel when Gaullists insisted on various preconditions being met including UK and US guarantees to the EDC and even the settlement of the future of the Saarland (Laniel's government included two Gaullist ministers and was dependent in part on Gaullist support). Opponents of the EDC were encouraged by the Juin Affair on 28 March 1954. Marshall Juin, Permanent Military Adviser to the French Government and Vice-President of the Supreme Council of the Armed Forces, was sacked for gross insubordination for saying in a speech to Reserve Officers that an alternative solution to the European army 'could and should be found'.

In the context of a worsening Indo-China crisis and mounting opposition to the EDC in France, Eden announced to the House of Commons on 14 April the Agreement on British co-operation with the EDC (signed in Paris the previous day). Eden said Britain was ready to place a British armoured division, stationed in Germany, within an EDC Corps and under EDC command when the Treaty came into effect (House of Commons Debates, 1953–54, vol. 526, cols 1142–45). This offer came too late to sway French opinion in favour of the EDC. Eden had warned Sir Christopher Steel, UK delegate at the Paris EDC talks, of this a month before but had told him not to reveal it to the French 'as it might only induce them to ask for more or for a written guarantee'. Eden's announcement was well received in the US and by it he hoped to avoid any blame for the probable demise of the scheme. Under Dulles' threat of 'agonising reappraisal' and the need to prevent the UK being the scapegoat for the EDC's failure, Eden offered a division of tanks for the European army. The timing was well judged – it came too late to improve the chance of ratification in France.

The Geneva Conference on Indo-China started on 26 April 1954 (where Eden and Molotov were co-chairmen). The long expected fall of Dien Bien Phu occurred on 7 May 1954 when the last French Legionnaire defenders surrendered, finally overrun by the Vietminh's human wave assaults. Laniel survived an immediate vote of confidence but his government fell on 12 June during the Indo-China Debate. On 16 June the forthcoming Washington Talks (scheduled for 25–26 June 1954) between the UK and US were announced. These informal talks were intended to repair Anglo-American relations which had been turbulent and badly damaged by the Geneva Conference. Eden and Dulles had had at least two rows in recent weeks. Dulles was furious that Britain refused to back American plans for 'united action' in support of the French in Indo-China and had to abandon the idea of military intervention there (bombing the hills around Dien Bien Phu and sending in Divisions of US marines). Eden was subsequently accused of appeasement of communist China and his efforts at diplomatic brokerage between parties at

Geneva were, he felt, misrepresented by US State Department officials and the American press as creating a 'Far Eastern Munich'. Dulles in a speech at Los Angeles on 11 June 1954 made pointed references to Britain's faint-heartedness.

Commenting on the forthcoming Washington Talks, the French newspaper *Le Monde*, on 17 June 1954, in the absence of a French government, referred to the humiliation of France,

> because the two main questions for discussion at Washington will be Indo-China and German rearmament in which French interest is second to none ... and that the Prime Minister [Churchill] will have a new opportunity to plead for an autonomous wehrmacht and may meet less American opposition than he did at Bermuda.

(The Bermuda Conference was in early December 1953 between France, UK and US.)

The weekend talks in Washington marked a rapprochement in Anglo-American relations. Agreement was reached on Eden's solution for Indo-China of partition along the 17th Parallel, establishing a joint 'study group' to consider alternatives to the EDC should it fail as well as a timetable for getting the EDC or alternative solutions through before November's mid-term elections in the United States. The US and UK seized the initiative over the EDC away from France as the Geneva Conference was moving towards an agreement. French diplomats two weeks later, in July, complained of an 'organised campaign of pressure against France', and of leaked 'hypothetical alternative policies' to the EDC (such as a return to Bizonia without France!) (Public Record Office (PRO), FO 371/112781, 7 July 1954).

It was recognised in the capitals of 'Little Europe', London and Washington, that once Laniel's government had gone there was no chance of a self-declared pro-EDC candidate winning an absolute majority of the National Assembly's votes (314) needed for investiture as Prime Minister. On 19 June 1954 Mendès-France (with 419 votes) became the first French Premier since 1952 not to commit himself to ratification but to promise a vote by a certain date. His government composed of Radicals and Gaullist ministers, was split on the EDC issue. The Socialist Party who voted him into office and called for ratification of the Treaty also refused to participate in his government! He was the first Prime Minister since 1947 that the Communist Party (99 votes) voted into office sensing the end of the EDC.

On 23 July Mendès-France's Indo-China settlement was approved by the National Assembly but on the issue of the EDC Mendès-France announced that his government was 'united only on one point namely that they disagreed completely with everyone else' (PRO FO 800/790, FR/54/5, 6 August 1954). Mendès-France pressed his allies for a two-month delay before putting the EDC to the vote as it was likely to fail so soon after the Indo-China settlement. Churchill, in a note to Eden, opposed any further postponements as they would 'alter the whole timetable for fulfilling the Bonn Convention as agreed by us with Ike in Washington' (PRO FO 800/779, EN/54/15).

On 6 August Mendès-France wanted to renegotiate the whole EDC Treaty, with complete disregard for the position of the Benelux and German governments, who had already ratified the treaty. Mendès-France wanted to remove the supranational components and equality of rights for Germany in the Treaty and in effect create 'a European Army for the Germans and a French Army for France'. Italy, poised to ratify the Treaty, backed off from doing so in the face of these French proposals. The disappointment and shock apparently killed Alcide de Gasperi, the Italian ex-Prime Minister (Fursdon, 1980, pp. 269, 280, 284–85). At the Brussels Conference on 19 August 1954, Mendès-France met to argue his case with the other EDC states. It was rejected as wholly unacceptable. Following this conference Mendès-France visited Churchill at Chartwell, who told him the Western Bloc 'could not agree to be governed by the impotence of the French Chamber in which we have no vote' (Kirkpatrick, 1959, p. 261). Yet Churchill also hinted to Mendès-France that Britain would pursue an alternative solution should the EDC fail, which was of some encouragement. Churchill also telegrammed Dulles after this meeting to report that Mendès-France was 'much keener about NATO ... as France would not be boxed up in civil and military affairs with a more active and powerful West Germany, whereas in the NATO system, the UK and US counter-balance Germany to proper proportions' (Fursdon 1980, p. 292; PRO FO 800/790 FR/54/28, 24 August 1954).

Following the Brussels Conference few realistically expected the EDC to survive a vote; it was generally discounted as a 'dead duck' by US State Department officials briefing the American press. On 30 August 1954 the long saga of the EDC ended; it died in the French National Assembly without even being accorded the dignity of a debate; a technical motion was passed to proceed to other business. Communists and Gaullist deputies got to their feet and sang *La Marseillaise* amid general uproar. Mendès-France abstained and his government remained neutral – it was not made an issue of confidence and was therefore not a resigning matter if it failed (Fursdon, 1980, pp. 296–97). Mendès-France stayed in office and the EDC was buried. Laniel's government had paradoxically survived a vote of confidence on the subject of a European army on 27 November 1953, which had encouraged Eisenhower and Dulles to believe in the EDC's eventual ratification. However, the issue then was of confidence, not the Treaty's ratification.

This French rejection of a French scheme was the cause of much bitterness, resentment and disappointment in the capitals of 'Little Europe' – and also in Washington. However, while generally regarded as a diplomatic defeat for the US, it was not a domestic political issue. Democrats and Republicans were similarly distressed. Dulles described it as a 'serious set back' and a 'tragedy' and said: 'US post war policies were framed on the assumption that Western Europe would at long last develop a unity which would make it immune from war between its members and defensible against aggression from without' (PRO FO 371 / 1090 1 28 August–4 September 1954).

In London, Washington and Bonn there had for some months been a growing apprehension regarding Konrad Adenauer's political future. French delays and prevarication had jeopardised his Western-orientated policy's survival and increased the danger of Germany drifting towards 'nationalism and neutrality' because of the political strain of enduring the agony of the EDC's living death. After 30 August the German predicament became an urgent matter (borne out by the Schleswig-Holstein September election results – seen as a rebuff to Adenauer's policy on the EDC) as the Bonn Contractual Agreement had collapsed along with the EDC and its associated plans, under Article 38, for an EPC. It was widely anticipated in the press that Britain and America would now restore German sovereignty and obtain a German contribution to defence even against French opposition.

After what Eden referred to as 'the entangling impediment' of the EDC was dead, he took the initiative to pursue Britain's preferred NATO solution for German rearmament and restoration of German sovereignty. The Americans had no alternative to the EDC prepared. Eden's plan, which he claimed he thought of in the bath, was to use the Brussels Treaty of 1948. An enlarged Brussels Treaty Organization (BTO) renamed Western European Union – would make West Germany's absorption into NATO more acceptable to France, providing a figleaf of political control as Britain and France were already members of the BTO. It was a non-supranational consultative body and Germany and Italy could be equal members. Dockrill has shown that, in fact, it was an old idea (Eden had mentioned it in Cabinet in December 1952). Eden's plan won UK Cabinet approval on 27 August 1954 (Fursdon, 1980, p. 313; Dockrill, 1991, p. 146).

Eden on 11 September embarked on his whirlwind diplomacy, making a flying circuit of Brussels, Bonn, Rome and Paris. His Brussels plan solution was received with some relief in the first three. Eden, in Paris, impressed on Mendès-France the dangers of driving Germany into the arms of Russia and the US into 'fortress America' (PRO FO 371/109101). Mendès-France subsequently announced the Brussels solution as his own idea.

On 28 September 1954 a nine-power conference started at Lancaster House, London, to resolve finally the vexed linked issues of German rearmament and restoration of German sovereignty based on Eden's plan. At the right psychological moment, Eden committed Britain's four divisions and the tactical air force stationed in West Germany to stay permanently in NATO for 50 years (and not to withdraw them without WEU approval). This was a commitment he had declined to give to the EDC, when requested by Schuman, in March 1954. Adenauer agreed to the 'ABC weapons policy' – of Germany not producing atomic, bacteriological and chemical weapons. France finally gave up her 'prolonged resistance against Germany's entry into NATO' (Fursdon, 1980, p. 325; Young, 1988, ch. 3, p. 99; Dockrill, 1991, pp. 146–50). Dulles pledged US support. Thirty-three days after the French rejection of the EDC, accords were signed in London and Paris resolving the joint issues of rearmament and restoration of sovereignty for Germany Thanks to Eden's statecraft Dulles could stage the first televised 'Cabinet meeting' at the White House to draw national attention to this foreign policy success (after setbacks with Indo-China and the EDC) as part of the mid--term Republican election campaign.

By 5 May 1955 the ratification process was completed (it still took two attempts in the French National Assembly in December 1954). West Germany attained full sovereignty, with the termination of the last vestiges of the allied occupation regime, and the new Bundeswehr entered NATO.

Once German rearmament in NATO was an accomplished fact it ceased to be a political issue in France. This also applied to the USSR. In 1955 West Germany and the USSR exchanged ambassadors.

A postscript to the 1950s European army scheme was the Franco-German plan for developing the WEU into a separate European defence pillar in autumn 1991, prior to the Maastricht European Council meeting. Britain's reaction was a faithful echo of her 1950s policy, insisting that any proposed WEU force should be autonomous, within NATO and outside EC control, 'linked to both and subordinated to neither'. Britain still did not want closer European co-operation to interfere with NATO nor encourage US withdrawal.

The eventual resolution of German rearmament confirms the substance of the old saw that 'NATO is all about keeping the Russians out, the Germans down, the Americans in and the French calm'.

The final irony for France was that it was not the Bundeswehr but the French army that proved the greater menace to the Fourth Republic in May 1958 (the threat of a military uprising code-named 'Resurrection' assisted General de Gaulle's return to power).

Why should so much attention be paid to an unsuccessful scheme? The EDC episode has a wider historical significance concerning the scope and motives for European integration. Nothing like it has been tried since. The hastily conceived European Union Treaty of 1992 did not attempt to recreate anything like the EPC or EDC. The only successful integration for 45 years has been economic. This suggests that the parameters for viable integration are fairly narrow, precluding, to date, non-economic supranational schemes.

The EDC is generally portrayed as an over-ambitious project in too sensitive an area that collapsed because it was such an idealistic and premature attempt at integration. However, was it a real attempt at integration or a French device for delay? The EDC may have collapsed but did it fail? From the standpoint of French national interests and security the outcome of the entire Pleven Plan–EDC episode, 1950–55, was not a failure at all. Fursdon, in conclusion, saw the EDC as 'the French device for keeping Germany out of NATO' (Fursdon, 1980, p. 337). It successfully delayed German rearmament and joining NATO for almost five years. Moreover, the European army scheme protected the Schuman Plan and embryonic ECSC as it prevented the restoration of German sovereignty by another means. The fact that the EDC and Bonn Agreements were inextricably linked meant that France managed to prevent the restoration of full German sovereignty between 1950 and 1955. Why was this important to the ECSC's success? When it came into effect economic controls over German coal and steel were to end and France promised to press for the disbandment of the International Authority of the Ruhr. However, if Germany had regained its sovereignty by supplying troops to NATO, as the US proposed in September 1950, this might well have destroyed any German interest in the ECSC or at best weakened the French negotiating position. Would West Germany have made economic concessions to France in the ECSC if she had less to gain politically?

The ECSC Treaty did not complete ratification until August 1952 and its Common Market only started to operate fully in 1953. The ECSC's supranational High Authority and other components were untried experimental arrangements. So French control over the restoration of full sovereignty through the EDC Treaty provided some political insurance for the ECSC throughout the early 1950s. It would obviously be fallacious to impute French motives for creating the EDC between 1950–52 based only on evidence of its failure in 1954–55. Nevertheless it was the case that only by postponing ratification, by not putting the Treaty to the vote in the National Assembly, could France prevent German rearmament and the restoration of full sovereignty, as after a vote, and regardless of the result, German rearmament and full powers would certainly follow, either through the EDC or the NATO solution.

What are the implications of the EDC's collapse for Lipgens' and Milward's explanations of European integration? Lipgens' view of the 1950s integration was that governments were putting European federalist ideas 'partly into effect', but there is no evidence for this at all (only the Americans and Italians were really interested in the prospects for political federation). The EDC episode revealed governments pursuing their own rather different national objectives and interests through diplomacy and bargaining, not co-operating together to construct an idealised conception of a federal Europe. Adenauer's overriding objective was the re-emergence of a full independent West German state: this was achieved and permitted through the architectural framework of the ECSC and the NATO/WEU solution.

The parallel sagas of the ECSC and EDC 1950–54 tend to confirm Milward's thesis that only economic integration is successful. Economic integration only occurs when nation states' economic plans and prospects depend on links with the West German economy. The Pleven Plan 1950, however, was conceived as a means to stop the American demand for swift West German rearmament and to protect the back of the Schuman Plan, which in turn was devised to safeguard the essential elements of the Monnet Plan. Military and civil integration as envisaged in the EDC Treaty was not an attractive political option in the early 1950s. Had the EDC come into force the supranational Board of Commissioners would decide where to deploy troops; German conscripts could have been stationed in France, Belgium and Holland.

Eden and the Foreign Office thought the end of the EDC and success of the 'Brussels Pact solution' for West German rearmament was a setback to 'federalists' and for supranational schemes in Western Europe. This was a major miscalculation. The demise of the EDC finally cleared the way for further negotiations on European economic integration. In fact, without the obstacle of the EDC they would probably have started much sooner.

In May 1955 West German sovereignty was restored and the WEU came into force, and in June the Messina Talks were held by the six 'Little Europe' states to consider establishing two new communities.

6 From the Common Market and the Treaties of Rome (1957) to the first enlargement (1973)

British hopes of stopping 'federalist' moves in Europe with the European Defence Community's failure and the success of the Western European Union were immediately quashed. Even before the ink was dry on the agreements concerning German sovereignty, in Paris in October 1954, parallel Franco-German negotiations were underway on their further economic co-operation or association. These included the possibility of German investment in the French Union (the French equivalent of the Commonwealth). By November 1954 the Americans were pressing 'Little Europe' to turn the WEU into a single trading area, an economic 'United States of Europe'. They envisaged a two-tier economic and political structure to balance the military unification of the WEU. One tier would be a 'Little Europe' of the six states, the other would be the UK with eventually perhaps the Scandinavians and others joining. (The stock reaction of the US to the creation of a new European organisation as seen previously with the OEEC and EPU was to try and widen its scope.)

British Foreign Office officials feared these initiatives might lead to the UK's exclusion from Europe and to a trade war with a new superstate, created under American and German auspices, while British forces were committed to its defence under NATO and the WEU. Four years later, in January 1958, under the Treaty of Rome, the European Economic Community (EEC) started to operate. Although far from being a superstate, Britain had indeed chosen to stay out of the EEC while its army and tactical airforce in West Germany defended its frontiers (*European Review,* 49, November 1954; 50, December 1954).

What exactly did the Treaties of Rome entail and how did this situation arise? The Treaties were signed by the six 'Little Europe' states on 25 March 1957. These established the EEC, a common market in manufactured goods with a Common Agricultural Policy (CAP) and Euratom a common market in nuclear materials providing equal access to stocks of uranium 233. The Treaty of Rome establishing the EEC with its 248 articles, protocols and appendices was, none the less, mainly a statement of intent, a programme of action, a timetable. It was not a detailed comprehensive blueprint of regulations, as there simply had not been enough time for the necessary detailed micro-planning and negotiations between June 1955 and March 1957. The EEC came into force on 1 January 1958 with a completion date set for full operation of 31 December 1969. The Treaty's actual provisions often consisted of general statements concerning objectives and intentions where the details would have to be worked on and agreed in the future. The original Treaty of 177 pages contained only five on agriculture and Article 43 concerning a common agricultural policy occupied less than one page – although the eventual CAP was to consume more than two-thirds of the EEC budget by the late 1970s. The Treaty of Rome actually left virtually everything to be done. It did not automatically deliver a common market but relied on governments to reach agreement later. The EEC spent the first year of its official existence setting up shop in Brussels and getting its administrative machinery working. By the end of 1958 it had designed an ambitious programme for economic and commercial expansion in Europe, and common welfare and social policy objectives. The removal of tariffs and quantity restrictions by the six to create a single common market was to take place in three stages of four years each, starting in 1958. In the first stage tariffs were to be reduced by 30 per cent, in the second four years by 60 per cent and abolished completely by the end of the third stage. All export subsidies, export taxes and revenue duties on imports had to go before the end of the first stage. Although there were difficult negotiations between 1958–60 regarding the internal trade of the Common Market, tariff cuts were made ahead of the Treaty's scheduled timetable. By the end of 1960 tariff cuts already amounted to 30 per cent, while at the end of 1963 a 60 per cent cut had been agreed. In 1961 the removal of all quotas on imports was speeded up so that all quantity restrictions on imports enforced by EEC members were abolished.

The administrative structure of the EEC was very similar to the ECSC. The three communities, the ECSC, EEC and Euratom, shared the same Assembly now called the European Parliament and Court of Justice. Since 1967 they have had a common Council of Ministers and Commission, so that the three communities were fused into one with a common set of institutions.

Although the preamble to the Treaty of Rome 1957 reaffirmed their determination 'to establish the foundations of an ever closer union among the European peoples', following the failure of the EDC the word 'federalism' was never mentioned. For the EEC emphasis was placed on short- and medium-term economic and commercial benefits rather than long-term political possibilities to avoid arousing the latent fears of nationalists. It was essentially a commercial treaty between six states embedded in another supranational community.

Two institutions were of crucial importance to this community. The Commission of the EEC was the central concept behind the integrated organisation of the EEC. The architect of this was Pierre Uri, a French economist and colleague of Jean Monnet. The Commission had a multifunctional purpose and role, it acted as the EEC's executive civil service and it espoused the communities' interest (commissioners took an oath to pursue community and not national interests). The commissioners' main role was to initiate policy ('the Commission proposes but the Council disposes'). It was also the guardian of the Treaties – an important policing role to avoid systemic collapse through non-compliance, ensuring that members kept their obligations by mediating between members' interests and the Treaties' rules. The EEC's Commission had no national equivalent, being much more than a neutral bureaucratic executive. Indeed, it was initially regarded by many as the 'engine' of the EEC and 'an ever closer union'. The nine-man Commission to run the EEC with Professor Walter Hallstein as its first President, was different from the ECSC's High Authority in a number of respects.

The six states wanted to retain as much power as possible in their own hands and take all major decisions on proposals originating from the Commission through the EEC's Council of Ministers. Decision-making power lay collectively with 'the Six' – France, West Germany, Italy and Benelux. The Commission and the Council of Ministers together constituted the supranational integrated element in the Rome Treaties. The six member states transferred decisions concerning the Common Market and atomic energy to a supranational Council of Ministers drawn from the six states whose decisions were binding on all and had to be followed.

Unlike the ECSC's High Authority the six countries reserved the right to name their own commissioners, so in the EEC they were national nominees. The Commission also was wholly dependent on financial contributions from member states (until 1970) whereas the High Authority of the ECSC was financially autonomous through its own sales taxes. The EEC's Commission exercised less power than Monnet's High Authority of the ECSC (the original Schuman plan for an ECSC did not even include a Council of Ministers). By 1957 Monnet's High Authority was considered too powerful by France and Belgium.

The European Parliament was never a legislature: it has not passed a law since it started in 1952 as the assembly of the ECSC. Between 1958–75 it had to be consulted by the Council of Ministers which was then free to ignore it. The Parliament could also dismiss en masse the Commission voting with a two-thirds majority, a drastic but somewhat empty political check as national governments, not the Parliament, would have made the reappointments. Since 1970 the EP has won more budgetary control over EEC non-compulsory expenditure (the CAP, coming under the Treaty of Rome 1957 and representing 70 per cent of the budget in 1980, was 'compulsory' and so excluded). In 1975 an Amendment Treaty enabled the EP to reject the EEC budget as a whole, which has occurred a number of times. A Court of Auditors was established in 1977 due to the EP's demand for a closer audit of EEC expenditure. In 1979 the first direct elections to the EP were held (previously representatives were sent by members' parliaments).

The Treaty of the European Union on 7 February 1992, in a gesture towards reducing the 'democratic deficit', gave the EP the power of 'co-decision' with the Council of Ministers over a limited number of issues (EU Treaty

1992, Article 189b) on internal market law, policies of research and development, training, education, health, consumer affairs. However, the key policies of agriculture (66 per cent of budget by 1986), fishing, foreign policies, competition and regional policies were all excluded. The EP since 1992 can 'request' the Commission to submit any proposal it wants where it considers new legislation is needed (EU Treaty 1992, Article 138b); whether the Commission is obliged to accede to such requests is another matter. While the EU Treaty also established an ombudsman, gave the EP more investigative powers and made the appointment of Commissioners and President subject to EP approval, these gains were mainly at the Commission's expense. Power in the EU still lies with the nation states in the Council of Ministers.

Why was the EEC a common market and not simply a Customs Union or free trade area (FTA)? Distinguishing between these three schemes provides the answer. An FTA abolishes customs duties and quotas between members; a Customs Union is the same as an FTA but also imposes a Common External Tariff (CET) on outsiders. A Customs Union was legal under GATT Article 24 providing the CET was no bigger than current duties and reduced to zero over time. Both FTAs and Customs Unions could be interdependent organisations. A common market was a Customs Union which also pursued common policies inside; accordingly a common market was an integrated supranational body simply because of these common policies.

Why did the Treaty of Rome 1957 establish an EEC with common policies in a common market and not just an FTA or Customs Union? The principal architect of the EEC, Pierre Uri, followed Friedrich List, the nineteenth-century German economist, in thinking that free trade in a technologically advanced era only made sense between countries whose industries were developed to the same extent. Simple free trade could not satisfy French national economic needs as much of French artisanal industry was internationally uncompetitive. Also, a free trade area would only cover trade in industrial goods not agriculture (which employed 28 per cent of the French labour force in 1955) nor would it accommodate France's colonies.

Moreover, simply opening frontiers to trade would be unfair as it would lead to distorted trade patterns as governments pursued different economic policies. Some heavily subsidised industrial exports, some had anti-monopoly laws, or imposed a heavy burden of social security costs on employers or followed deflationary policies. Free trade was considered insufficient as differences in national economic policies had to be dealt with. Consequently a common set of rules for a common market was devised so that member states would not 'play the same economic game by different rules'. This has always been the logic behind the Common Market's regulations on, for example, competition policy, the Common Agricultural Policy and the harmonisation of social security payments and benefits. Lynch shows that the French car industry's prices were much higher than her competitors due to higher wages and social charges (Lynch, 1993, p. 79). It was therefore considered essential to try to equalise social security costs (which in France could amount to as much as 40 per cent of the employers' wage costs) so that no 'unfair' burden was imposed on industries in a common market.

Similarly, there could be no simple free trade in arable, livestock and dairy products within a Customs Union because agricultural subsidies and protection varied so much between the six. Something else had to be devised – the French were insistent on the creation of a Common Agricultural Policy within the Treaty of Rome 1957, with common prices, protection and subsidies within 'Little Europe'.

The objective behind creating a common market was that it would lead to one large amalgamated economy of 170 million consumers at the end of a 12–15-year transition period. Six national economic systems would then, it was thought, be fused effectively into one domestic economy through common policies, common rules, the free movement of goods, labour and capital.

Pierre Uri and other architects of the Common Market 1955–57 expected that national responsibility for economic prosperity and full employment would be assumed by a supranational EEC, resulting in fiscal, monetary and even political union. In reality it took 40 years for the European Community to embark on a process leading to Economic and Monetary Union (EMU) by 1999 under the timetable established at the Maastricht Summit and under the Treaty on European Union 1992. However, back in 1970 EMU was supposed to be attained within a decade.

How did the move towards a common market and Euratom start? Monnet by 1955 had become enthusiastic about the collective commercial development of atomic energy by 'the Six', given the success of the ECSC. Joint European action on the nuclear front was an attractive prospect in the mid-1950s as it would reduce dependence on Middle East oil and American coal. Gas and oil extraction in the Sahara had not begun and North Sea natural gas off Holland had yet to be discovered. Nuclear power seemed to be the fuel of the future. Western Europe appeared short of energy resources at this time, a fact demonstrated vividly by the Arab oil embargo in the wake of the 1956 Suez crisis. The peaceful use of atomic energy became a matter of high priority with the cutting off of Europe's oil supplies. Collective co-operation in atomic energy made sense as the Six could pool their technical expertise and knowledge, and use Belgian uranium in the Congo, with Germany sharing the cost of building separators and reactors.

Jacques Beyen, the Dutch Foreign Minister, had proposed the formation of a common market in 1952 (combining it with the EDC/ EPC schemes). He revived the idea in early 1955 in response to Mendès-France's proposed 'Franco-German economic committee' of December 1954, that was intended to bind the two economies more closely together (Lynch, 1993, pp. 75–76). Beyen could not allow Benelux to be excluded, as while there was some substance in Walter Lippman's colourful description in 1962 of the EEC as 'a bargain between French agriculture and German industry' the reality was more complex. In 1957 the Netherlands supplied more agricultural products to Germany than France, and imported more German vehicles and machinery than the French.

Initially the French Foreign Ministry was not keen on the idea of a common market and for many West European statesmen it seemed almost inconceivable that the French could ever be converted to anything approaching free trade. However, as we shall show, the French economic ministries came to regard a common market as the solution for France's economic predicaments. The reverse was true in Germany where the Foreign Ministry and Chancellor Adenauer were enthusiastic about the political benefits whereas the Economic Minister Ludwig Erhard was very much opposed to a common market, seeing harmonisation of social charges as a threat to German competitiveness (Milward, 1992, p. 213).

Consequently there were internal departmental arguments in both France and Germany over the merits of a common market, 1955–57, and also much hard bargaining between the six states over the terms of the Rome Treaties.

Following discussions between Monnet, Beyen and Spaak (Belgium's Foreign Minister 1954–57) both the idea for a common market and Euratom were to be formally proposed at the Messina Conference of the six foreign ministers in June 1955. Monnet and Spaak were much more positive about Euratom than a common market but Beyen was insistent that it was both or neither. The six foreign ministers were meeting in Sicily to appoint Rene Mayer as Monnet's successor as President of the ECSC's High Authority. This was because France was the only ECSC member that did not want Monnet to serve a second five-year term as ECSC's President. Monnet had effectively become persona non grata within French governing circles following a dispute with Mendès-France over the dilution of supranational controls in late 1954. Monnet, who really wanted to continue in the post, resigned and set up the 'Action Committee of all the Non-Communist Political Parties and Trade Unions of the Six', as a pressure group for further European integration.

Spaak and Beyen's paper on the dual proposal formed the basis of the conference communiqué to establish a common market and Euratom. Messina in 'Euro-mythology' is regarded as the starting point for '*la relance europénne*' after the EDC's collapse and the birthplace of the Common Market.

A small team was assembled under Spaak's chairmanship to study the schemes and draw up plans, including experts from the ECSC in Luxembourg such as Monnet's right-hand man, the imaginative French economist Pierre Uri. Another Frenchman, Robert Marjolin, resigned as Secretary-General of the OEEC to take part. The German team included Adenauer's mentor on foreign affairs, the Permanent Under-Secretary of Foreign Affairs, Professor Walter Hallstein. The British sent as their representative a Board of Trade official Russell Bretherton, a former economics don at Wadham College, Oxford. He was initially briefed to try and steer the talks towards an OEEC free-trade area framework for West European commerce and trade. When this failed the UK became only an observer at the talks and finally left to try and undermine the proceedings (Young, 1989, p. 210). In May 1956 the Spaak Report (mainly written by Pierre Uri) was submitted to another Foreign Ministers' conference in Venice and broadly approved. The same team was then consigned to the Chateau de Val Duchesse outside Brussels to draw up a Treaty. The Spaak Report emphasised the necessity of fusing separate national markets as 'the strength of a large market is its ability to reconcile mass production with the absence of monopoly'. It went on to argue that the 'advantages of a common market cannot be obtained ... unless measures are taken to put an end to practices whereby competition between producers is distorted; and unless co-operation is established between the states to ensure monetary stability, economic expansion and social progress'. The Spaak Report's proposal for a common market went much further than Britain's simple aim of a free trade area. The whole process of establishing the EEC and Euratom took place extraordinarily quickly and, compared with the EDC episode, relatively painlessly. The Treaty of Rome was signed on 25 March 1957 and ratified by the six parliaments by July 1957.

Why did the six governments of 'Little Europe' sign what was essentially a commercial treaty, and their parliaments subsequently ratify it? The obvious reason was because it was the right thing to do. What they had decided to create proved to be a mutually beneficial political and economic framework for the continued expansion of trade, industrial and agricultural growth in Western Europe.

There was diplomatic pressure from the OEEC to reduce tariffs and quotas on intra-European trade and also move to full currency convertibility. The US pressed for yet another attempt at European unity. Although in 1954–55 the Foreign Offices of 'the Six' believed that French agricultural and industrial interests would never accept a common market, attitudes had and were changing in France because of economic circumstances. By 1957 France recognised that a common market in 'Little Europe' was the right commercial framework for French national economic and diplomatic objectives.

French experience in the ECSC revealed that anxiety over their supposed industrial inferiority and lack of competitiveness (because of a heavy social-security bill) had been exaggerated. Also, since 1946 the French economy had been modernised under successive four-year reconstruction plans and the largest and most modern firms were becoming more export-minded. Exports were considered vital to continued growth and expansion. In a sense this modern export sector in France had the worst of both worlds as they were faced with competition from Volkswagen and Grundig in export markets while bearing the cost of measures intended to coddle artisanal old-fashioned businesses in France. The export sector had competition in the export markets but not at home where it could have revitalised antiquated French business. The dynamic export-orientated element of French industry was attracted to the EEC and had considerable influence with the French civil service. French Economic Ministries were eventually convinced that to complete the modernisation of French industry, the whole manufacturing sector, including protected artisanal industries, should receive shock therapy by being immersed in a competitive common market.

A common market also looked an increasingly attractive solution to the problems facing the French government with the Departments and Territories of Metropolitan France (Dom-Toms). Even before the Dutch proposed a common market in 1955 French officials in October 1954 were discussing the possibility of Germany investing in their Dom-Toms because France alone could no longer afford to. Moreover, the proposed full convertibility of currencies would end the main protection French goods enjoyed in the Franc Area of the Dom-Toms, and an OEEC agreement in 1954 to open up colonial trade to all members also threatened France's commercial monopoly of Dom-Toms' trade. Frances Lynch has shown that French goods cost 19 per cent more in the Dom-Toms and so cross-subsidised cheap French exports to the rest of the world. Algeria was a particularly big market, taking 21 per cent of French car exports in 1954 (Lynch, 1993, p. 71). Lynch showed French planners recognised that with the OEEC agreement ending France's monopoly of Dom-Tom commerce there could be advantages in linking the French Union's Dom-Toms with 'Little Europe'. By doing so France might gain the quid pro quo of Germany and the others' net contributions to French colonial investment in return for open markets.

This was indeed the case. The EEC's Overseas Development Fund had $581.25m to invest between 1958–63. Both France and Germany contributed $200m each to this fund, yet France's African Dom-Toms received the bulk of the money, some $511.25m (Mahotière, 1961, p. 34).

The third reason for the French conversion towards a common market was that under the second Monnet Plan it was planned to increase agricultural output by 20 per cent (Lynch, 1993, pp. 75–76). France contained 47 per cent of 'Little Europe's' agricultural land and even in 1961 farming employed 20 per cent of the French workforce. French agriculture was under-mechanised so there was potential for a massive growth in production (an increase in output per man or per hectare), which would increase output well beyond the demands of the French market. Without secure markets this expansion could not proceed as it would only result in falling prices and farm incomes. The whole point of this French government plan was to raise the rural standard of living fairly quickly. In the mid-1950s West Germany imported a third of its food and, as Lynch has shown, France was negotiating to sell 2m tonnes of wheat per annum for three years to West Germany in 1954. However, Germany was insisting on full reciprocity, exporting goods to the same value that French quota restrictions currently excluded (a case of 'I'll eat your wheat if you drive my Volkswagens'). If France accepted the German demand for reciprocity France would almost certainly have to extend it to countries like Switzerland and Britain, which up to then had imported French wheat without requiring reciprocity

When Beyen proposed fresh talks about starting a common market in 1955 the consequences for France and particularly increased competition for

French industry, were little different to what the Germans were demanding in return for buying French wheat (Lynch, 1993, p. 77). For French officials in the Economic Ministries concerned with planning, the Dom-Toms and agriculture, a common market began to look an attractive policy option in 1954–55. France's diverse national economic objectives might best be secured through an integrated common market framework rather than any other arrangement.

This again tends to confirm Milward's thesis that economic integration occurs when it is needed by nation states and when national policy objectives depended on links with West Germany. Only when attainment of national economic objectives hinged on a German connection then integration and supranational organisations (ECSC and EEC) followed.

Although the Common Market was a Dutch initiative the Treaty of Rome 1957 largely reflected French preoccupations. France was in a very strong bargaining position as no one wanted the French National Assembly to reject a second Treaty and without France nothing could happen. However, any rejection by France of the Common Market would have wrecked its policy of economic rapprochement and co-operation with Germany adopted in 1948–49. In contrast to the powerful French opposition to the EDC, strong political support was mobilised in favour of the EEC in France. Jean Monnet and his 'Action Committee' were prominent here. This was an organisation of political parties not individuals; the logic being that if the main political parties and trade unions could be won over to the idea of European economic integration, few governments could resist the pressure. A key conversion was that of Eric Ollenhauer and his German SPD party, which made it easier for French Prime Minister Guy Mollet's Socialist Party (the SFIO) to forget its schism over the EDC and accept the new EEC initiative, as it was backed by the other socialist parties of 'the Six'.

Also Maurice Fauré, in charge of European Affairs at the Quai d'Orsay and elected by a rural district, kept in close contact with French agricultural leaders during the negotiations. French agriculture's eventual conversion was of critical importance for French parliamentary acceptance of the Treaty – without it the Treaty would have failed. In July 1957, the French Assemblée Nationale voted by a comfortable majority – including all the socialist and most of the rural votes – to accept the Treaty of Rome. In the German Bundestag both the CDU and the SPD voted almost unanimously in favour.

Although for France the main reason for signing the Treaty of Rome was economic, a supranational common market would help guarantee the peace of Western Europe as the continued growth of trade and prosperity should enhance both its internal and external security. Moreover, a common market might provide a platform for the reassertion of French regional leadership in Western Europe.

In West Germany's case, however, the reason for agreeing to the Rome Treaties was largely political. Ludwig Erhard, West Germany's Economics Minister, strongly opposed a common market on economic grounds. He preferred a free-trade area in which German industry would flourish. It was Konrad Adenauer who persuaded Erhard to acquiesce with the arrangements for a common market. Adenauer's main aim was to achieve a reconciliation between West Germany and its West European neighbours; France was crucial to this. Adenauer, just as with the ECSC and EDC previously, insisted on being an equal partner with equal status, and was determined to continue his West-orientated policy of embedding the Federal Republic in Western Europe.

Nevertheless, there was a great deal of hard bargaining particularly over the French demand for harmonisation of social-security costs, which Erhard considered a threat to German manufacturing competitiveness (Milward, 1992, pp. 212–13). Erhard believed that Adenauer's foreign policy would impose at French insistence a crippling burden of additional social security costs on the German economy. For example, France had a 40-hour week (compared to 45 hours in Germany), longer holidays and, in principle, equal pay for women. France insisted that the automatic timetable of tariff reductions at the end of the first stage was in fact conditional on progress in standardisation of such measures and costs. Negotiations eventually became deadlocked on 22 October 1956, only to be resolved at an Adenauer–Mollet meeting on 6 November. Between these two dates events in Hungary (where the USSR crushed a popular uprising against communism) and in Egypt where Anglo-French forces invaded, in collusion with Israel, made this Franco-German dispute about overtime pay look rather trivial. Adenauer and Mollet on 6 November swiftly resolved all outstanding disagreements delaying Treaty completion (Milward, 1992, pp. 214–15).

The old orthodox view of the significance of the Suez crisis was that it had a decisive effect on the French, propelling them into an agreement with Germany. To force the British to withdraw the Americans precipitated a sterling crisis. The pound sterling, unlike the French franc, was convertible to dollars and therefore vulnerable to American financial pressure. The US traded sterling for dollars, UK reserves fell by \$50m and the UK was brought to heel by the Americans. The traditional view was that France therefore saw Britain as a weak unreliable partner, subservient to the Americans and therefore signed up with the Federal Republic of Germany instead. Milward's research shows that this view, though neat, was not fact. Both leaders, irrespective of British behaviour, had moved towards agreement prior to Suez. On 6 November, Adenauer and Mollet agreed so quickly they barely bothered to read the document (Milward, 1992, p. 215).

Although this smoothed the way for the EEC coming into existence, there were another four years of argument after 1958 over the CAP The first moves were made at the Stresa Conference in 1958 and with the EEC Commission's proposals in 1960 to merge six different systems of agriculture into one common policy. Some states, like the Netherlands, had an expansive, aggressive policy; others, like Germany, were protective and defensive towards their agriculture (using direct subsidies to farmers, quotas and bilateral arrangements to insulate their small peasant farmers). The CAP, which France was insistent on and which involved years of argument between de Gaulle, Adenauer and Erhard, led to the abolition of all these protective measures in Germany and elsewhere. Instead there was to be a free exchange of agricultural goods combined with a uniform minimum level of prices and a guaranteed market (through storing and dumping of surpluses, exercising 'community preference', i.e. prioritising the purchase and guaranteeing a market for EEC produce and imposing big duties (agricultural levies) on competitive imports into the EEC). The CAP evolved into a highly regulated and protected market. If prices were not fixed according to sound economic criteria, enormous imbalances in production would arise. Cereal prices were vitally significant being a staple food and animal feedstuff, thereby affecting the prices indirectly of all animal products (milk, eggs, meat).

The price of corn was only agreed in 1964. Germany demanded a high price (as this was vital for their peasants' living standards) which meant an average price increase of 18 per cent in the EEC. In France it meant a 30 per cent price increase. France also had the greatest potential to increase production. From 1964 the guiding principles behind the CAP – high prices and a guaranteed market – could consequently only result in time in over-production and 'structural surpluses' (Priebe, 1973, pp. 312–14).

Adenauer's motives for co-operating with a 'French-style' common market were basically political, yet the arguments over the precise arrangements were invariably economic. However, West Germany benefited enormously from both the Common Market and the CAP. West German GNP per head between 1958–72 grew by 178 per cent, in France by 185 per cent, in UK (who pulled out of the EEC process) by only 140 per cent and in Italy by 180 per cent.

Was it the expectation of such growth that encouraged the Italian government to sign the Rome Treaties? In fact, in all six states in 1955–58 predictions of economic doom were as common as optimistic forecasts concerning the effect of a common market. In Italy, which had the highest tariff barrier in Western Europe, the fear was that its car and refrigerator industries would be destroyed by free market competition from Germany. In fact, Italy was extremely successful in selling cars and refrigerators in the EEC.

According to Federico Romero, Italy's main objective in the EEC was to encourage 'rational productive emigration'. They needed to export their unemployment, particularly from the underdeveloped south. Italy wanted and tried to win acceptance for the 'free circulation of labour' inside the EEC to complement the principle of a 'free movement of goods'. The government's main goal was an open European labour market to drain off Italy's massive unemployment (Romero, 1993, pp. 38–39). They failed to achieve this in 1957 because the other five members' priority was the antithesis of this: to safeguard jobs for their national workforce. A 'common labour policy' and the free market for labour that Italy wanted conflicted with the other states' goals of controlling immigration and protecting domestic employment. Moreover, it would seem that the Italians made an error in 1955–57 in not negotiating an

EEC 'community preference' for EEC labour. The growing demand for labour in the 1960s boom meant non-EEC Turkish and Portuguese migrants entered the EEC, particularly in Germany and Holland. There was no Treaty obligation to give priority to EEC migrants that would have benefited Italy (Romero, 1993, p. 54). Article 49 of the Rome Treaty made the free movement of labour an objective to be achieved in three stages by 1 July 1968 when work permits were abolished.

The regulations facilitating this were devised between 1961 and 1968. Regulation 15/61 allowed the free movement of labour only if there was no suitable worker available from the regular labour force of the other state. Nonetheless, it was thought that by late 1961 Germany had one million foreign workers in its farms and factories – the largest portion being Italian. Italy also needed EEC help with its economic development; the European Investment Bank and European Social Fund (ESF) were concessions to Italy. One of the first ESF schemes was the redeployment of 10,000 Italian workers to Germany and Holland to take up jobs in building, catering and industry. The ESF paid half the expense incurred by governments or employers' organisations to resettle or retrain workers; the ESF also helped provide lodgings and ensured they benefited from German and Dutch social security schemes (Mahotière, 1961, p. 356).

Although Italy won these concessions from the EEC it failed in its ambitious objective of getting 'Little Europe' to share the burden of its unemployment in the late 1950s (Romero, 1993, p. 57).

Britain's refusal to join the EEC at the start is now seen as one of the biggest mistakes of post-war international statesmanship. Although there were previous occasions when the UK declined to take a lead or participate in supranational bodies, the major error was in 1955–56 when the Conservative government under Anthony Eden entered and then left the Spaak Committee's talks. The EEC only started to function in 1958, yet already by December 1960 the Conservative Prime Minister, Harold Macmillan, had changed his mind and decided to join a club whose rules Britain had not helped to write. Britain's two applications to join were then vetoed by de Gaulle in 1963 and 1967. De Gaulle held the key and he locked Britain out. Britain only entered the EEC in 1973 after de Gaulle had resigned as French President in 1969. It had taken Britain 13 years to become a member.

How could such a miscalculation have been made? What factors explain Britain's ineptitude? Traditional explanations invariably pointed to Britain's insularity. As an island and also a maritime power she combined a 'Little Englander' outlook with global responsibilities. Also, the old balance of power doctrine meant that Britain's instinctive reflex was to throw its weight against any new power bloc that emerged in Europe (Napoleon III, Hitler, Stalin – and now the EEC?). Moreover it is often argued that Britain's wartime experience, 1940–41, reinforced its faith in its own national sovereignty and parliamentary tradition. In contrast, 'the Six', who were defeated and occupied and then collaborated, embarked on economic integration. As a result a psychological gulf existed between countries like Britain, Sweden, Switzerland and 'the Six' simply because of their different experience of the war (Beddington-Behrens, 1966, p. 17).

Nevertheless, while there is truth in such observations we have to remember that Ernest Bevin (Foreign Minister 1945–51) encouraged European unity before 1948–49, as Chapter 3 showed. After 1949, with the US firmly committed to West Europe's defence, Britain reverted to a policy of 'limited liability' towards Europe, discouraged any initiative that might encourage the Americans to pull out and focused on its global problems.

Britain was still the third greatest global power in 1945 with 1.5 million men in its armed forces around the world. Atomic bomb tests in 1952 reinforced Britain's self-image as one of the Big Three globally and not as one of the Big Three in Europe. The reality though was that the UK could no longer afford its global role, having lost 25 per cent of its wealth in World War II (cf. 15 per cent in World War I). Defence spending equalled 28.5 per cent of total government expenditure in 1953, which meant very high tax rates (Churchill paid 19s. 6d. in the pound tax on the royalties from his war memoirs). Global defence commitments of 'UK World Power Inc. Ltd. Co.' were a big financial burden on an overloaded ailing economy, and the hundreds of thousands of men in the forces also strained the manpower budget as they were only consumers and not producing anything to sell. In retrospect, the UK's self-image in the early 1950s was a delusion, she was a medium-ranked power not comparable to the US or USSR. Colonial and foreign affairs were given too high a priority by Britain's governing class. Considerable attention was devoted to closing down the Empire but scant thought was given to Britain's economic and political future without one. Both Eden, Prime Minister from 1955 to 1957, and R.A. Butler (Chancellor) admitted they were 'bored by European issues' and Harold Macmillan, Foreign Secretary, failed to pay Europe sufficient attention. On 11 November 1955 it was the Economic Policy Committee, and not even the full Cabinet, that decided against joining the EEC; neither Eden nor Macmillan were present (Young, 1989, pp. 213, 217).

France prioritised Europe rather than its *vocation mondiale* from 1950 as it had to construct a framework safely to accommodate West Germany and provide access to its coal and markets. Britain was unable to make a similar volte face in policy until after the failures of Suez in 1956 and the last Four Power talks in Paris in 1960 (following this the two superpowers never asked Britain and France to their summit meetings again). These setbacks meant that in governing circles the painful reality of Britain's position as a declining power was indisputable and the policy changed. By then it was too late to join the EEC at its outset. Britain had 'missed the European bus' for three fundamental reasons: an absence of any forethought; a bad error of judgement in adopted policy; and a misplaced confidence and belief in the Commonwealth's commercial significance as an alternative to the EEC.

A key factor in Britain missing its opportunities in Europe was that no one gave it any serious thought at the Foreign Office between 1949 and 1955. The

Foreign Office was overwhelmed by problems and paperwork; the number of incoming papers in 1913 was 68,000 but by 1950 it was 630,000 (they doubled between 1939–50). When Eden became Foreign Secretary in 1951 he said 'the workload had killed Bevin, destroyed Morrison and now he understood why'. Eden was seriously ill within two years (Adamthwaite, 1988, p. 3). The British Foreign Office's conduct of foreign affairs traditionally followed the 'shop-keeper' approach (dealing with things as they turned up in a pragmatic fashion), not the more 'heroic' approach of framing realistic objectives and pursuing them rigorously at others' expense if necessary. The British tradition was bereft of vision, thought or any sense of direction. It was not just Eden who was responsible: successive Permanent Under-Secretaries who ran the Foreign Office admitted that they were 'permanently overtaken by events' and adopted a purely 'day to day approach' (Adamthwaite, 1988, p. 17).

Sir Ivone Kirkpatrick, in charge of the Foreign Office when Eden was Foreign Secretary 1951–55, said in his memoirs that there was 'little time to think, look ahead and make wise long term plans' (Kirkpatrick, 1959, p. 267) and he admitted that he had little time or interest in 'research, analysis or prolonged discussion'. This amounts to a systemic failure in foreign-policy formation. Britain missed her chances as no one in the mid-1950s thought about where Britain should be or what would be in her best interests 10 or 15 years ahead. Churchill's general conception of Britain's foreign-policy position (that Eden also endorsed) was that she lay at the centre of three inter-locking circles of influence: with the US, the Commonwealth and Europe. Between 1949 and 1961 Britain avoided too close a connection with Europe, not wanting to jeopardise the special relationship with the US (ironic given US policy towards European integration) or weaken Britain's connections with the Commonwealth. Prioritising these 'two circles of influence' was understandable in the late 1940s as Europe was poor, weak and discredited.

By the mid-1950s, however, Anglo-American relations were more often strained than special, commercial and military ties with the Commonwealth had weakened while Western Europe recovered quickly and continued to develop as the fastest growing market outside the US.

Nevertheless Foreign Office policy continued as before, determined to avoid any further loosening of ties with the US and the Commonwealth.

These two Foreign Office priorities were a major reason for the government's fateful decision in November 1955 to leave the Spaak Committee's negotiations on a common market. Originally, in June 1955, Britain was a full participant, represented by Russell Bretherton of the Board of Trade. He was briefed to try to steer the talks away from a common market to turning the OEEC into a free trade area. When he failed to do this the Foreign Office disengaged from the talks before Britain became associated with the final report. The Foreign Office tried to disrupt and divide 'the Six' by working on the tensions and differences of opinion between Adenauer and Erhard tempting them to abandon supranationalism for a free trade area. This failed but upset 'the Six' as it was seen as sabotage.

John Young's research in Cabinet, Foreign Office and Board of Trade papers revealed that while the Common Market was generally seen as being bad for British interests all the reports warned that if a common market formed Britain would have to join it, having had no say in its original structure, otherwise as a powerful economic bloc it would operate against Britain's interests. Sir Frank Lee of the Board of Trade even argued that the balance of advantage lay in joining the Common Market at the start (Young, 1989, pp. 206–12). However, the Cabinet decision not to join left Britain with a negative, inept and potentially dangerous policy of staying out while recognising that if a common market was established it would have to be in it! The vital moment of entering the Common Market at the start was missed in November 1955 when the rules were drawn up. British officials and ministers gambled that the Germans could be persuaded to join a free-trade area, that the French would never accept a common market, and that 'the Six' had recently failed with the EDC.

The Foreign Office assumed that 'the Six' had federalist intentions and so misread the economic motives behind the Spaak Committee talks. The advice of Gladwyn Jebb, Britain's Ambassador in Paris, was that the Common Market would never happen.

Britain's miscalculation in 1955 appears extremely erroneous especially as officials realised already that the UK's power was declining, that Commonwealth trade was likely to fall and that if a common market succeeded it would harm Britain's interests, making membership essential (Young, 1989, p. 219). This decision, though wrong in retrospect, was not controversial at the time (a decision to enter would have surprised everyone including 'the Six'). Public opinion was not in favour of entry in 1955–56. However, apart from the Liberal Party this was still the case in December 1960 when Macmillan changed his mind. So it does not absolve Eden's government (1955–56) for a failure in decision-making and leadership.

In May 1956, meeting in Venice, 'the Six' finally approved the Spaak Committee's reports and decided to press on with draft Treaties. When the UK realised that the EEC was likely to come about there was consternation in the Foreign Office. Other states such as Switzerland, Sweden and Portugal pressured Britain to mount a counter-initiative to the Common Market. Britain duly proposed talks with 'the Six' to convert the 16-state OEEC into a free trade zone. However 'the Six' refused talks until the Common Market was established.

Negotiations in the Intergovernmental Committee of the OEEC formed under the Chairmanship of Reginald Maudling, British Paymaster-General, were held in 1958 to discuss creating a wider free-trade area for manufactured goods. However there was nothing in the idea that appealed to France. Agriculture would not be included and France had food surpluses to export. Also OEEC members would benefit from EEC tariff reductions while accepting none of the obligations under the Rome Treaties.

Olivier Wormser, Head of the Economic Department of the French Foreign Office, saw these negotiations as an ill-conceived device whereby Britain could have access to a tariff-lowering EEC market on easy terms. Wormser also suspected that Britain wished to wreck the EEC from within, having failed to sabotage it from without (Mahotière, 1961, p. 68). General de Gaulle, who had taken over as the French President, disliked the EEC but detested free trade, which had no compensating political advantage for France. Moreover he didn't want to risk France playing a subordinate role to Britain again, as in World War II, or see Britain challenge French leadership in Western Europe. On 14 November 1958 the General's new Foreign Minister, M. Couve de Murville, was instructed to issue a press statement rejecting the OEEC free-trade area plan incorporating the EEC.

Following this French rebuff Britain embarked on 'Plan G', Whitehall's scheme for setting up a European Free Trade Area (EFTA), as a rival orga-nisation to the EEC. Plans A to F also existed (see Ellison, 2000).The EFTA Treaty was signed in Stockholm on 20 November 1959 and came into force following ratification in May 1960. It established a headquarters of 80 staff in Geneva (compared with 3,000 for the EEC in Brussels). EFTA was made up of most of the OEEC states that had not joined the Common Market (Brit-ain, Norway, Sweden, Denmark, Austria, Switzerland and Portugal). News-paper headlines announced that Europe was now at 'sixes and sevens'. Greece, Turkey, Spain and Ireland originally attempted to establish some special relationship with the EEC. Finland became an associate EFTA member in 1961 and Iceland joined EFTA in 1970.

EFTA aimed to reduce tariffs between members in stages at a similar rate to the EEC and free trade was completed in December 1966. EFTA undoubt-edly benefited small states like Sweden and Switzerland with low tariffs as they gained access to the heavily protected big market of Britain. For Britain EFTA was a completely lopsided commercial arrangement. Britain provided 51 million of EFTA's population of 89 million. Britain was the only big market. EFTA countries took only 10 per cent of British exports in 1960 and were never going to be a substitute for the EEC. The market of 'the Six' was 170 million.

However, Britain never intended EFTA to be an end in itself. Plan G was to demonstrate that an FTA could operate and thereby persuade 'the Six' into an association with 'the seven' creating a big free-trade Europe of the OEEC states. Reginald Maudling, now the President of the Board of Trade in the UK, tried to bring this about in 1960 and so prevent the permanent division of Western Europe into two rival economic blocs.

It was a complete failure. An EEC commission report written by Jean-François Deniau, a French Inspector of Finances, condemned the Maudling 'Pan-European' solution. It argued that free trade could only be effective if there was a common policy to ensure 'fair' competition, that agriculture must be included, a regional policy devised and a CET established. Maudling's plan was also condemned by the Americans. Mr Dillon from the US Treasury explained that whereas the EEC was acceptable to the US, the simple free-trade plan was not, because it had no compensatory political benefits; both schemes were potentially harmful to US trade. The UK's policy on Europe was consequently in complete ruin.

By an impressive feat of incompetence British officials and ministers had succeeded in bringing about the very situation they were so anxious to avoid six years before: exclusion from the EEC with the prospect of a trade war, while Britain's NATO forces in Germany helped defend its commercial rival the EEC.

Although EFTA had only come into force in May 1960, Harold Macmillan, during Christmas 1960, decided to reverse his policy and make a bid to enter the EEC. This was finally announced to the House of Commons on 31 July 1961 after much surreptitious preparatory footwork in Europe, the Conservative Party, the Commonwealth and Britain. Why did this change in direction occur?

It had been recognised in 1955 that if the EEC came about Britain would have to be part of it. Having failed twice to gain access in 1958 and 1960 by trying to set up a large free-trade zone Britain had no option but to actually join. The commercial success of the EEC made this an urgent matter. The EEC's productivity increased by 19 per cent between 1957–61, faster than the US or UK (at 13 and 12 per cent respectively). The GNP of 'the Six' increased by 27 per cent in real terms between 1957–61 (compared with 18 per cent in US and 14 per cent in UK). How much of this growth was due to the Common Market is hard to say. Their economies had been growing very rapidly before 1958, in fact industrial output in 'Little Europe' increased by over 90 per cent between 1950–60 compared to 39 per cent in the US and 29 per cent in Britain. Growth rates of individual EEC members varied greatly between 1958 and 1963, Italy's GNP rose by 59 per cent compared to Belgium's 15 per cent. Nevertheless, as Professor Walter Hallstein, the first President of the EEC Commission, remarked, 'It may be objected that these growth figures are no index of the success of the Common Market; but my reply would be that they certainly show that it has not failed'.

French fears of industrial competition in the EEC had given way to the enthusiastic exploitation of the benefits of a very large common market. French industry was helped considerably by de Gaulle's 17 per cent devaluation of the franc which gave them a competitive edge that ensured commercial success. This was important as it meant there was little recourse to the battery of safeguards and escape clauses built into the Rome Treaty at French insistence that would otherwise have restricted the pace of development within the EEC. As a Belgian diplomat remarked: 'we are condemned to succeed'. Although supranational schemes were an anathema to General de Gaulle (French President 1958–69) who believed in the sanctity of the nation state and 'L'Europe des Patries', he nevertheless agreed to honour French commitments to the Treaty of Rome. The early success of the EEC convinced de Gaulle that it could serve French political interests, with French leadership and ideas and a close alliance with West Germany laying the foundations of a new Europe. This would restore to France '*la grandeur*' after the pain of decolonisation and '*l'héroisme de l'abandon*'. A 'Paris–Bonn Axis', with France riding the German horse, would ensure French regional leadership in Western Europe, restore French prominence politically and diplomatically and provide a sense of mission post-decolonisation.

The other two tenets of de Gaulle's foreign policy were linked to this, the development of '*la force de frappe*', an independent nuclear strike-force, and an unswerving hostility to American leadership. De Gaulle detested the passive acceptance of American protection that, in his view, reduced Europe to 'protectorate status'. De Gaulle's objective was to replace America with France in German affections. Britain's problem in the 1960s was that de Gaulle knew that Britain would always side with the US in his struggle with America. Nevertheless, US investment in the EEC increased by 81 per cent between 1956 and 1961, growing fastest in Germany and Italy. Between 1958 and 1961, 608 American firms established themselves in the EEC as opposed to 235 in the rest of Europe. Industrial agreements and mergers between firms in the EEC rose from 50 in June 1959 to 190 by February 1962. By July 1963 customs duties between EEC states had been reduced by 60 per cent from the 1957 level. Britain was faced with the CET which resulted in Dutch and German tariffs being higher than in 1957 and France's slightly lower. Britain had excluded itself from a dynamic Customs Union of 170 million. Even in 1971 although the average CET was about 8.5 per cent (and the UK tariff 10 per cent) for some products the EEC's protective duty was very high. Britain's commercial vehicles faced a 22 per cent duty, 18 per cent on organic chemicals, 16–18 per cent on plastics, 18 per cent on tractors and 14 per cent on diesel engines (HMSO, 1971, p. 21).

Macmillan reversed policy in 1960 because the reality was dawning that the Commonwealth was not an important market for the type of high-quality goods in which Britain specialised. Newly decolonised states in Asia and Africa might have large populations but were underdeveloped and so provided a poor market for British exports. They were also often ill-disposed towards the old metropolitan power in the early years of independence. Canada, Australia and New Zealand were large, rich territories but their combined population was only 30 million. South Africa left the Commonwealth in May 1961 before it was expelled (following the Sharpeville massacre, March 1960). British exports to the Commonwealth fell from 47 per cent to 42 per cent of total UK exports in 1950–60 and this trend was to continue. For example, in Australia (with a population of 10 million) manufactured imports from the UK accounted for 70 per cent of its total imports in 1954. By 1960 they were under 50 per cent. The Australian–Japanese Trade Agreement of July 1957 meant an increase in Japanese imports into Australia. Between 1950 and 1960 Britain's trade with the Sterling Area as a whole rose by only 9 per cent and other countries by 19 per cent, whereas the share of total UK exports going to the EEC rose from 14 per cent in 1958 to 21 per cent in 1964.

There had been a substantial deterioration in both Britain's international economic and political position between 1956 and 1961. Failure at Suez in 1956 confirmed that Britain was no longer a world power. The US began to see the EEC, and in particular Bonn, as a strong and dynamic ally. John F. Kennedy (US President 1961–63) relied less upon Britain as a mentor in foreign affairs. The failure of the Paris Four Power summit in 1960 which Macmillan had arranged shook him badly, as from then on the two superpowers only conducted bilateral talks.

Events had demonstrated Britain's inability politically and financially to sustain an independent role: the long-preferred two circles of influence – the Commonwealth and the 'special relationship' with the US – had lost credibility. Europe, in the shape of the EEC, was the last resort. Britain had nowhere else to go. The idea of joining the EEC was therefore not popular in Britain as it signified national failure.

Jean Monnet's famous remark was proved correct: 'There is one thing you British will never understand: an idea. And there is one thing you are supremely good at grasping: a hard fact. We will have to build Europe without you; but then you will come in and join us.' Over Christmas 1960, Macmillan was facing up to the hard facts. In spite of Britain's cavalier treatment of her EFTA partners, Denmark was relieved to learn of Britain's intention to join the EEC, and Ireland also announced its intention to apply. Sweden and Switzerland were not pleased.

From 1961 to 1963 Britain pioneered negotiations for entry for Denmark, Ireland and Norway. Henri Spaak led the EEC's team of negotiators and Sir Pierson Dixon, Britain's Ambassador in Paris, Sir Eric Roll, former Economics Professor at Hull and Edward Heath led the British side. Monnet wanted Macmillan to accept the Treaty of Rome and, once inside, ensure that Commonwealth interests were safeguarded. However, the Government could not appear to be abandoning the Commonwealth given that 'the Six' would not agree to the UK maintaining indefinite preferential trading links with the Commonwealth.

There was no alternative to negotiation over every conceivable tropical and temperate traded commodity. Zero duty on tea, cricket bats and polo sticks was easily agreed. There was a great deal of argument over Canadian tinned salmon, Australian canned fruit, Cypriot sultanas and – critically – New Zealand lamb and dairy exports. There were long, difficult all-night negotiating sessions on British agriculture. On 14 January 1963, in the midst of these negotiations, General de Gaulle called a press conference and unilaterally rejected Britain's application for membership. This shock announcement astounded the five other EEC states and the Commission. Macmillan though had been warned of this possibility by de Gaulle in 1962. Although Article 237 of the Treaty of Rome invited others to join, the irony was that Spaak (who was leading the negotiations) insisted in 1957 that Article 237 should allow any of the six states to block the entry of a new member. The original reason for this was that socialists were worried that some future right-wing majority on the Council of Ministers might admit fascist Spain and Portugal.

Why did General de Gaulle veto British entry? There is evidence that what de Gaulle wanted from Britain was an offer of nuclear partnership allowing the two countries to work together and so save France a fortune on defence-research costs. De Gaulle was too proud to ask Macmillan directly for this and while the idea had also occurred to Macmillan, he never suggested it either. However, during the Brussels negotiations on British entry, Macmillan met Kennedy at Nassau and signed the Polaris deal which put Britain's nuclear force into a NATO grouping, and marked the end of Britain's fully independent nuclear deterrent.

De Gaulle was never consulted about this and took great exception to it. He considered that the Anglo-American special relationship operated to the detriment of France. He regarded Britain as America's 'Trojan Horse' in Europe (allowing greater US penetration of the Common Market) and feared that the EEC could be subsumed in a colossal Atlantic grouping under US control. Kennedy's Philadelphia Address on 4 July 1962 referred to a two-pillar Atlantic Partnership between the US and a United Europe. De Gaulle hated this conception and saw Britain, aligned with the US, as insufficiently European and so unsuited for EEC membership. De Gaulle wanted to shut Western Europe into a fortress, with France holding the key, a prospect that was unappealing to both the Benelux states and the European Commission.

French industry was averse to British entry to the EEC and a public opinion poll in January 1963 showed that 61 per cent of Frenchmen considered the Franco-German Treaty of 22 January 1963 desirable. When asked with which country France should have closest ties, 40 per cent said Germany and only 25 per cent said Britain. French public opinion had changed markedly in the ten years since the EDC collapsed. Furthermore, it was extremely doubtful that de Gaulle was prepared to share the leadership of Western Europe with the UK, or risk being subordinate to Britain, and Macmillan had said in 1961 that 'we can lead better from within'. De Gaulle avoided isolation despite his unilateral rejection of UK membership as he retained the support of Konrad Adenauer, the 87-year-old Chancellor of the FRG.

The Franco-German Treaty was negotiated from September 1962 and signed on 22 January 1963. For Adenauer reconciliation with France was of prime importance. The Treaty was a French attempt to constrain permanently the scope of West Germany's independent action; it stipulated regular consultations with France on all important questions of foreign policy and common interests in order to achieve as much 'similarly directed activity as possible'. The effect of this Treaty was largely nullified though in May 1963 when the Bundestag (the FRG's Parliament) ratified into law a preamble to the Treaty confirming its faith in the Western Alliance and the need to integrate the EEC and the Atlantic Alliance, West Germany refused to accept permanent French leadership at the expense of its relations with the US.

Ludwig Erhard, who succeeded Adenauer as Chancellor in 1963, did not share de Gaulle's views on Europe, was unimpressed by the *'force de frappe'* and regarded Germany's relations with the US as being most important. De Gaulle threatened to walk out of the EEC unless Germany agreed the Common Grain Price. This had to be settled before the GATT (Kennedy Round) of tariff-cutting negotiations started. Erhard was enthusiastic about the commercial prospects of this, wanting greater access to the US market for German manufacturers. In December 1964 the grain price was agreed. This was the first major decision taken in the EEC since the abrupt termination of the enlargement negotiations in January 1963.

Following this in 1965 the European Commission proposed a 'package' of measures concerning the financing of the Common Agricultural Policy and the whole EEC. It proposed that funds collected from both the levies on agricultural imports and the CETs should be used directly to finance the EEC in place of the direct contribution made by member states. Dutch concern over the need for democratic political control of EEC funds meant that the Treaty of Rome was to be amended to give the European Parliament budgetary powers. The EEC's President at the time, Professor Walter Hallstein, was a federalist and regarded the Commission as a proto-European government. If the Council of Ministers approved the Commission's proposal, the Commission and Parliament's powers would be strengthened at the expense of the Council. The proposed package angered de Gaulle, who was strongly opposed to any strengthening of parliamentary powers that threatened the power of member states. A state of deadlock existed at the Council meeting of 30 June 1965 and the French commenced their boycott of the EEC on 6 July, the 'empty chair' policy. For the next six months France did not attend Council meetings and no decisions could be taken on any major EEC issue. The French boycott was a blatant infringement of Article 5 of the Rome Treaty.

De Gaulle precipitated this crisis and boycott to stop the automatic introduction of majority voting on 1 January 1966. Previously, when the EEC back in 1961 moved from Stage 1 to Stage 2 (under the Rome Treaty's timetable at the end of 1961) agreement was needed both on CAP and that Stage 1 had been completed. This required unanimous agreement which proved enormously difficult. Five minutes before the set deadline on 31 December 1961 the Ministers had to 'stop the clock' at 11.55 p.m. and carried on negotiating until they agreed on 13 January 1962. However, the transition by 31 December 1965 from Stage 2 to Stage 3 of the Rome Treaty was to be an entirely automatic process that required no vote as specified in Treaty of Rome 1957 Article 8.3.

In the third stage 'qualified majority voting' was to be introduced into the Council of Ministers. France, Germany and Italy were to have four votes, Belgium and Netherlands two, and Luxembourg one. A two-thirds majority,

12 out of 17 votes, would be needed for Commission proposals to succeed. This would mean a big country could only stop a proposal if it was supported by another country (other than Luxembourg). It was this that de Gaulle intended to stop. More recent research has shown that this 1965 crisis was bound up with French insistence on a final agreement on implementing CAP (see Milward, 2000, p. 77); Moravcsik (2000)) which required German compliance with reducing minimum cereal prices (see Treaty of Rome (1957) Article 40(2); 44(2) that minimum cereal prices 'shall not be applied to form an obstacle' to trade; and fn.c, p. 98).

De Gaulle's heavy-handed treatment of the EEC and the other five member states by a boycott that paralysed the Community from mid-1965 to early 1966 was a direct challenge to the institutional machinery of the 1957 Treaty. It ended in January 1966 with the 'Luxembourg Compromise'. The original Commission 'package' of proposed reforms was shelved. Neither France nor the other five states would change their position on majority voting so they agreed to disagree over the French insistence on a veto where 'vital national interests' were at stake. This compromise simply postponed a resolution of the issue. Margaret Thatcher (British Prime Minister 1979–90) tried unsuccessfully during the Falklands crisis to exercise the veto against a majority vote agreeing new farm prices in 1982. Under French pressure the EEC argued it was not applicable and refused to allow Britain to invoke the Luxembourg proceedings in this case. Higher farm prices appeared to be the quid pro quo for EEC support of Britain against Argentina. De Gaulle's action in 1965–66 had nevertheless resulted in unanimity becoming normal practice in EEC decision-making for the next 15 years.

In addition to retaining its veto, France had ten complaints about the Commission that required resolution – all were intended to clip its wings and reduce it to a functional executive body. The 'striped pants clause' was designed to curb the Commission President's ceremonial prerogative in receiving Ambassadors' credentials from diplomatic missions to the EEC. The result of such complaints and the compromise was that in future the Commission, having been intimidated, would be more restrained and less ambitious in its proposals. The French had won their point. De Gaulle had showed that if he did not get his way the Community's business could be stopped, which effectively meant that the EEC had to operate within parameters set by France. It also meant that power within the EEC did not ultimately lie with the Council of Ministers (and member governments) but with any strong, single government.

In 1967 Harold Wilson (Labour Prime Minister 1964–70) reapplied for membership without insisting on all the special treatment and safeguards for the Commonwealth that Macmillan had. In November 1967 a balance of payments crisis led to the pound being devalued. This provided de Gaulle with an excuse to oppose opening negotiations, arguing that Britain should solve her economic difficulties first. For a second time de Gaulle unilaterally rejected British membership without consulting France's partners. The

Commission and the other five states refused to accept this French diktat and proposed alternative ways to involve Britain in the WEU to discuss the development of a common foreign policy. This precipitated the temporary withdrawal by France from the WEU.

For France's five partners British membership of the EEC became crucial in the 1960s as Gaullist France excluded Britain in order to assert its hegemony. French obstruction to enlargement and development within the EEC, and her apparent indifference to isolation, only ceased with de Gaulle's resignation as President of France in April 1969. De Gaulle's brutal handling of the EEC was designed to extract the maximum economic benefit for France while using it as a vehicle to advance his own policies in Europe, with France – not the supranational EEC – as regional leader. Moreover, de Gaulle both demonstrated and ensured that the nation state remained dominant, retaining full economic and political control (in everything except trade and agriculture). This effectively destroyed the theory formulated by E.B. Haas (1958) and current in the 1960s, namely that an automatic spillover from successful economic to political integration would occur.

De Gaulle's successor as President, Georges Pompidou (1969–74) at his first Press Conference on 10 July 1969, switched policy and said he had no objection to British membership. In December 1969 on Pompidou's initiative an EEC heads of state summit was held at The Hague where a package was agreed to complete, deepen and enlarge the EEC. The final transition arrangements, as laid down in the Rome Treaty, were completed 18 months early. Full operation of the Customs Union was scheduled for 31 December 1969. The arrangements (shelved three years before) for financing the CAP were agreed and for direct funding of the EEC from its 'own resources' (revenue from agricultural import levies and a proportion of VAT payments) rather than from states' annual 'membership fee'.

They also agreed to try and revitalise Euratom, which unlike the EEC had not been a success. In the mid-1950s uranium was thought to be scarce and so needed to be shared whereas it proved to be quite abundant. Euratom failed too because de Gaulle's government opposed it and although it had spent a lot on research and development (R&D) it had no strategy for exploiting the products developed.

In anticipating enlargement with Britain's membership a European Regional Development Fund was to be formed and the Lomé Convention widened, covering EEC trade and aid relations with ex-colonies. Apart from agreeing to start negotiations on enlargement with Britain, Norway, Ireland and Denmark, The Hague summit also commissioned the Werner Committee to report in 1970 on establishing a Monetary Union by 1980.

Why did Pompidou change course and agree to Britain's entry? By 1969 France was uneasy about the economic and increasingly political strength of West Germany and alarmed by its 'Ostpolitik' (Eastern Policy). Britain's membership would be a counterweight to growing German influence in the EEC. The development of *détente* between the superpowers from the mid-1960s (rather than Cold War rivalry and an arms race) following the Cuban missile crisis of 1962 enabled West Germany to embark on its Ostpolitik: trying to improve relations and the atmosphere with Eastern Europe. After the Soviet Union crushed the Czechoslavakian democratisation process under Alexander Dubček (1968–69) – 'the Prague spring' – West Germany's Ostpolitik continued but on Soviet terms. West Germany had to pay a political price, recognise East Germany, the 1945 borders and compensate victims of the Nazis in Eastern Europe. Willy Brandt's (Chancellor 1969–74) inaugural speech on 28 October 1969 recognised East Germany as a separate state – reversing 20 years of policy – and referred to Germany as 'one nation, two states'. The following August 1970 West Germany signed with the USSR the Treaty of Moscow, and in December 1970 the Treaty of Warsaw with Poland.

West Germany's NATO and EEC partners in Western Europe had misgivings about these developments and France was surprised at West Germany embarking on an independent diplomatic initiative eastwards when it had previously pursued a purely Western-orientated policy. West Germany, hitherto an 'economic giant but political pygmy', was now using its economic strength as a political lever with Eastern Europe (through trade agreements). Ostpolitik raised new fears of West Germany being 'Finlandised' (having to remain permanently friendly to the USSR) or of having agreed a new 'Rapallo Treaty', signed by the USSR and Germany in 1922 pledging closer co-operation and establishing better relations that was both a challenge and a warning to France and Britain at the time.

Such fears were soon shown to be groundless. In fact Willy Brandt only felt sufficiently secure to pursue Ostpolitik because West Germany was so firmly embedded in the Western framework of the EEC and NATO. Nevertheless, Pompidou's response in 1969 was to bring Britain into the EEC to counterbalance West German influence. Twenty years earlier, in 1949, the emergence of a West German state had meant a complete change in French policy towards Germany (see Chapters 3 and 4) with the start of a Franco-German economic alliance. In 1989 the collapse of the Berlin Wall (9 November 1989) and the imminent prospect of German reunification meant that François Mitterrand (French President 1981–95) contemplated a closer Anglo-French co-operation with Margaret Thatcher. Both were uncomfortable about a rapidly reunified Germany. Mitterand apparently told Thatcher at the Strasbourg European Council 1989 'that at moments of great danger in the past France had always established special relations with Britain and he felt that such a time had come again' (Thatcher, 1993, p. 796). However, Mitterand was finally unwilling to abandon 40 years of close Franco-German co-operation. Instead, following German reunification and the complete collapse of Soviet power in Eastern Europe, the Treaty on European Union was agreed at the Maastricht European Council in December 1991. The French dash to European Union in the autumn of 1991 was intended to curb German power, to tie a united big Germany down in European Union and try and stop Germany translating its economic and financial power into political dominance. Helmut Kohl (Chancellor West Germany 1982–90 and Germany 1990–98) agreed to Maastricht's 'three pillars' of Economic and Monetary Union; co-ordination of foreign and security policy; and co-operation over 'justice and home affairs'. Kohl wished to stabilise his Western relations to reassure EEC partners following reunification by portraying it as 'German unity in European Union'.

Whenever French anxieties have been raised over the 'German question' circa 1949, 1969 and 1989, the response was either to launch initiatives for further integration, develop closer relations with Britain or both.

EEC enlargement negotiations with Ireland, Norway, Denmark and Britain started in June 1970. Britain and the EEC had agreed the terms by June 1971. Britain's tariffs were to be eliminated in five stages of 20 per cent reductions, the last reduction being in July 1977. This meant a four-and-a-half-year transition period to full membership. Britain was in a weak bargaining position. Edward Heath's Conservative Government (1970–74) was in no position to refuse the terms of entry. Britain had nowhere else to go.

Britain, Denmark and Ireland joined the Common Market in January 1973, 15 years after its establishment. (Norway withdrew its application following a referendum in 1972.) How did exclusion from the EEC affect the Danish and British economies? Denmark was a big supplier of meat to Germany in the 1950s. However, the Community preference rule meant that much of this market was lost once the CAP was established. Danish exports to the FRG in 1972 were 75 per cent of their 1962 value while the value of Dutch exports had increased fourfold and French fivefold (Milward, 1992, p. 315). Between 1958–71 the growth of output in the EEC was 98 per cent, in Britain it was only 43 per cent. Britain was bottom of the OECD growth league in the 1960s and 1970s. The EEC growth rate was 5.4 per cent, Britain's was 2.8 per cent at best. The compounded effect over ten years was to raise the EEC standard of living (allowing for population changes) by 74 per cent compared with Britain's 31 per cent. Whereas in 1960 Britain had a standard of living higher than any EEC state, by 1970 it was lower than all EEC states except Italy *(Economist,*14 August 1971). By 1980 Britain's standard of living had slipped below Italy's.

Although not the only cause of Britain's malaise in the 1960s, being outside the largest fastest-growing European market was a major factor. British manufacturers treated Europe in the 1950s as of secondary importance, preferring to focus on less competitive soft markets. The result was that manufacturers of consumer durables avoided competition in Europe with Italian, German and French producers. British firms, through avoiding competition, became less competitive, as they were not driven to improve design, raise productivity, undertake technological innovation and investment to the same extent as European firms. Between 1959 and 1969 in the EEC 24 per cent of GNP was invested, in the UK it was 17 per cent. Moreover, within the Common Market, if a country's consumption of manufactures fell its manufacturers' output need not fall, as it might compensate by selling more to the rest of the EEC's Common Market (Milward, 1992, pp. 419–22). Britain could not do this and was faced with recurrent balance of payments crises and 'stop-go' policies.

By 1970 Britain was the only major car market where there had been no net growth since 1963 and car sales in 1970 were substantially below 1964. In 1969 West Germany's new car registrations were double Britain's. Both British manufacturers and the government in the 1950s had ignored the fact that Europe was the only big market in the world economy which bought the small and medium-sized cars that Britain manufactured. Membership of the EEC would have provided British car makers and other manufacturers with the security of permanent access to a market of 230 million. The Commonwealth and American markets did not offer this. Import surcharges on British car exports were imposed (e.g. Canada 1960, US 1971) whenever an importer was in economic difficulties. Australia adopted import substitution policies to encourage its own car assembly plants. British cars faced a 35 per cent imperial preference duty (other states 45 per cent) but component parts for assembly in Australia only had a 7 per cent duty to encourage foreign car makers to manufacture in Australia. General Motors and the British Motor Corporation did so, which hit British car exports again (Barber and Reed, 1973, p. 276).

By the late 1960s Ford UK and British Leyland both turned to the European market as Britain had become the smallest and most stagnant domestic market of any major car producer. From 1967 Ford integrated its European car making operations (making, for example, automatic transmissions at its Bordeaux plant). Ford also concentrated investment in Germany, rather than Britain, in order to supply the expansive German and EEC market. The British government's 1971 White Paper on *The UK and the European Communities*, by stating the advantages of membership, implicitly acknowledged the disadvantages of remaining outside the EEC for 15 years. It emphasised the benefits of a market of 300 million to spread R&D costs across bigger production runs, achieve greater economies of scale and specialisation. In the late 1960s Italian producers of refrigerators, Zanussi and Ignis, considered their optimal plant size, given the Common Market, was to make 800,000 p.a. while UK producers thought in terms of plants for 200,000 p.a. Italian machines, therefore, because of economies of scale, cost 15 per cent less to make. In 1966 three big independent UK companies were making computers – Elliott-Automation, International Computers and Tabulators (ICT), and English Electric – and were subject to intense US competition (they had 40 per cent of the UK market). In Europe the US had 89 per cent of the market. The UK's computer industry, unlike the United States', was thus handicapped by its restricted domestic market and was unable to meet the enormous development costs. The danger in the 1960s was that the whole UK and European computer market might fall into US hands (Beddington-Behrens, 1966, p. 554).

Bringing UK high-technology industry into the EEC might have enabled Western Europe to compete more effectively against the American and Japanese electronics, jet aircraft and aero-engine industries. Both Britain and the EEC were afraid of American predominance in advanced technology industries in the late 1960s and early 1970s.

What effect did enlargement have on the EEC? It was beneficial economically as Britain, being a mature industrial economy, would be a net contributor to the EEC's budget. Britain imported 70 per cent of its food and had only 3 per cent of its labour force in agriculture – once inside the EEC, CAP preference rules meant Britain's 58 million consumers would be a big market gain for the EEC's farmers. Ireland and Denmark had small populations and were easily absorbed.

Enlargement from six to nine did make agreement in the Council of Ministers more difficult, given the need for unanimity following the Luxembourg Compromise. The EEC has been described as being in the 'doldrums' from the mid-1960s to the early 1980s (Pinder, 1983, p. 30) because there were few new initiatives and no further successful integration. Although the objective of EMU was inspired by recurrent international monetary crises and financial turbulence (in 1967 sterling's devaluation; in 1968 the dollar, gold and French franc crises), the breakdown of the Bretton Woods system of fixed exchange rates between 1971–73 and the oil price shock of 1973–74 resulted in EEC member states pursuing different monetary and foreign exchange policies rather than attempting to co-ordinate them as the EEC Commission wanted. The Werner Report's (1970) aim of creating a common currency by 1980 had been wrecked by 1973. All six member states were resistant to any transfer of control of economic or monetary policy to a supranational body.

7   EMU, the first stage (1973) to the EU (1991)

The year 1973 marked the end of the 'long post-war boom', 1945–73, the break-up of the international monetary system based on fixed exchange rates and the Yom Kippur war in the Middle East. This war resulted in an energy crisis, with a massive oil price increase from $2 per barrel mid-1973 to $10 in 1974 and $12 in 1975. The effect was worldwide economic recession, unemployment and inflation. The combination of inflation and stagnation ('stagflation') had several implications for the EEC in the 1970s. It challenged governments' policies and techniques for managing their economies. Orthodox Keynesian demand management, spending one's way out of unemployment and recession, would not work but simply cause more inflation and so worsen the problem. With such uncertainty the nine EEC states were not prepared to risk experimentation with EMU, which required the transfer of economic and monetary instruments from national to supranational control, when faced with balance of payments crises and inflation. The original scheme to establish full economic and monetary union (EMU) within ten years was hatched at the Hague Summit in December 1969. Both France and Germany initially enjoyed taking the credit for getting the scheme going. Only just over a year later in January 1971 each was blaming the other for launching Europe towards EMU without first having worked out where it would lead to politically.

EMU was originally inspired by recurrent international monetary crises and the financial turbulence of the late 1960s. In 1967 sterling's devaluation (which ended Harold Wilson's Labour Government's attempt to enter the EEC) was followed in 1968 by crises affecting the US dollar, gold and the French franc. EMU was originally presented as a solution to recurrent monetary crises by supposedly creating a zone of monetary stability within the EEC (Dedman, 1998). However, it was clear by January 1971 that France was back-peddling vigorously on full EMU itself – apparently all the French really wanted was common banking and credit arrangements following the monetary upheavals of 1968.

France wanted to stick at just the first stage of EMU, which was limited to regular economic coordination meetings and a scheme to bind the dollar values of the six EEC currencies more tightly to each other. Thus the 1973 arrangement was known as 'the snake in the tunnel' whereby they agreed to float their currencies against the dollar and try to keep the six currencies' fluctuations between each other to a small margin. The aim was to reduce exchange rate fluctuations, which were reducing the value of French exports of farm products under the CAP.

France also wanted to give the appearance of the EEC acting together in monetary affairs. Denis Healey, Britain's Chancellor of the Exchequer, subsequently remarked in 1975 that the EEC was adept at dressing up a 'coincidence of policies as a coordination of policies'.

A third and perhaps more important French motive was to make Germany's large foreign-exchange reserves available to prop up the EEC's weaker currencies, like the French franc. In principle some $2 billion should then have been generally available as a medium-term credit facility for use during exchange-rate crises.

However, West Germany and other EEC members, notably the Dutch, professed to want a common currency for member countries, or at least to move to fixed exchange rates between all the Six. Dr Karl Schiller, the West German Economics Minister in 1971, refused to let France renege on the original plan. Three months of open wrangling followed inside the EEC which was finally 'resolved' in February 1971 with the compromise statement that the 'declared aim' was to reach full EMS during the next ten years. However, this declared intent did not carry the same weight as a full 'decision' under EEC law. The wording of this 1971 agreement was completely free of the idealistic supranational rhetoric seen in the original outline for EMU drawn up by Pierre Werner, the Luxembourg Prime Minster, only a year before.

In 1971 Willy Brandt, the West German Chancellor, eventually gave way on EMU, disowning his Economics Minister who wanted to see the 1957 Treaty of Rome revised to permit the creation of a European Federal Reserve Bank by a fixed date. Brandt let France off the supranational hook – only a vague pledge to achieve full economic union by 1980 or soon after remained. However, a diplomatic 'side payment', for which EEC internal diplomacy is renowned, was that President Pompidou agreed to support Brandt's Ostpolitik in return. This was important for Germany as their American allies were, at best, lukewarm about Ostpolitik by 1971 and French help was needed to push for an agreement over Berlin – so essential to Brandt's foreign policy at that time.

Interestingly, as previously observed, the timing of initiatives for monetary union in both the 1970s and 1990s was linked to Germany's Eastern policies of the time. Ostpolitik played a role in triggering Monetary Union attempts, as well as encouraging the Common Market's enlargement. West Germany's growing links with Communist Eastern Europe between 1969 and 1971 began to alarm France and others. It looked as if its economic feet had outgrown its Common Market boots. British entry would make the CM bigger and EMU would give that CM a wider role tying member states more closely together.

For France the combined weight of Britain and herself might stop Willy Brandt playing balance of power games in the middle of Europe. Also the fact that Willy Brandt was willing to stand up to France in 1971 was a sign of a shift to more equal bargaining power between France and West Germany inside the EEC. Both France and West Germany, in fact, saw the UK's EEC membership in 1970 as a useful balance and counterweight to the other.

The demise of the 1970s EMU initiative is usually explained by the oil price shock of 1973–75, when the price went up from $2 to $12 a barrel, leading to global economic recession, the worst world slump since the 1930s, and rising unemployment with inflation at the same time. Governments, unsure of what to do, were not prepared to experiment with Stages 2 or 3 of EMU. France of course only wanted Stage 1 anyway, yet the oil price rise reversed progress even here. France left the snake in 1974 in order to devalue, rejoined in 1975 only to leave again in 1976.

The verdict of Marjolin's EEC report on the first stage of EMU in March 1975 was that Europe was no nearer to Monetary Union than in 1969 ' … and had probably moved backwards as national economic and monetary policies have never in twenty-five years been more divergent than today'. In August 1975 the UK and Ireland were reining back their economies to combat price inflation, while others were expanding in order to combat unemployment. Sterling and the lira slipped out of the 'snake'. (The same currencies were again in crisis in 1992 with the ERM, the snake's successor.) When the nine EEC Finance Ministers held a crisis meeting in Venice in August 1975 one of them was quoted (unnamed) by *The Economist* as insisting that the final communiqué very sensibly and a little cynically contained ' … a paragraph of bullshit at the end to say how confident we all are' (Dedman, 1998).

Roy Jenkins in 1977, apparently to counter the tedium of being President of the European Commission, re-launched the EMU project. This was greeted with considerable scepticism particularly by François Xavier Ortoli, the Finance Commissioner, who thought it wholly unrealistic. Events were to prove him correct.

Chancellor Helmut Schmidt and President Valéry Giscard d'Estaing, despite opposition from the UK and Italy and with considerable fanfare, announced a new fast track to EMU at Bremen in 1978.

The European Monetary system (EMS) with an Exchange Rate Mechanism (ERM) replaced 'the snake in the tunnel'. It was felt that the worst effects of the 1973–74 oil price shock were now over. The EMS should provide a zone of monetary stability to benefit community trade.

Yet when France took over the Presidency of the EEC council of Ministers the following January 1979, its first move was to delay the immediate planned start of the EMS until it could extract a promise from its partners to settle French grievances over common farm prices (a 20 per cent gap having opened up between French and German prices). The EEC was then beset by a whole string of crises in 1979–80 over the budget, Spanish entry into the EEC, farm prices, the second OPEC oil price shock (doubling the price of oil) and budget contributions. Amid all this EMU was again postponed.

Completion of the EMS originally scheduled for March 1981, including a European Monetary Fund with central bank powers, was abandoned at the Luxembourg European Council meeting in April 1980. However, irrespective of the role of OPEC and oil prices in wrecking attempts at EMU and EMS, to have been successful would have meant a commitment to harmonise national economic and monetary policies. There was no sign of such policy convergence before 1984 as EEC members had different economic priorities: Germany to reduce inflation, France and Italy to reduce unemployment (Donges, 1981, pp. 20–24).

Another failure of EEC states to act together, with a community response, was during the 1973 oil crisis itself. The EEC did nothing to help defend Holland, a member state, when subjected to an Arab oil embargo (because it was considered pro-Israeli). Instead EEC members, notably France and Britain, moved quickly to make bilateral deals for oil with Arab states in the Gulf, in order to safeguard their own national oil supplies. The major oil companies helped Holland more than the EEC through supplying them by the clandestine diversion of oil shipments. The energy crises revealed the inability of the EEC to act collectively as a 'community' with a common strategy towards OPEC's oil price increases 1973–75 and a shameful unwillingness to defend the Dutch and so jeopardise Anglo-Arab and Franco-Arab relations. The EEC looked like a community where economic integration and co-operation worked well in the commercially buoyant 1950s and 1960s but as soon as economic conditions got rough in the 1970s it was every member for itself.

This failure to act together highlighted the rudimentary level of foreign policy coordination or political cooperation that existed in 1973, despite the EEC recently establishing a means to do so. At the 1969 Hague Summit efforts were made to improve economic and political cooperation.

European Political Cooperation (EPC) had its origins in the subsequent Davignon Report 1970. As the Belgian Foreign Minister, Davignon was commissioned to report on ways of increasing EEC coordination in foreign policy 'to bring nearer the day when Europe can speak with one voice'. The EPC operated outside the EEC's institutional framework, as the EEC's remit was limited to economic matters and foreign trade policy. The ambition was to improve mutual understanding of member states' position on issues and cooperate with a view to aligning foreign policies in the same direction wherever possible. EEC foreign ministers were to meet twice a year to tackle questions on political cooperation.

The worst effect of the 1970s recession was that it threatened the whole operational success and integrity of a single common market by the growth of a new protectionism between member states and by the EEC with non-members. During the 1970s most EEC governments resorted to subsidising ailing industries during the recession. Such 'state aids' distorted competition in the Common Market but were justified by national governments to the EEC Commission on policy grounds (regional, employment or industrial restructuring). In 1975 the British government got the EEC Commission's reluctant agreement to a £1,500m rescue plan for British Leyland.

However, the main problems were protectionist devices known as non-tariff barriers (NTBs) that proliferated in the 1970s. Member governments' different regulations concerning safety, public health, environmental protection were used as NTBs. A single market, for instance, in gas central heating boilers and cars was breaking up through the enforcement of different national safety regulations (e.g. Italy specified laminated car windscreens, Germany toughened glass). The EEC Commission attempted to harmonise such regulations into common EEC directives. In 1977 common EEC standards for cars were set. Harmonising different specifications was a slow process – on average only seven directives were negotiated per year.

The EEC as a whole became more selectively protectionist in the 1970s, notably in protecting the EEC textile and shoe industries from Third World competition by, for example, the Multifibre Agreement in 1974 (renewed in 1978 and 1981). The EEC also organised crisis cartels to help entire manufacturing sectors in distress, like the steel restructuring programme of 1977 reinforced by compulsory price and production controls in 1980 under the Treaty of Paris, Article 58. Only Ireland and West Germany did not use 'voluntary export restraints' to limit the number of imported Japanese cars. This encouraged the Japanese to build 'screwdriver' and then manufacturing plants in the EEC, mostly in Britain.

Britain's problem in 1973 was that she joined at the end of the long boom and had to adjust to the EEC and the heavy costs of membership at a difficult time. In February 1974 a new Labour government tried to negotiate 'new and fairer methods of financing the budget'. The UK Treasury estimated that while Britain would pay 24 per cent of the Community budget by 1980 its share of community GNP would be 14 per cent. At the Dublin Summit in March 1975 all they achieved was a 'budget correcting mechanism' which provided for a refund (of up to 3 per cent of the budget) if budget contributions were significantly beyond Britain's share of EEC GNP. In April 1975 a Commission Report on EMU written by Robert Marjolin (ex-Vice-President of the EEC) reported on its complete failure. This helped both the Labour government in its negotiations in 1974–75, and also the pro-EEC lobby win a 2:1 majority in favour (the government itself was supposedly neutral (Morland 2009) in Britain's referendum on EEC membership in June 1975, as it meant little prospect of further costly supranationalism (only in the Shetlands and Western Isles were there majorities against).

At the Fontainebleau Summit of June 1984 Margaret Thatcher eventually achieved 'financial justice' with a 50 per cent rebate reducing Britain's contribution from £1,000m to £500m p.a. The issue of Britain's 'budgetary imbalance' (as the EEC called it) and the connected rising cost of the CAP were both most time-consuming for the Council and represented the major preoccupation of the EEC between 1980–84. This cleared the way for further developments leading to the Single European Act (SEA) 1986 and the Iberian enlargement.

The key motive behind the Single European Act was to rescue the dynamic benefits of one large single market for European industry and commerce. The result of neoprotectionism in the 1970s was that the EEC had become less dynamic. The EEC was growing more slowly than Japan and the newly industrialised countries (NICs) of the Pacific Rim (South Korea, Taiwan, Hong Kong, Singapore). The EEC seemed, at least compared to these 'Asian Tigers', to be suffering from 'euro sclerosis', and the danger was that its industries might be 'rolled over' by competitive Japanese and American transnational corporations. The tendency of some EEC states (France and Italy especially) to select and protect leading firms as 'national champions', feather-bedding them through public contracts meant that these companies focused on their domestic market, eroding the EEC's large Common Market. By the late 1970s and early 1980s more economists, government officials and politicians recognised that to compete with Japan, the US and NICs, European companies needed to be globally competitive and treat the EEC as their 'home base'.

The European Council Meeting in Milan, June 1985, considered the EEC Commission's White Paper 'Completing the Single Market' and decided under Article 236 of the Treaty of Rome (1957) to convene a conference to consider a Treaty amendment. The result was the SEA signed 17 February 1986. Lord Cockfield, the Commissioner responsible for the internal market, was inspired in his White Paper by the Court of Justice's 'Cassis de Dijon' ruling of 1979 (a drink excluded from Germany on grounds that its alcoholic content was too high for wine but too low for spirits). The ruling introduced the new principle of 'mutual recognition' of national specifications so that 'legal manufacture meant legal circulation' throughout the EEC (if it was considered safe for Frenchmen to drink it was safe for Germans or anyone else in the EEC). Lord Cockfield and EEC President Jacques Delors aimed to develop this principle (that by-passed much of the need to harmonise regulations and standards for every product) and create a single internal market by '1992' with free movement of goods, people, services and capital. The 1985 White Paper listed 300 items that required resolution to complete the Single Market, including wholesale eradication of the NTBs whether technical, physical or fiscal. It meant dispensing with most customs' formalities and reducing the costs of frontier delays for lorries; harmonising VAT rates; opening up public procurement through state contracts to EC competition.

While the SEA did introduce procedural changes for political cooperation and the coordination of foreign policy and a slight enhancement of the European Parliament's role and looked ahead towards creating EMU, the main constitutional change was to extend qualified majority voting (QMV) over all internal market legislation. This change meant that for the first time, under the SEA 1986, all 'harmonisation' agreements were made by QMV, not unanimity. For a measure to pass into EC law required 8 of the 12 states or

54 out of 77 votes. Harmonisation of regulations (on, for example, EC car exhaust emissions) became a quicker process and over 90 per cent of the 1985 White Paper's '1992' agenda was achieved by that date.

The other reason for introducing QMV was to avoid complete deadlock in EC decision-making if an enlarged EC of 12, including Spain and Portugal, had to achieve unanimity.

The SEA had implications resulting in procedural changes for EPC. The EPC was codified under Title III of the SEA 1987 but still remained strictly outside the EC framework as Title III was not a constitutional document. National governments had no intention to relinquish sovereignty over national foreign policy. However, they did agree to a new limited obligation 'to inform and consult each other on any foreign-policy matter of general intent' before taking unilateral action! The EPC also acquired a 'presidency' that rotated every 6 months and a Brussels based permanent secretariat under the SEA. Foreign ministers were going to meet four times a year from now on and might be called together in a crisis within 48 hours at the request of at least three governments. There was however no real obligation to cooperate in the coordination of foreign policies. The hope was that through these regular gatherings, the habit of cooperation might eventually become the norm. However, the reality over time was that the EPC served more as a forum for foreign-policy declarations not for synchronised action. Such declarations too had little impact as the need for consensus inevitably resulted in vague pronouncements that represented the lowest common denominator on which all 12 could agree.

Spain and Portugal joined the EC in 1986 after eight years of negotiations (1978–86). Greece had joined in 1981 (following six years of negotiations). Applications for membership followed their return to democracy after years of dictatorship. Why did it take so long to negotiate Spanish entry? It proved much harder for the EEC to absorb a big, less-developed agricultural state because of the CAP, which provided free access to the European market at guaranteed prices. Spain would increase the EC's population by 20 per cent but GDP by only 10 per cent. Spain had surpluses in olive oil and citrus fruit to add to the EC's surplus. When Spain applied to join in 1977 the EEC budget was already under strain: the CAP took 80 per cent of the budget, whereas both Regional Aid and the Social Fund together accounted for 8 per cent. Spain's admission might wreck the EEC's budgetary and CAP arrangements unless reforms were made to both as Spain would also draw on Regional Development Funds. In 1984 a start was made to limit the upward growth of agricultural expenditure in the CAP through production quotas. By 1992 60 per cent of the EU budget was spent on the CAP and 28 per cent on Regional Aid.

Spain also had a huge fishing fleet – 50 per cent of the size of the total EEC fleet in 1980. Fishing was a highly sensitive matter in the EEC (of the 302 boats caught fishing illegally in EC waters in 1983–84, only five were not Spanish). The Common Fisheries Policy dating from 1971 required revision

prior to Spanish entry. A new policy was agreed in 1983. Spain proved difficult to include in the EEC because of the sensitivity of the existing members
for their own national interests (whether fishing; citrus fruits and olive oil
producers; the dispute with Britain over Gibraltar; or competition from
Spain's steel and textile industries).

Absorbing a small agricultural state like Greece in 1981 was not too problematic; it only added 7 per cent to the EEC budget. Yet any future absorption of Poland's population of 35 million with 8.5 million farmers into current
CAP arrangements and the EU would, it was estimated, increase the EU
budget by 20 per cent. Turkey (population 52 million), an associate since 1963
with an application for full membership turned down in 1989, signed a Customs Union agreement with the EU on 5 March 1992. This excludes agriculture, which employed 55 per cent of Turkey's labour force.

The other associated attraction of full EU membership for small states is
that they had a disproportionate voting power and influence in the Council of
Ministers. Both Austria and Sweden, would eventually have four votes each in
1995. Germany, with a population of 80 million, had ten votes under 1986
arrangements. (These conventions date back to 1957 and favoured the small
states of 'the Six'.)

For the EU's neighbouring non-members, being outside the EU club and
Single Market nevertheless means conforming to EU standards, regulations
and laws. This is necessary both for any exports into the EU and because of
the eventual requirements of 'acquis communitaire', if they were ever to join
the EU club. So EU membership meant states were better able to protect their
national economic interests inside, and participate in making decisions which
would still have affected them even if they had remained outside. For small
states, membership accorded them a disproportionate political weight to their
population size in decisions.

Even though the Norwegian and Swiss electorates in 1994 and 1992
respectively rejected closer connections with 'the twelve', their governments
and main political parties all favoured membership. This was not surprising
given that the EU's Single Market had in 1995 348 million people (cf. 259m in
the US and 125m in Japan) and the EU accounted for 40 per cent of world trade.

The '1992' Single Market objective lead directly to the creation of the
European Economic Area (EEA) composed of the EEC and EFTA. EFTA
had been founded only as a reaction to the EEC. As EFTA's Deputy Director,
Per Mannes, said in 1989, 'EFTA was a result; it never had a political objective'. Yet EFTA was the EEC's major trading partner (well ahead of Japan
and USA) and the EEC was even more important to EFTA accounting for
more than half its imports and exports. This mutual dependency had given
rise from 1984 to talk of establishing a European Economic Space. Claude
Cheysson, the French Foreign Minister at the time suggested that this EES be
composed of the 18 states in the two groups. By 1984 EFTA and EEC had
created a tariff free zone in most manufactured goods. The EEC's plans for a

Single Market for 1992 suddenly eclipsed any talk of the EES, and came as something of a shock to EFTA members. George Reisch, Secretary General of EFTA, was reported in 1989 saying, 'Suddenly, European integration had a vision, a clear program (sic) and a timetable. But EFTA countries were excluded from that vision'.

Alarm sounded in EFTA states, even though industrial free trade already largely existed between EC and EFTA. EFTA feared being discriminated against on the grounds of not being in the EC: by EEC consumers, firms and governments.

The EC's '1992' programme gained momentum through the 1980s, the downfall of communism in 1989 reflected a growing confidence in the EC viewed as the stable centre of Europe, while all around was in disarray. The EC too was seen by Eastern European (EE) states as their ticket to economic stability and eventual affluence. EFTA states (Austria, Finland, Iceland, Norway, Sweden, Switzerland and Lichtenstein) did not want to miss possible trade opportunities, which lay in Eastern Europe, by not joining the '1992' club. Why didn't the seven EFTA states simply apply to join the EC 1989–90, rather than enter this EEA? Initially in 1989 this was because four of them were neutral states and so had political and ideological reservations about EC membership. Jacque Delors, President of the Commission and the EC were also worried about admitting these countries for the very same reasons, and that the rationale for the EEA was to keep EFTA states at arm's length. Delors was concerned that the neutrals as members could 'neutralise' the EC and block or wreck future developments of Common Foreign and Security Policy (CFSP). Norway and Iceland were also very concerned about their fishing industry. Negotiations started in 1990 and the European Economic Area Treaty was signed on 21 October 1991.

This agreement extended most of the Single Market's principles to the EFTA countries once the 1000 page Treaty, plus 12,000 pages of annexes (European directives which constituted the EC's 'acquis') had been incorporated into their statute books and also ratified by all 19 parliaments and the Community's bodies. EC regulations covering the 'four freedoms': free movement, of labour, goods, services, capital would then apply to EFTA. Under the deal EFTA countries adopted a raft of community regulations including those on company law, consumer protection, mergers and state aid amongst others. The EEA was the world's biggest free trade area (FTA) with a 19 country market of 380m people stretching from the Arctic to the Mediterranean representing 46 per cent of world trade, 68 per cent of the 19 nations' total trade was with each other. The EFTA states also agreed to contribute 'cohesion' money to the EC's poorer states, a fund was established of 500m ECU for grants and 1.5bn in soft loans over a five-year period to assist development in certain regions of the EC. EFTA remained outside CAP and CFP. The EEA was not set up as a CU so border controls, 'rules of origin' procedures still applied to goods arriving from EFTA though with all formalities greatly simplified. There were no changes in EFTA's external trade policies.

Sweden and Austria (2 of the 4 neutral EFTA members) had already formally applied for EC status prior to the EEA Treaty being signed; entry negotiations were meant to start in 1992 ready to join in 1995. Three EFTA states were to follow Finland, Switzerland and Norway (Iceland and Lichtenstein did not intend to). In referendums in 1992 Switzerland and in 1994 Norway's population rejected membership.

Communism's collapse, withdrawal of Soviet forces and the end of Cold War rivalry meant that neutrality was no longer an important or even relevant issue. Opinions in the USA varied concerning the EEA. Some at the time saw the agreement as a further opening up of trade under the Single Market. Others feared that the deadlocked GATT talks over agriculture in the Uruguay Round presaged more 'Fortress Europe' protectionism. However, the EEA, given the liberal trade regimes of EFTA meant that it would have been more difficult for the EC to isolate itself from competition and market forces associated with world trade even if inclined to. For Japanese and US companies the EEA meant the chance of gaining access to an enormous market with harmonised standards via the EFTA countries with their lower tariffs. It was conceivable that the non-European companies might even benefit disproportionately from this accord. For some EFTA states the EEA was seen as a 'stepping stone' to EC membership (Austria, Sweden et al.). For the EC the EEA was conceived as a way of sidestepping any immediate enlargement of the EC to provide breathing space to complete the 1992 process and further deepen the EC first through the process of monetary and political union before enlargement. Events in Eastern Europe, the creation of EEA and the emergence of new fragile democracies worked against this policy spurring on countries to join the EC club.

The EEA effectively confirmed a sort of secondary citizenship status on non-EC members by permitting economic integration, allowing states to be governed by rules they didn't make while not exempting them from contributing funds to help other EC people poorer than themselves to conform to the rules. This was the EEA's great limitation for EFTA members who had no vote on community law even when directly affected by it. It was no surprise that full EC membership, even if requiring a subscription, looked preferable.

The EEA was described portentously by Jacques Delors as an 'important pawn in the architecture of the great Europe'. EFTA applications for EC membership altered perceptions of the EEA to that of an ante-chamber where states enjoy some benefits but find it unappealing as a permanent abode, the acquisition of the 'acquis' to be in the EEA was a big vital step to full membership. This was also to apply to EE countries too. An Austrian diplomat said 'we are much less worried about the details of the EEA than we once were, because we now regard it as a short term arrangement leading to full membership, not a structure that is meant to endure'. Collapse of Eastern Europe's dictatorships transformed the meaning of the principle of neutrality.

Austria and Finland had once been pressurised by the Soviet Union but that had ended and they were no longer constrained in their foreign policy. Even Sweden and Switzerland whose neutrality long pre-dated the Cold War since 1947, were reconsidering their stance given that Europe was no longer composed of mutually hostile states and alliances but by countries determined to voluntarily join together. Neutrality ceased to be a major obstacle to a widening of the EC.

Applications for full membership came from EFTA members and Eastern Europe (EE), Turkey and Morocco. The Commission originally envisaged EE integration in three steps: that Poland, Hungary and Czechoslovakia could initially use the EFTA entity to create a FTA together, acquiring more experience of market conditions, join the EEA and face a wider more competitive market prior to full membership of EC so using EEA as a sort of 'laboratory'. This was Delors' concept of 3 concentric circles to complete the experiment of converting from command economies to capitalism.

There were strong reactions from Eastern countries to this FTA and EEA transitional idea. Poland claimed the EEA was an obstacle in their present negotiations for a preferential trade agreement. The EEA was seen as a structure to hold EE away from EC until they were healthy enough to join the by then 'deepened' EC.

Hungary also rejected the EEA 'waiting room' proposal insisting that the only way to save democracy in the EE countries was to become members of EC without this transitional period. EE states really needed agreement to eventual entry in order to maintain their new western orientation and ensure democratic progress was maintained. Moreover, the more certain their eventual membership appeared the more confident foreign firms would be to invest.

In March 1990 Jacques Delors, President of the Commission, complained to MEPs about their slow progress in completing the Single Market legal process – at least 100 pieces of legislation were held up and behind schedule. It was inevitable that the difficult intractable issues would be the last to be resolved, such as the complex and highly vexed issue of the EC's banana imports.

However, as the 1992 deadline approached the EC's big challenge for most politicians was not to complete the Single Market but how to cope with the growing throng of states waiting at the EC's door to join. The EC could not cope and would face financial and institutional collapse if all who wanted to join were rapidly admitted. How and when to enlarge the EC had become a major pressing issue brought about by the swift collapse of communism and the regime changes in EE.

In June 1989 Poland's Solidarity Trade Union won the election. In October 1989, Hungary's Communist Party voted to dissolve itself. In November, mass protests in Czechoslovakia forced the collapse of the communist regime and also in Bulgaria and Albania. In Romania in December 1989 protests began in Timisoara and five days later President Ceausescu along with his wife had been executed by firing squad. East Germany, the DDR, underwent the most stunning sudden transformation in less than 18 months, when in May 1989 Hungary opened the Hungarian–Austrian border allowing East Germans to escape to West Germany. In a few weeks 1 per cent of the East German population had left. In October anti-government protests over-shadowed the DDR's 40th anniversary celebrations and Honecker, CP leader, was removed from office. On 9 November 1989 the Berlin Wall was opened. The irony was that the wall was built because people were leaving and it also came down because people were leaving!

To staunch the flow of refugees the East Germans thought that once people knew they were free to leave they would stay put. They still left fearing a reversal of the policy. Within eight months (and after free elections in East Germany) East and West Germany had achieved currency union followed three months later (3rd November 1990) by complete unification of the two Germanys with a new constitution, a new parliament and five new Lander (states). The whole process took less than 18 months!

All of this occurred fundamentally because President Gorbachev's policy of reform in the USSR which spread to other regimes meant that any residual will to repress dissent had evaporated long ago. From the Communist point of view the rot had set in with the failure to confront Polish Solidarity in 1980s. During pro-democracy demonstrations throughout the Warsaw Pact's member states, Red Army units were ordered to take no part and remain neutral in their bases. The USSR's Foreign Minister Edward Shevardnadze displayed rare refreshing humour by referring to their 'Sinatra Doctrine' (as opposed to the Brezhnev Doctrine) that countries should do things their way!

This was in stark contrast to the Chinese Communist government ruthlessly crushing what they termed 'hooligans' and 'counter revolutionaries' in Tiananmen Square in June 1989. Hundreds of pro-democracy demonstrators were killed or wounded by the tanks and troops of the Peoples Liberation Army. The Chinese regime had the will and was still prepared to react just as the Warsaw Pact and Red Army had once done in Hungary in 1956 and Czechoslovakia in 1968.

East Germany automatically joined the EC as part of a reunited Germany, Article 227 of the Treaty of Rome 1957 anticipated German reunification. Enlargement was seen as a mere fulfilment of the Treaty of Rome by Germany. Hungary though, in January 1990, made it clear that they did not look kindly on East Germany getting such preferential treatment by the EC. It certainly made any refusal to allow in other ex-Communist states all the more politically and morally indefensible.

Post-1989 the Central and Eastern European (CEE) states expectation was that the EC would become their trade anchor, a security anchor and a modernisation anchor. 'Nobody has previously taken the road that leads from Socialism to Capitalism and we are setting out to do just that' said Lech Walensa (*Observer* 31/12/89). There was no experience of the wholesale transformation required in moving from a Stalinist centrally planned socialist command economy to a liberal market economy. Poland, Hungary and Czechoslovakia abolished price controls in early 1990 freeing prices so that the market was able to self-regulate by prices moving up or down according to supply and demand. Prices were then able to emerge that reflected the real value of a good. This was a first step to a free market economy. In Poland only about 10 per cent of prices were still fixed and only where state monopolies continued (rents, public utilities, public transport fares).

Fixed prices under state socialism did not reflect the true cost of the good and led to price distortion. Food, for example, was priced far too cheaply so that stocks were quickly snapped up and shelves stayed empty. Inflation was artificially repressed by price controls. Inflation rose between 30 and 60 per cent in 1991 and remained at 30 per cent in 1992.

There were also shortages of basic goods and fuel, balance of payment deficits and growing indebtedness. Problems arose too because of the abandonment of Comecon (Communism's version of the 'common market') which was based on a barter system of state trading. The breakdown occurred as states decided to settle accounts in hard currency even before full currency convertibility was achieved. However, this did serve to stimulate trade with market economies instead so furthering liberalisation. Consumers had to tighten their belts as GDP fell. The problem initially for these transitional economies was that conditions deteriorated further as a result of change which meant some questioned the merits of free markets. This though was not allowed to slow down the transition process and most people calmly waited for a better future. In the long term their prospects were good as their manufacturing sectors had a huge advantage in lower labour costs.

Poland, Hungary and Czechoslovakia held free multi-party elections in 1990, a prerequisite for economic liberalism. By 1991 these three countries had restructured their economies to a great extent; in 1989 they had no capital market, no banking system and no experience in monetary control. As well as creating such infrastructure, new systems of civil law and the law of contract had to be adopted to enable the ownership and transfer of property and 'freedom of contract' implemented to ensure competition and a free market. These were also essential prerequisites to encourage FDI and closer relations with the EC.

It was not reform of their systems that was needed but a complete root and branch transformation. The feared consequences of failure to transform themselves were the risks of nationalistic upheaval, political backlash, economic collapse and mass emigration. The Italians were already contending with Albanian boat people. The EC and other Western states through helping to sustain economic transition by providing economic, technical, managerial and financial aid effectively counteracted such threats. The aid provided was not simply for the benefit of transition states but was in the EC's interests too. To avoid chaos on its Eastern border the EC could not afford to be a passive observer of historic changes but helped shape events and influence the outcome. *The Economist* (7/12/91) summed it up as 'Europe's future stability and prosperity will depend upon how Western Europe's grown up democracies treat Eastern Europe's foundling states appearing on their Eastern doorstep'.

How exactly did the EC treat them? What did the EC and 'free world' do? Initially the EC signed what came to be known subsequently as 'First Generation' Trade and Cooperation Agreements. These were negotiated with every CEE state between 1988 and 1990, following the early phase of political change in EE inspired by President Gorbachev's post-1985 reforms in the USSR. These agreements were very limited in scope because Western Europe remained protectionist and restricted imports through quotas on the 'sensitive' products of steel, textiles and agricultural goods. These of course were the very same products that CEE specialised in, had a comparative advantage in (as costs of production and prices were lower) and needed to export. Joint cooperative ventures were possible but proved difficult to arrange with Western Multi-National Enterprises (MNEs) in transition economies. VW and Skoda cooperated in modernising the Czechoslovakian car market and aimed to produce to Western standards by 1992. There were cooperative ventures too in Poland between Dutch and German food-processing companies. Tampax was one of the few ventures early on to start a factory in the USSR but they had to repatriate profits in the form of raw cotton.

Other aid initiatives were more useful. The UK Foreign Office in 1989 started 'know-how' Funds for Poland, Hungary and Czechoslovakia to transfer UK know-how and skills in production and management. Eligibility for assistance was conditional on progress in moving to liberal democracy and market economies. UK banks (which had built up experience because of Margaret Thatcher's privatisation of loss-making state-run nationalised industries in the UK) became involved in the privatisation process in EE, more than German banks which were involved with their Eastern Landers transformation.

Under the EC's initiative in December 1989 the European Bank of Reconstruction and Development (EBRD) was set up. Financed by 42 countries it again made its loans dependent on clients' democratic development. Initially its funding, 13 billion ECU, was a drop in the ocean yet its significance was in using Western public money to help develop the private sector in EE and the Soviet Union. Exposure of public money to risky investment in the earliest stages of transition from a Stalinist system (before Western private capital was ready to risk doing so) was justified as a 'public good' through encouraging democracy and the market economy.

The Phare Programme (Poland, Hungary Assistance to the Restructuring of the Economies) was set up in July 1989 by the G7 in Paris and the EC was charged with the task of coordinating assistance from the G24 group of states. It was to provide emergency help to Poland and Hungary and was extended in 1990 to Bulgaria, Czechoslovakia, Romania and Yugoslavia. By March 1991 aid had come to include writing-off over 50 per cent of Poland's official debt. The TEMPUS Programme (Trans Europe Mobility Programme for University Students) started in May 1990 initially with three years funding for academic exchanges for students and teachers to spend a year in EC universities.

The East European states had joined GATT, IMF and World Bank and quite logically they wanted full membership of the EC too. How did the EC respond to this? Was there a membership common policy and strategy? In fact inside the EC there were two opposite approaches. Advocates of a 'broadening' approach favoured closer cooperation with reforming CEE favoured states. Germany was particularly interested in the integration of its Eastern neighbours. The UK was in favour of this too. The German government proposed that these countries (Poland, Hungary and Czech Republic) should be given 'associate status', recognised as a stage before full membership.

An alternative strategy shared by the President of the EC Commission, Jacques Delors and southern EC members aimed to intensify the homogeneity of the 12 existing members, i.e. 'deepen' the community before any enlargement, and postpone any decision about offering associate status to countries queuing up to join. Their argument was that the EC couldn't absorb EE states as it was still struggling to deal with the recent Iberian enlargement (Spain and Portugal) and in particular absorb two poor states Portugal and (even the comparatively new member) Greece, which joined in 1981. Whereas in fact Greece, as a small country added only 7 per cent to the EEC's budget.

These Mediterranean states supported the EC Commission's and Jacques Delors' view as they feared that their aid payments would be re-allocated to the even poorer CEE states. Jacques Delors thought that enlargement would result in two unattractive outcomes; it would considerably increase Germany's influence in the EC and it would threaten his goal of political integration in Europe. In a speech in Bruges, October 1989, Delors said ' ... the community's institutions had to be reformed to respond to the acceleration of history' and that ' ... the only satisfactory and acceptable response to the German Question is the reinforcement of certain federalist traits'. For Delors a more Federal Europe would contain and counterbalance a united Germany. He believed that this vision of a political union would be endangered and swamped if and when further states were admitted to the EC. Delors' own view, in March 1990, was that the EC could not afford to enlarge now or for years to come; it had to complete its move to the Single Market, Monetary Union and political integration before adding new members.

Jacques Delors, President of the European Commission, was prepared to ignore the reality and needs of EE states clamouring for membership. His concern was to focus on 'completion' and 'deepening' the existing EC's agenda and so disregard the requirements and demands of those queuing for entry.

Delors' conception of three concentric circles, as mentioned earlier, might have been a logical gradual sequential route to eventual membership but it had no appeal for EE applicants. Delors envisaged a Europe separated into three parts, the inner core of 12 EC states; the second circle of EFTA and

Association Agreement states; an outer circle of CEE, Malta and Cyprus and Trade and Cooperation Agreement countries. Some movement was envisaged from outer to middle circle. Delors' lack of sensitivity was seen here in his bundling the CEE transition economies in with the fringe microstates of Malta and Cyprus. Poland, Hungary and Czechoslovakia saw an EFTA-type transitional zone as a 'waiting room' and they were determined to avoid being pushed into another 'poor man's club'. They wanted the EC to promise them eventual full membership and thereby effectively grant them 'political membership' quickly and so eventual economic membership in the Association Agreements, the second Generation Trade and Cooperation Agreements. They did not want to be held in the limbo of a free-trade zone between themselves and the EC while their economic standards and indices improved. An expectation of full economic membership would provide EE states (in 1990/91) with a definite objective and goal to aim at. Such an offer within a reasonable timescale would bolster political stability and help deter any attempt at reversion to any authoritarian alternative to a democratic market economy.

Contrary to Delors' priorities outlined above in October 1989, the European Council (of heads of governments) in Strasbourg December 1989 recognised the need for the EC to be more welcoming, positive and integrationist, declaring that 'the EC is and must remain a point of reference and influence. It remains the cornerstone of a new European architecture and in it's will to openness a mooring for the future European equilibrium.'

The reality was that ultimately Delors lost. Exactly two years later in December 1991, Delors' original modus operandi had clearly been rejected with the conclusion of new, second generation, European Agreements granting associate membership status to Poland, Hungary and Czechoslovakia with early talks leading to integration much more certain. Delors admitted some widening would have to occur somehow and in January 1992 said that, 'It is essential to prepare a structure for Europe which I expect will have 25 members'.

Before looking at this particular outcome of Association Agreements and guarantees and promises it is necessary to consider other countries' positions on the 'deepen' or 'widen' dichotomy and indeed their changing positions, in order to appreciate what determined the fates and futures of the EC and EE at this climacteric point, 1989–91.

Spain and Portugal and other Southern European states suddenly felt eclipsed by EE appearing as the region of new political progress and economic promise (*Guardian Weekly*, 8/8/90). This shift aroused fears that the stream of foreign investments could dry up and EC funds be diverted to backward areas in the East. Non-European firms, in 1990, had already started looking at EE to invest in rather than Mediterranean states. Suzuki Motors suspended studies in January 1990, of locating a car plant in Portugal and at the same time announced it would invest in a plant in Hungary (one was not a replacement for the other Suzuki claimed, but there weren't funds for both projects!). Volkswagen had planned a \$5.7 billion investment in Catalonia, near Barcelona, over seven years but then announced its next project would be in the East German city of Karl Marx Stadt and also opened talks with Skoda, the Czech car maker, on a possible joint venture there. Jordi Pujol, President of Catalonia's regional government (in 1990) confirmed that FDI delegations that used to visit the Southern Mediterranean area had now shifted attention to include Berlin and Eastern Europe. Pedro Solbes, Spain's Secretary of State for Europe predicted that the full impact would be felt after four or five years; once infrastructure improvements and better legal systems in the East were in place these would further encourage foreign investment. (*Guardian Weekly* 8/4/90).

Structural funding was a big issue though for the Spanish and Portuguese. They feared that East Germany would get a lot of help at their expense; Brussels claimed that this help would be from new funding at least until 1993. Such facts and fears explains Southern Mediterranean support for the Delors Commission's view of first deepen then much later widen the EC.

Eastern enlargement meant the balance in the EU tilted eastwards. Small peripheral states such as Ireland and Greece feared that their influence inside the EU, as well as their cohesion and structural funding, would shrink. In 1993 Ireland's GDP per head was still 20 per cent below the EU average and its share of structural funds (worth £1 billion in 1993 equal to 2 per cent of Ireland's GDP) would decline sharply when the funding package expired in 1999. Eastern enlargement meant agreements with current members would be unpicked by the Commission. Of course Ireland would be a 'victim' of its own success; as a fast growing Celtic Tiger it was less eligible for EC largesse. In fact Ireland's growth was due more to its sound macroeconomic conditions which meant FDI into Ireland was three times bigger than EC structural funds 1986–91 (*Economist* 3/8/96).

The UK was keen to widen the EC. It wanted, 1989–90, to admit countries quickly especially as the UK believed the seven EFTA states thought broadly in much the same way as themselves and were sympathetic to the UK's stance on most issues. Such support might possibly even shift the balance of power inside the EC, away from the Paris–Bonn axis. A wider EC could eventually perhaps result in an EC that was mostly a FTA. In other words, widening might produce some dilution or loosening of integration. John Major, Britain's Prime Minister in 1991, wanted to see the Czech Republic, Hungary and Poland in the EC within ten years; and thought that ' ... far from deepening the EC the irresistible logic of wider membership is to abandon grand designs for Europe and stick to Free Trade' (*Sunday Times* (*ST*) 27/10/91).

Margaret Thatcher, who was Prime Minister of Britain from 1979 to November 1990, resigned following a leadership contest (caused by a bitter internecine ideological battle over Europe in the Parliamentary Conservative Party, i.e. between fellow MPs). She failed to win outright on the first ballot and was then persuaded by men in suits to quit. Thatcher had referred since 1988 to the 'nightmare' of a Federal Europe; whereas the European

Parliament called for swift moves to bring about a United Europe. Thatcher, who had signed the SEA in 1986 and championed the concept of a single market, nevertheless denounced the 'bureaucratic centralism' of the EC. Within the European Parliament a majority of Conservative MEPs were Europhiles locked into a ferocious argument with the 'Blue Circle Group' of MEPs (known as 'Blue Rinse Group' to their critics) who were Thatcherite. Michael Heseltine, deputy Tory Leader, was a keen Europhile, critic and rival to Thatcher. The divisions between the factions had as much or more to do with posture and attitude than substance or basic positions on issues. John Major (Thatcher's chosen successor as Prime Minister and leader of the Conservative Party) and Douglas Hurd, Foreign Minster under both Thatcher and Major, were no less opposed to Euro-federalism or the UK joining EMU than Margaret Thatcher but were much more diplomatic and not as negative or hostile in tone in dealing with fellow European Community partners. (*Independent* 27/6/91).

The long-held original French position on the dichotomous issue of EU strategy: to 'widen' or 'deepen' was that if membership grew, especially if it included neutral states, the EC would never be able to deepen with respect to building a European Defence policy.

Germany held the view that deepening and widening were not mutually exclusive. The Germans wanted a Federal Europe but also to let in EFTA and the CEE states as soon as their economies would fit. FRG President Richard von Weizsacker argued that a bigger EC would accelerate not block the emergence of political union. For the Germans a Federal Europe would resemble an enlarged FRG and for Germany it only meant an additional layer of government on top of their national government tier, and was wholly non-controversial.

Germany of course was preoccupied with all the ramifications of reunification from 1989; detailed complex multi-national negotiations on many issues were simultaneously conducted at a rapid pace. Richard Helms (ex US, CIA chief) described German reunification as a 'runaway freight train' (*Guardian* 4/3/90) with other parties being out-manoeuvred all along the line by the speed of reunification. Chancellor Kohl managed to win (it was said at the time) all the time along what proved to be an 'open road to unification' (*ST* 22/4/90).

Of course only a year before the whole idea of reunification appeared to be a complete non-starter. There were some bumps along the way though. There was acrimony when Kohl appeared to be setting conditions for the final definitive German recognition of the Oder–Neisse frontier with Poland. This upset and alarmed Thatcher (who played up the border plans) and Mitterand as well as the Poles. Hans Dieter Genscher, the FRG's Foreign Minister and President von Weizsacker repeatedly said as reassurance that only present borders mattered, not the 1937 ones. The whole episode was an electoral ploy, seemingly, by Chancellor Kohl as there were 8–10m. voters in Germany whose families had come from and had roots in the disputed areas of Silesia (once German and now Polish). The SPD was expected to win the election in the East but it was Kohl's CDU that was returned to power.

The border issue worsened Franco-German relations; they were already in poor shape before East Germany's collapse but they then worsened considerably. France was no longer the most powerful partner, no longer the guide and condescending helper to the defeated nation, West Germany. Germany's economic and political weight had turned France into a more supplicant state that needed answers.

As noted above the stock French reaction to any move or German initiative independent of France, whether in the 1950s or 1990s, was to seek closer ties to the UK or embark on some further integration initiative in Europe or both together. Initially Mitterand contemplated closer links with Thatcher's UK but ultimately rejected these in favour of a drive to further European integration, re-energising the Franco-German axis and engine for change in the EC.

Relations became quarrelsome and acrimonious when Kohl seemed to be setting conditions over the recognition of the Oder–Neisse line. Mitterand, whilst outwardly, publicly welcoming German unity, nevertheless tried to throw obstacles in its path and West Germany's newspapers reacted negatively to these acts (*ST* 22/4/90). Mitterrand's visit to East Germany was seen as a French attempt to encourage their retaining a separate identity. Mitterand flew to Kiev to talk to Gorbachev in December 1989 (and was unsuccessful in getting him to block reunification as he'd already agreed to it); in the German press this visit was seen as an attempt to surround and tame the German giant. Resentment in Bonn increased further when Paris invited Polish leaders to visit at the height of the Oder–Neisse controversy and then Paris received Oskar Lafontaine, the German SPD leader when it seemed the East Germans would vote SPD (they voted for Kohl's CDU).

This breakdown in relations over German unity really hurt. The Germans were resentful and the French aggrieved at being ignored by the inattentive and preoccupied Kohl. Whereas Brandt and Pompidou could detest and avoid each other as far as possible back in the 1970s (according to Roger de Weck in the liberal weekly *Die Zeit*), this was not possible in 1989–90. Germany had to be seen to be in agreement and moving together in the same direction at such a time. Kohl, also acting out of personal conviction, knew that he needed to show firm European solidarity while German reunification was negotiated. In a phone conversation to President Mitterand in March 1990 he made a bold proposal regarding European unity. This conversation marked the start of a reconciliation and a new chapter in the uneasy Franco-German relationship and a turnaround in French policy following weeks of suspicion and acrimony.

According to newspaper reports at the time, Mitterand, in a French TV interview, almost apologised for his misdirected foreign policy (*Guardian* 27/3/90). Mitterand had led efforts to slow down unification which had not brought about a closer understanding with Margaret Thatcher (as she expected) but had undermined the Paris–Bonn axis. Mitterand, in the TV interview, fairly accurately in fact, forecast the downfall of Thatcher. Bonn and Paris he announced were ready to fix a timetable for EMU and re-launch moves to Political Union. Mitterand said on TV that a big step to Political Union would be taken in 1993 (the year the SM started to operate from 1/1/93). Mitterand also said that France would set the pace in the next three to four years as West Germany was preoccupied (weakened) by absorbing Eastern Germany.

Chancellor Kohl, interviewed on French TV (29/3/90), said that the aim of the joint proposal was to work towards the ' ... United States of Europe, when the hour of truth strikes Europe ... we'll see who'll be ready to turn over national jurisdiction and rights to Europe ... we're ready' (*Le Monde* 31/3/90). This was Kohl and Mitterand deliberately throwing down the gauntlet to Margaret Thatcher and Douglas Hurd. The Franco-German Declaration in favour of both EMU and Political Union marked a reconciliation between the two states. Mitterand and Kohl's call for European Political Union and EMU by 1st January 1993 (a wholly unrealistic and fantastic objective) was a deliberately provocative and headline-grabbing opening gambit by the two leaders. They were urging the most dramatic shake-up in Western Europe's economic and political geography for half a century and clearly presented Mrs Thatcher with the shocking prospect of her 'nightmare' becoming a reality. She appeared to face a stark choice and challenge of whether to be a part or not of a USE. Kohl and Mitterand said they would push for fast and full EMU and for political reforms to turn the EC into something like a Federal Political Union. Their declared objective was for EMU and Political Union to take effect on 1/1/93! (*Guardian* 20/4/90).

The Irish Prime Minister, Charles Haughey, would host the EC Summit in Dublin on 28 April 1990 and France and Germany were pressing hard for Monetary and Political Union. The UK Foreign Office in London treated this news with disdain. Margaret Thatcher was predictably very hostile and Douglas Hurd, the Foreign Secretary, said there was no question of the UK agreeing to a centralised government in Europe (*ST* 22/4/90). Chancellor Helmut Kohl, President François Mitterand and President of the European Commission Jacques Delors were together thrusting ahead towards more European integration in April 1990. These three all believed a reunified Germany had to be tied up in an 'integrated Federal Europe' before it was too late, that was before Germany discovered a taste for using her new power independently (*Independent* 8/6/92). This was a fear commonly held by the older generation of European leaders that Mitterand, Delors and Kohl came from. It was also shared by Mrs Thatcher but she of course wanted a different solution to the German question. In fact this attitude (less commonly found among a younger generation of leaders) was really quite insulting to the new Germany, which had proved to be a model ally over the decades since 1945.

Germany was intent on there being a strong Treaty at Maastricht on Political Union, making Political Union a condition for a deal on Economic and

Monetary Union. Bonn insisted on more power for the EP in order to bring the EC under democratic control and eventually elections for the President of Europe by the end of the twentieth century. The German position of not moving on EMU without clear progress on Political Union was quite logical as monetary economists et al. doubted that one could survive without the other. Moreover the Deutschmark and monetary stability were Germany's most prized achievements since World War II. 'Politically and emotionally it was the family silver' (*Independent* 26/10/91).

Mitterand wanted an Intergovernmental Conference on Monetary Union to report by 1991. Kohl was non-committal on this and pressed for a 'maximalist Federal agenda as a prerequisite'. For Kohl and Germany to entrust monetary stability to other Europeans (many of whom had shown feckless even reckless monetary behaviour in the past) was out of the question unless there were solid real institutional guarantees and clear political gains to be had, moving to Political Union. 'Political Union' meant different things to different people. Delors argued that there was an 'irresistible logic for swift Federation' as an EC of 19 or more states could not function on present lines, it was hard enough with just 12. Delors wanted more power vested centrally immediately and ultimately Federalism. Others doubted the wisdom of creating exclusive political and monetary links at Maastricht while the future shape of the EC was uncertain. The UK chose 'Political Union' to mean enhanced political cooperation between sovereign governments, not federation. Helmut Kohl's initial very strong views on a Federal Europe meant he demanded a timetable for federalising reforms or rather what he called 'evolutionary clauses' in the Treaty document.

Prior to the Dublin European Council Summit in April 1990 the UK Foreign Secretary was highly sceptical about the seriousness and feasibility of the Franco-German Declaration. Douglas Hurd said that the UK was not the only country to have reservations about Political Union. When pressed by the interviewer he said (in what was a provocative statement for the French) ' ... we know the inherent improbability of the French accepting a central government or parliament' (*ST* 22/4/90). Hurd's doubts about French convictions were to prove wholly correct eighteen months later at Maastricht.

The Draft Treaty on European Union took shape after the Dublin Summit 1990. Months of argument and negotiations ensued; positions changed and opening gambits were watered down, initial expectations and aspirations were scaled back. The Maastricht Treaty transformed and pooled national sovereignty in 12 policy areas most being decided supranationally by qualified majority votes. These included consumer protection, free movement of labour, rights of professionals throughout the EU, training young workers, environmental protection and the Social Chapter on Workers' Rights (there were only three pages on this to be completed over time). The eventual treaty followed a French design put forward by François Mitterand of three pillars: economic and monetary union; internal security; foreign and defence policy. France's priority at Maastricht was to seek more EC powers over employment law and industrial policy and also on a European Defence identity. Germany's eventual short-term priorities were more powers for the European Parliament including the European Parliament having veto powers over all EC laws not decided unanimously by the Council of Ministers. Britain ensured that not all European cooperation was channelled via the Treaty of Rome, i.e. under supranational control, as Jacques Delors wanted. Supranational institutional responsibility was essential for Single Market matters and in EC's World Trade negotiations but definitely not for foreign and security policy or interior/justice affairs. Jacques Delors had tried to fuse these three pillars into one under supranational control but this approach was not acceptable to Britain, France (as Douglas Hurd had predicted long before) and some others and so was not adopted.

Douglas Hurd, speaking in a House of Commons debate on Britain's role in Europe in June 1991, said he liked a Europe in which separate pillars of cooperation are maintained; keeping intergovernmental cooperation and the institutions of the Treaty of Rome separate was an important element in the government's vision of Europe. It would be necessary to check that the pillars really were kept separate. He reported that the term 'Federal Goal' had been inserted into the draft Treaty recently partly to placate those who had lost the argument. (*Independent* 27/6/91). Elsewhere though a Dutch diplomat had said the term was inserted as it was known that the UK would want to remove it and so would have to concede on something else to do so! John Major got the subsidiarity principle adopted: that decisions should be taken at the right level as close to the citizens as possible. Also that countries should be allowed to act on their own even if a common policy had been agreed ' ... in cases of imperative need'.

Douglas Hurd, speaking in parliament, said that there was ' ... no possibility of being pushed into a Treaty which is repugnant to us', and to rebut diehard Thatcherite Europhobes, that ' ... History would deal harshly with us if we retreated into some form of querulous isolation, worried always at the prospect of being outwitted by clever foreigners, acting always as a brake on the ideas of others without putting forward ideas of our own' (*Independent* 27/6/91).

The UK agreed to accept the Treaty of Maastricht on the basis that it had the option to decide on entry to EMU in the future. Britain, like Germany, was adamant that states entering Monetary Union must have similar rates of inflation, budget deficits and public debt : GDP ratios. It was essential for such economic convergence of European economies to occur Pre-Economic and Monetary Union. These conditions became the eventual Maastricht preconditions for countries joining EMU, the 'convergence criteria' for EMU.

By November 1991 Germany had substantially scaled down its expectations of the Maastricht Summit on European integration and the proposed Treaty on Political Union in the 'face of widespread resistance'. Chancellor Helmut Kohl had dropped his long-standing demand that the Treaty should embrace a common policy for interior and legal matters like immigration.

Kohl had been won round and now accepted Britain and others' view that these matters (at least initially) should be dealt with by cooperation between states (*Independent* 26/11/91).

In a Sunday night TV interview in France, Kohl indicated that a more pragmatic and less visionary approach to European political union would be adopted. Inter-governmental cooperation would co-exist with common institutions, and that there would only be a partial shift of powers to Europe with national parliaments responsible for most legislation. This conception corresponded closely with the UK's ideas of 'gradualist institutional reform' which apparently got a surprisingly favourable reception in Germany (*Independent* 26/11/91).

Jacques Delors condemned the Draft Treaty in a speech to MEPs at the European Parliament just days before Kohl's TV appearance, as an ambiguous cynical compromise to assuage UK's anti-Federalist fears and to some extent French concerns. The 'hybrid Treaty' was a model of 'organised schizophrenia' despite being grandly re-branded as the European Union, as it mixed the communitaire approach (supranational) and the intergovernmental approach (sovereign states remaining supreme). The concessions won by the UK corresponded exactly to Douglas Hurd's view that ' … those that believe in integration on federal rails will be disappointed. The future lay with government to government cooperation' (*Independent* 21/11/91).

Elizabeth Guigou, France's Minister for European Affairs, also rejected the idea that France was moving inexorably towards a federalism that effaces national identities (in an interview in the *Observer* 8/12/91): 'No one should imagine that Europe is going to be turned into the United States of America. We are not going to plough under the centuries' old traditions of Britain and France and other countries of the EC to transform them into Dakota and Kansas.'

French and UK positions on Europe were often closer than they appeared. *Le Monde* concluded that France was glad to hide its low opinion of the usefulness of the European Parliament behind that of Britain, which had an even lower regard for it. Britain's European partners were used to relying on Britain being 'the brake' on anything too fanciful or fantastic and some argued that as such the UK provided a cohesive force in the EC as the 'focus of community irritation without which real divisions might emerge if the UK were left behind'. No one wanted to back the UK into a corner. The opt-outs ensured that the UK could sign the Treaty (*Independent* 28/10/91; *ST* 27/10/91).

Maastricht was more than a constitutional Treaty: it was a redesign of the EC, now re-branded as the EU. It incorporated the staged, timetabled objective of a single currency to be achieved by 1999, with an embryonic central bank (the European Monetary Institute (EMI)) to be established under Stage 2, 1 January 1994, along with adopting a narrow band for the ERM.

The entire populace of the EU's member states were, in a psychologically symbolic move, to become citizens of the EU with a common passport and with working and voting rights throughout the EU. A fledgling foreign policy and embryonic defence policy for the EU were both issues to be settled by intergovernmental cooperation, outside the remit of the Treaty of Rome. The EU's legal tentacles were to extend into many new areas. The 'mad dash to Maastricht' was, according to Jonathan Eyal (Director RUSI, *Independent* 2/8/93), predicated on France's belief that only by erasing the Deutschmark would Germany be deprived of the ability to translate economic power into political power in the centre of Europe. France tried to force the new united Germany into its old political agenda – whereas according to Eyal's view, they should have focused on accommodating new Germany into a new enlarged EC. Everything else was sacrificed to achieve this French objective (wholly shared by Jacques Delors) ignoring and relegating EE enlargement to a distant future.

François Mitterand and the French government wanted to pour concrete in the form of Monetary Union and a single currency over the big feet of a unified Germany to embed them in EMU and prevent any future delinquent outbursts (*Independent* 2/8/93).

When Elizabeth Guigou, France's Foreign Minister for European Affairs, was interviewed in December 1991, she did not deny the feverish haste in the run-up to Maastricht. She justified it by the threats to peace in EE and ' ... the lack of instruments to cope with a crisis that could plunge the old continent back into what Mitterand called "tribal Europe"' (*Observer* 8/12/91).

However, it must be said that Chancellor Helmut Kohl at the time (1990–91), willingly participated in this shared project and even suggested it in a phone conversation back in March 1990. Kohl wanted to anchor united Germany firmly in the West. For Chancellor Kohl the unification of Germany and the unification of Europe went together. Kohl could see the strains on German prosperity and social cohesion from absorbing and renovating the East; the resurgence of ethnic nationalism in EE and the disintegration of the USSR and signs of hatred and skinhead violence closer to home.

However, John Major, Chancellor of the Exchequer and then Prime Minister of Britain, saw things differently. He was born in 1943 and so not from this older generation of leaders. Margaret Thatcher considered German unity as unthinkable and out of the question in 1989 and Delors' blueprint for the EU as simply confirming German hegemony in the EC. John Major did not share this experience, fear and distrust of Germany which appeared a model of constitutional democracy and good behaviour. He had developed a good rapport and working relationship with Helmut Kohl, whereas Mrs Thatcher was barely on speaking terms (Peter Jenkins, *Independent* 20/10/91).

This good relationship was to prove important following the Danish rejection of the Maastricht Treaty in a referendum in June 1992 by a majority of 24,000 against the Treaty (*The Economist* 6/6/92). *The Economist* summarised the general view that 'Maastricht was a rushed job, bounced upon the community by the governments of France and Germany to fulfil their dream of European Union before its basis in cold war Europe vanished'. For this liberal weekly magazine the mistake was not the goal but the ' … immoderate manner of its pursuit. Europe's single market is not even up and running yet'. The detailed plan for monetary union offered more than enough to be getting on with. The community was marching into areas of centralised law making, particularly on social policy, which scoffed at its own principle of 'subsidiarity'. 'Above all there was the whiff of coercion in the air of governments frog-marching public opinion along or of "saving the Germans from themselves". Coercion was Comecon's most damaging ingredient' (*The Economist* 6/6/92).

For Delors and Mitterand Denmark's rejection was an embarrassing result but John Major (who was about to take over the Chairmanship of the EC's Council of Ministers for the next six months) was concerned about Chancellor Kohl's position. If the Maastricht Treaty disappeared Kohl's European policy would have failed and his government's future could be at risk. Kohl was at the centre of the UK's Europe policy, he was Major's most important ally, sympathetic to UK interests, and should be supported. It fell to John Major to salvage the Maastricht Treaty as the incumbent EU President until December 1992. Although Maastricht was perhaps regarded as an impulsive blunder with an absurdly unrealistic timetable caused by needless French panic over German reunification; the UK government wanted to avoid its total breakdown. This might lead to the formation of an inner European group of France, Germany and Benelux, which might move to a real political and monetary union of a sort the UK could neither join nor comfortably keep out of. So it was in the UK's interest to maintain Kohl's European position and the existing Maastricht Treaty and so discourage any federalistic *démarche* of a Europe of the five.

Jacques Delors was widely blamed, condemned for contributing to the Danes' rejection by continuing clumsily by calculation to make federalist speeches about the EU's future shape and reducing the influence of small states (*Independent* 8/6/92; *The Economist* 6/6/92).

Major and Kohl considered that rapid moves to enlargement would reassure the Danes if the EU grew to seventeen states including (subject to referendums) Switzerland and Norway, Austria, Sweden and Finland – states that tended to view the future in much the same way as the UK and Denmark. An 'Alpine-Arctic' enlargement in 1995 helped secure a second positive vote in Denmark by a whisper in 1993. In France their Maastricht Referendum was carried by barely a 1 per cent majority. When it looked as if the French would reject it, Mitterand (having kept the news secret for years) announced on TV the night before the vote that he had cancer. It's thought that the sympathy vote secured a majority. In the UK, with no referendum, it passed through the Commons by a two-vote majority.

However, Chancellor Kohl, in December 1991, by agreeing to less at Maastricht than his opening gambit of a federal Europe had not given up this original objective. Maastricht was simply the start of a United States of Europe (USE). He was reported (10/12/91) as saying 'The most important thing is that it is clear that what we are doing is irrevocable, on the way to political union we are now crossing the Rubicon. There is no going back.'

As well as the Maastricht Treaty the Association Agreements were signed on 16 December 1991, following a year of difficult negotiations with Poland, Hungary and Czechoslovakia. These eventually gave them desperately needed access to European markets and hard currency. The significance was political and even psychological as well as economic. The Czech negotiator Zenon Pireck saw it as a further step to being a fully fledged member of the EU. EC officials cautioned that the agreement was not a 'free ticket' to membership which would need to be negotiated; however the preamble made explicit reference to the fact that ' ... bearing in mind the ultimate objective of the three countries is to become full community members ... this agreement will help reach this'. This was what the three states wanted, clear recognition of future membership. Kohl had 'promised' them membership, grateful to Hungary for its role in hastening the end of East Germany by opening its frontiers and to Vaclav Havel, Czechoslovakian President, who (unlike President Mitterand) said in Berlin that Germany had a right to unity, to the dismay of East German communists.

Apart from Germany and Britain who were keen on enlargement there was a growing recognition among the richer EC members that the extra budget money they would be spending on EE would otherwise be spent on them anyway as aid. Moreover, confidence in eventual EC membership could help steady democracy in these old communist states, as it had done for post-dictatorship Spain and Portugal.

The 1991 Association Agreements would in time give free access to EC markets for all goods including agriculture products. This had proved difficult to negotiate as France was hostile to cheap meat flooding an already saturated market but eventually fell into line after pressure from other EC states. Spain waged a similar campaign to protect its steel industry and got some protective safeguards. There would also be free movement of people and full implementation of all categories would be within ten years! However they escaped Delors' intended fate for them in the outermost 'concentric circle' waiting room, as the reality was that Delors was overruled with the conclusion of these European Agreements with early integration now more probable.

The potential trade benefits and particularly export opportunities to the three CEE states were enormous, as in 1991 only 2.2 per cent of EC imports were East European manufactured goods. It was vitally important that the EC reduced its protectionism especially in sectors like processed foods because CAP excluded Poland and Czechoslovakia, who were hit hard by this as they had been very dependent on food exports to USSR. They had lost this big customer and failed to gain access to another market pre-1991 Agreements. It was also important for clothes and other low-cost manufacturers and basic staple products that EE had a comparative advantage in. The danger in the EC's protectionism up until 1991 was that it delayed EE economic adjustment and so might have provoked social upheaval and unrest. The abolition of trade barriers was of mutual benefit to EE and the EC, with its almost completely open frontiers and future possibilities of an almost unlimited flow of goods, services, capital and labour.

Events between 1991 and 1993 overshadowed the start of the Single Market. Successive ERM crises in 1992–93 and the Yugoslavia crisis and civil wars severely tested two of the pillars of the Maastricht Treaty, EMU and the CFSP. Germany was to play a crucial part in these crises: the immense expenditure involved in its own 'Eastern enlargement' of the GDR strained the ERM to breaking point and Germany insisted, against most of the EC states, on recognition of the breakaway republics of Slovenia and Croatia.

8 From Single Market (1992) to single currency (2002)

The years 1992–93 were not good ones for the EU (despite the achievement of a Single Market by January 1993) in so far as the two main elements of Maastricht, cooperation in foreign and security policy and Monetary Union, appeared to fail their first tests. These setbacks were largely due to German policy. In the Maastricht talks Germany wanted to see majority voting on at least some aspects of foreign and security policy. The UK opposed voting on foreign policy, and extension of EU power over foreign policy, as the UK believed no European government should find itself compelled or forbidden to use its forces. One reason for the German government's eagerness on this issue was the desire to escape from its domestic and constitutional difficulties over the use of force. The British thought they should instead solve this internally and not expect Brussels and the EU to do the job for them. The EU's fledgling CFSP was expected to emerge through discussion and mutually agreed intergovernmental decision. Yet in December 1991 Germany declared it would recognise Croatia and Slovenia within weeks regardless of what other states in the EC wanted. In the face of this threat of unilateral German action and the need to maintain some outward semblance of unity, however false, the EU reluctantly and half-heartedly recognised Slovenia and Croatia on 15 January 1992 and Bosnia on 6 April. This was accompanied by anguished recriminations and warnings that recognition would further inflame the Yugoslavian situation. Britain and France supported by Greece, Portugal and the Netherlands had agreed that premature recognition would provoke Serbia, especially the Yugoslavian Federal Army to step up their attacks on Croatia and break off their talks with the UN envoy Cyrus Vance, for the deployment of UN blue helmets.

Why did Germany insist on recognition? The Yugoslavian crisis worsened considerably in mid-1991 and Kohl wanted to recognise these two states then but was persuaded to delay this by Mitterand. These putative fledgling independent states craved and pleaded for recognition. Germany felt that they themselves had benefited from the principle of self-determination to legitimise reunification and so others should not be denied. Germany supported eventually by Denmark and Italy wanted to accelerate the recognition process because of the principle of self-determination and because they thought any further delay in recognising Croatia and Slovenia would only encourage aggression by Serbian and the Yugoslav national army. Chancellor Kohl was also pressing for the early entry of Austria into the EU (achieved in the 'Arctic-Alpine' enlargement 1995, which admitted Sweden and Finland too). Kohl was effectively resurrecting an old zone of German influence that stretched from the Baltic to the Adriatic; a zone that had been dismantled twice before in 1918 and 1945. Germany could not remain indifferent to EE's collapse and tried to establish stability where it could in the face of the withdrawal of Soviet influence, regime change and the Warsaw Pact's dissolution. Germany was 'filling' part of the vacuum left behind. Moreover Kohl in 1991, had against the Bundesbank's advice, traded in the Deutschmark for the euro, so facilitating the French goal of EMU. He was, however, disappointed and dissatisfied that the crafty guileful Mitterand had not done more to deliver or help achieve political union but had in fact aligned himself with the British. Kohl realised in December 1991 that France would not co-sponsor the political federation of Europe that he wanted and insisted upon as the quid pro quo for EMU. This helps to explain Kohl's rebellious foreign policy over the Balkans in 1991.

For Mitterand it was a heavy blow when Chancellor Kohl broke ranks for the first time and the EU and France were forced to fall into line behind the Germans over recognition. From then on, in the last four years of his second Presidency, Mitterand was preoccupied in Franco-German relations with trying to regain the initiative. Resorting to dramatic happenings and gimmicks supposedly pregnant with symbolism; being photographed holding Kohl's hand at Verdun; German troops in the Bastille Day Parade. Given the wanton and reckless violence of the Yugoslavian civil wars seen nightly on TV, public opinion did not react against recognition even if they had noticed.

Germany, though, had prioritised its national interest at the expense of any attempt to achieve an agreed common policy. The EC itself was also deficient as Kramer (*JCMS* 31/2/93) has shown. From early 1991 the EC was negotiating a trade and cooperation agreement with Yugoslavia in Belgrade, yet it failed to appreciate the seriousness of Yugoslavia's problems and was completely unable to use negotiations on trade as a lever to achieve the EC's preferred long-term aim of keeping the Yugoslavian federation intact (Heinz Kramer 'The EC response to new Eastern Europe' *JCMS* 31/2/93 fn.27).

By October 1991 the EC was threatening economic sanctions, a complete trade ban against Yugoslavia, if the latest peace accord signed in The Hague was not observed. Successive ceasefires having previously collapsed (*Independent* 7/10/91), Yugoslavia's civil wars were not spontaneous eruptions of ancestral, tribal animosity although the region as a whole reputedly enjoyed reopening old wounds and parading their victim status. The wars were started by Serb, Slovene, Croat and Bosnian independence leaders. Among these Slobodan Milosevic, Serbian President, was the *eminence grise* behind the carnage, ethnic-cleansing genocide. (A. Russell, *Telegraph* 6/10/00). No Western organisation, power, authority or force could have prevented the

Yugoslavian civil wars. (S. Eyal, *Independent* 30/9/92). Milosevic primed and armed the Croatian Serbs. He bolstered Radovan Karadzic, the Bosnian Serb leader. As President of Serbia, Milosevic delivered a rabble-rousing speech to hundreds of Serbs in Kosovo. He instigated and lost four wars (in Croatia 1991, Bosnia 1992–95, repression in Kosovo; and in 1999 in a 78-day air war with NATO lost control of Kosovo). He saw Yugoslavia shrink from six to two states, and reduced a once proud Serbia to a pariah status in less than a decade. Milosevic signed the Dayton Peace Plan in 1995 ending the war in Bosnia and was acclaimed briefly as a peacemaker by the West! Milosevic was a sly, ruthless multifaceted politician (communist, pan-Serb nationalist, the 'Butcher of the Balkans', rabble-rouser, statesman, defendant in the International Criminal Court at the Hague). Milosevic deceived diplomats and envoys (*DT* 6/10/00).

It was with Milosevic and his nationalist Serb henchmen that the EC assumed the prime role of bringing calm and order to the region. The CSCE and the Council of Europe were sidelined despite perhaps being better placed to discuss and maybe help resolve territorial disputes as CSCE did include USSR and other communist East European states. As it was, little Luxembourg in the rotating Presidency of the EC had the nerve and effrontery to inform Croatia and Slovenia that they were too small to be 'viable' independent states (J. Eyal, *DT* 30/9/92). Jacques Poos, the then Luxembourg Foreign Minister, flew into Belgrade claiming vaingloriously 'this is the hour of Europe, not the hour of the Americans', almost as the first shots were fired. Of course what was to finally stop Serb aggression was American-led NATO military intervention; nothing else succeeded. Brussels threatened dire consequences if ceasefires negotiated with EC envoys were not kept. Milosevic correctly assessed that the EU might bark but couldn't bite and carried on fighting. The EC's conference on Yugoslavia under the Chairmanship of Lord Carrington got nowhere. The EC blundered into the Yugoslavian conflict despite being a wholly civilian soft power whose limitations were only too apparent once serious fighting was under way. The EC monitors (observers) were never intended to stop violence and were almost wholly ineffectual. Failure to find a peace agreement or maintain a ceasefire showed the EC lacked diplomatic power.

In October 1991, partly in response to these developments and also in the lead-up to Maastricht, a Franco-German proposal for a Eurocorps was announced, intended as the embryonic future multinational European Army. Paradoxically like the EDC scheme of 1950 to counter Soviet communist expansion, this new proposal was made as communism disintegrated. Mitterand envisaged European Defence becoming the direct responsibility of the EC with the WEU (whose members were all in the EC) being Europe's defence pillar. The UK et al. Atlanticists were very much opposed to this and insisted (in a faithful echo of her preference in the 1950s) that the proposed WEU force should be autonomous, constituted within NATO and outside EC control but 'linked to both and subordinated to neither' (Dedman and Fleay, 1992).

The EU passed responsibility in Yugoslavia over to the UN. The UN used NATO peacekeepers on the ground. The US refused to supply ground troops and Germany was constitutionally unable to do so. The UN failed to protect civilians in Srebrenica, Sarajevo or elsewhere, (European-led) NATO forces were humiliated when four hundred troops were taken hostage, and it took six weeks to deploy the Rapid Reaction Force. The European-led NATO role was as subcontractor to the UN, its operations limited to fulfilling UN resolutions. UN approval was required for NATO air strikes. European states like UK and France were reluctant to get too embroiled in Yugoslavia. Foreign Ministers had long memories concerning the nineteenth-century 'Eastern Question'; arguably the opening shot of the Great War was fired here; and the French had had a Foreign Minister shot in the Balkans in the 1930s. Like Bismarck all were wary of the Balkans trap. Bismarck memorably quipped that the area was not worth 'the bones of one Pomeranian Grenadier' and that ' ... one must give these sheep stealers plainly to understand that European governments have no need to harness themselves to their lusts and rivalries'.

For President Clinton and the US administration this was not the 'Eastern Question' but, as they saw it, a fire in the heart of Europe 400 miles south of Munich and five hundred miles north of Athens. The US let Europeans take the lead in NATO's involvement there but considered them far too timid.

The US wanted to assist Bosnia via a 'strike and lift' strategy (bomb Serb forces and lift the arms embargo on Muslims fighting there). The Europeans led by Douglas Hurd cautioned against this policy. As Kramer said, far from there being a new security order in Europe, post-communism, of interlocking institutions it was more a case of the UN, NATO, CSCE et al. in Yugoslavia making a 'disorder of inter-blocking institutions' (Kramer, 1993).

In the end a combination of ground troops, air power (including American) and economic sanctions by 1993–94 brought the fighting to an end in Croatia, around Sarajevo and in Central Bosnia. The use of bombs drove the Serbs to the Dayton talks. In 1999 Milosevic's refusal to sign a peace plan for Kosovo led to a 78-day air war (NATO bombing from 15,000 feet) ensuring he lost control of Kosovo and had to allow NATO ground troops into Kosovo, ultimately an operation that was an unqualified success in saving lives. It also showed what could have been achieved by earlier intervention.

The second reason why the years 1992–93 were not good ones for the EU was that successive currency crises within the ERM 1992–93 (September 1992, February 1993 and August 1993) threatened the entire EMU project and overshadowed the start of the Single Market in 1993. The ERM was at the very heart of the Maastricht Treaty, part of a long-term French goal of getting their hands on the Bundesbank via EMU and European Central Bank (ECB) and wresting political control of interest rate and exchange rates away from Germany and Bundesbank via monetary integration (see Connelly, 1995;

Dyson 1994, p. 306). The ERM system of fixed exchange rates was originally established in 1979 with Italy, Belgium, Holland, Ireland and Luxembourg taking part in a Franco-German initiative the aim of which was to restrict fluctuations among participating currencies and achieve monetary stability in the wake of a collapsing $USD (Dyson, 1994, p. 313). A middle exchange rate was fixed and some maximum permitted variations of +/-2¼ per cent was allowed within this band. Under ERM rules the participating Central Banks cooperated and colluded in buying and selling currencies to keep them within this narrow band, in order to avoid problems of 'competitive devaluation' and also with changes to the real values of CAP payments and other transfers inside the EC.

The independent Bundesbank, guardian of the DM that had never devalued and also markets were certain would never devalue within the ERM, was seen by all as the anchor of the ERM system. From this certainty everything else flowed. The ERM was effectively a 'DM-zone'. Early on there had been revaluations and currency realignments (changing their relative values) in the European Monetary System (EMS). From 1983 though (following the currency crisis and ERM realignment) France followed a 'Franc-fort' policy crucial to its long-term goal of regaining some control in setting interest rates. From 1987 (and yet another currency crisis and ERM realignment) to 1992 there were no more realignments. A huge amount of political capital was expended on the monetary virility symbol of the Franc-fort. The policy was very painful for the French economy as it meant disinflation and a high interest rate (higher than the Bundesbank's) as the French Franc was not as strong as the Deutschmark and so there was a higher risk involved in holding it. The Franc-fort meant the subordination of French domestic monetary policy interests to French foreign economic policy aims. The Franc-fort policy elevated France (it believed) to co-leadership status at least with Germany in the EC. It became 'impossible' for the French to devalue the Franc as this would necessitate abandoning the Franc-fort policy that French corporations, trade unions as well as the government had bought into. To devalue the Franc would have revealed the policy to be fundamentally flawed and misconceived as domestic economic policy. It was not possible for a French government to openly accept permanent membership of a DM-zone. The Franco-German pact since 1951 was based on equality of status, even though in practice it meant decades of French leadership. However, France was not prepared to accept German leadership and so be relegated to a follower role, hence the Franc-fort policy.

In reality France was pursuing a similar economic policy to its *bloc d'or* policy of the 1930s when France remained on the Gold Standard after the UK and USA had abandoned it, with highly deflationary effects. The Franc-fort necessitated a high interest rate and resulted in unemployment of 12 per cent. Mitterand may have persuaded Kohl to adopt EMU at Maastricht but the independent Bundesbank took a different view. Other sources might convey an impression that Maastricht saw governments' institutions cooperating harmoniously in the construction of Monetary Union. In reality the Governor of the Bundesbank, Dr Schlesinger, hated the ERM and the whole EMU project although he had little choice except to act as Kohl's agent in delivering EMU.

Problems within the ERM only really arose because of German reunification's induced inflation. By 1994 the German Unity Fund had spent DM115 billion. In 1991 25 per cent of the Federal German Budget was spent in the East (over DM90 billion) financed by government borrowing. Germany also paid out DM50 billion to the states of the former Soviet Union for withdrawing forces from East Germany. The cost of moving the German parliament and government apparatus to Berlin from Bonn was put at DM100 billion spread over a decade. There were other costs too; compensating former property owners in East Germany; debts of East German firms that could not be sold off and more. The point was that these expenditures were not covered by any increase in GDP due to enlargement. German GDP only rose by 10 per cent with reunification but German population rose by 27 per cent. Public sector debt in 1992 rose consequently from 5 per cent to 7 per cent of German GDP and this pushed up inflation from 4 to 5 per cent which meant that the Bundesbank's interest rates increased to combat inflation.

In the 1980s the FRG had had a current account surplus (due to an export surplus); this changed in the first quarter of 1991 when Germany's current account became negative (a net importer) and international investors became nervous. Uncertainty had increased by 1992 as Germany was unable to meet all the Maastricht criteria for joining the single currency due to high inflation and budget deficits.

Higher German interest rates meant that the UK and other ERM states' interest rates were higher still. By June 1992 the UK base rate was 10 per cent (and it had been even higher at 15 per cent, October 89–October 90). This meant that classic interest-rate sensitive areas of the economy (like housing) were depressed tipping the UK into recession. Base rates were estimated to be between 1 per cent and 2 per cent higher because of the ERM (T. Congdon, Lothian Foundation, 1992). Overall EU growth was estimated to be 0.5 per cent lower because of the ERM. John Major had forced the UK into the ERM in 1990 and took Britain to the brink of bankruptcy in 1992.

The ERM was a trap because markets came to suspect that the fixed exchange rates were unrealistic and wrong given that there had been no changes in the system or realignments in 1987–92. The UK had had to devalue before in 1947 and 1967 and the markets began testing sterling's fixed exchange rate. This was a safe 'one way bet'; speculators could not lose. Suspecting a future depreciation, speculators sold sterling to buy Deutschmarks. When sterling was forced to devalue they would buy back more sterling with the more valuable Deutschmarks, making a good risk-free profit. If sterling didn't devalue speculators were still holding Deutschmarks and lost nothing.

The ERM/sterling crisis of September 1992 was preceded by a run on the Finnish Markka which had been pegged to the ERM as their own version of a Markka-fort policy. The Markka shadowed the ERM but without any of its support mechanisms. Finnish interest rates were forced up to 18 per cent but the speculation meant Finland abandoned the peg and the Markka fell by 15 per cent in value giving speculators a big immediate profit. The Italian lira then became a target as markets had heard rumours of ERM realignments and massive intervention was required to defend the peg which ultimately led to unilateral devaluation. Markets then saw sterling as the one-way bet, on 15 September sterling sold heavily as foreign-exchange markets and the pound closed barely above its ERM floor. In the midst of the crisis during an early evening meeting (15 September 1992) of Bank of England and Treasury officials to discuss strategy for the next day (some advised putting the rate up to 12 per cent before the markets opened). The Governor of the Bank of England, Robin Leigh-Pemberton, read out loud a message from his press office. Dr Helmut Schlesinger, President of the Bundesbank, had given an interview casting doubt about whether existing parities (exchange rates) would hold – a very clear hint that he thought sterling would depreciate. The meeting was stunned by this devastating indiscretion and public admission that the game was nearly up. The end came the following afternoon at 2.15 p.m. after interest rates were briefly hiked to 15 per cent which didn't work and ERM membership was suspended. Britain had spent £11 billion in reserves, 50 per cent of its total trying to defend its fixed rate (Will Hutton, *Guardian* 1/12/92). Interestingly, the day Hutton's piece appeared on the 'History of Black Wednesday', Schlesinger made a scathing attack on the ERM calling it 'a machine for enriching speculators', which of course it was, especially for George Soros' hedge fund.

Dr Helmut Schlesinger, the hard-nosed President of the Bundesbank, blamed by the British government for sabotaging the pound sterling in September 1992, refused the following year, in August 1993, to reduce Germany's discount rate (the DM rate being the 'floor' for all other rates) to save the French Franc and the ERM. Schlesinger supposedly refused to reduce the rate as it would have undermined the Bundesbank's credibility and corrupt it's principle of using interest rate changes only to maintain price stability. Hans Tietmeyer, his deputy, argued in favour of the wider European interest and reducing the rate to help the French Franc. Schlesinger was quoted as saying that 'domestically there was no clear indication to support another reduction in interest rates'. Germany's domestic interests had apparently come first. There was shocked amazement in Paris dealing rooms that the Bundesbank had left their discount rate unchanged in France's hour of need. Dealers were left stunned and incredulous. Article 109 of the Maastricht Treaty specified that until the start of the third stage of EMU member states were supposed to treat exchange-rate policy as a matter of common interest,

Since the 1980s the Franc-fort and the link between the Franc and the Mark had been the cornerstone of Paris's economic policy and was the string holding the Paris–Bonn axis together. (This bond in Franco-German bargaining relations is often described as bound by 'cords of steel' (Dyson, 1994,

p. 339).) However, the whistle blower and ex-Monetary Commissioner of the EU Bernard Connelly (1995) pointed out that Schlesinger refused to act to defend the French Franc as he was enraged by Mitterrand's treachery over the ECB. In a TV broadcast before the French Referendum on the Maastricht Treaty in 1992 (which was also quite anti-German in tone) Mitterand said the ECB would not be left in the control of central bankers but politicians would decide monetary policy especially exchange-rate policy. ECB technocrats would apply the decisions of the European Council, the ECB would not really be independent. Mitterrand's interpretation was diametrically opposed to the Bundesbank's and effectively amounted to a 're-writing' of the Maastricht Treaty. Schlesinger (perhaps ignoring its context?) was according to Connelly deliberately punishing France for such treachery.

At the time the EMU project looked seriously, perhaps fatally damaged. The ERM had in any case generated the worst slump in the UK and else-where since the early 1980s with stagflation in the UK. In France the economy only had 2 per cent inflation but an interest rate of 13 per cent meant high unemployment of three million plus, over 12 per cent of the labour force. Germany's economic conditions were worsening yet decades of DM currency stability meant investors happily held on to DMs, so other currencies had to pay higher interest rates to attract funds. The reunification of the FRG and GDR, as we have seen, meant public spending increased dramatically and therefore inflation. The Bundesbank responded by increasing the interest rate to its highest level in thirty years. All other ERM state's interest rates needed to be higher still.

One possible solution to this predicament would have been to allow the DM to rise sharply in value (a revaluation) as then Germany's import prices would be reduced, inflation would fall and the Bundesbank could lower its interest rate. This was unacceptable to France as the Franc-fort policy since 1983 was effectively holy writ (a strategy widely supported in corporatist France determined not to use devaluation again as a solution to the country's economic problems). Only this could deliver monetary union which would give France real influence again over their own interest rate. Regaining some economic control was referred to as 'symetrie' in French political circles but there was nothing symmetrical about it as their intention was French control over German monetary policy by controlling the ECB (*The Economist* 31/5/ 1997). This strategy would be imperilled by French devaluation via a DM revaluation. So France ruled out a general ERM realignment against the DM, as ten years of monetary policy and deflationary economic pain would have been for nothing.

Such inflexibility meant that the ERM snapped because it would not bend. Anglo-Saxon speculators were blamed but in the end it was large French corporations that were the big sellers of the FF, effectively putting profit before sentiment. The ERM's narrow bands of 2.25 per cent were widened to 15 per cent to prevent any further speculation. Effectively the ERM ceased to exist in practice; it still existed in name but with such incredibly wide buffers was somewhat meaningless. This change to the ERM shut off the quick route to EMU, as for the third stage to start in 1997 required the previous two years at least to be in the narrow band of the ERM. The Bundesbank sabotaged the ERM and the Franc-fort policy that France, by being more German than the Germans, hoped they might neutralise the Bundesbank's overbearing influence on the economies of France and the rest of Europe.

The FF suffered its fate not because its value was thought too high (3.4180 FF to the DM was its floor) but because the recession hit the French economy so severely and it desperately needed lower interest rates. The money markets knew this. The Bundesbank by insisting that German inflation didn't allow it to cut its interest rate signalled that France could only get interest rates down by leaving the ERM.

This is precisely what happened to sterling after its ERM exit a year before. Interest rates fell to 6 per cent, the pound : DM parity fell from DM3 to DM2.4 and economic recovery was under way (David Smith, *ST* 1/8/93). George Soros, the Hungarian-born fund manager, had supported the French position writing in *Le Figaro* but given the Bundesbank's inaction and the run on the FF it was futile to preserve the ERM and he felt free to sell the Franc. Soros apparently said that ' ... for France to stay [in ERM] would be like a battered wife to go back from the hospital to her husband' (*ST* 1/8/93).

Yet this is precisely what happened. For France (unlike the UK) there was no alternative to Plan A. Mitterand was in London for a scheduled Anglo-French economic summit just after the debacle and dismissed the Franc's troubles and the whole affair insisting that everything was still on track for EMU. Whether feigned or not he displayed considerable sang-froid. Towards the end of his Presidency when asked in an interview 'What was the greatest quality a President of France should possess?' Mitterand said 'indifference'.

The British government regarded the ERM as dead (if not yet buried) a view generally shared by banks' economists, dealers and pundits in the UK press. EU officials in Brussels and the French thought otherwise; they were of course proved correct.

The French Prime Minister, Edouard Balladur, also displayed 'stunning aplomb' in public, refusing to acknowledge that a crisis ever existed. He declared the loosening of the older ERM's tight bands to be a tremendous victory for French monetary rigour, and congratulated his friends the Germans for their dedication to the European ideal! He promptly went on holiday leaving French interest rates unchanged. (*ST* 8/8/93). Observers of the previous week's tumultuous ERM drama, wrongly predicting the demise of Maastricht and the Franco-German axis, were mystified by these bravura performances. With French interest rates remaining unchanged the FF promptly recovered to within a few centimes of its previous ERM floor against the Mark (albeit in an ERM with incredibly wide and unbreakable bands, allowing very big variation in exchange rates).

Balladur was helped too by the fact that his most dangerous economic critics kept quiet. People such as Phillipe Seguin, Speaker in the French

National Assembly, left on holiday saying nothing, perhaps out of a sense of patriotic solidarity (*Observer* 8/8/93).

The struggle and rivalry within the EMU process persisted through the 1990s due to incompatible objectives of the Bundesbank on one hand, the German government insisting on a 'hard' euro while the French wanted a 'soft' euro. Arguments continued over the location of the ECB and who was to be the Governor of the ECB and other issues such as a Stability and Growth Pact.

These two episodes in 1992–93, concerning the CFSP in Yugoslavia and the ERM crises, demonstrated Germany's considerable economic and political weight inside the EU and the battered and frayed state of the Franco-German alliance in the ERM. France nonetheless remained wedded to this, there being no other way to alter the asymmetric control of monetary policy in the EU. Only Germany had something to lose and nothing to gain, from EMU and the death of the DM, namely its freedom or full autonomy to set interest rates. The Bundesbank, many German politicians and public opinion were dismayed by the prospect of Germany becoming like everyone else, unable to solely determine its own rate of interest and especially dismayed at losing their only iconomatic symbol of national pride. This was why Kohl promised Germany that he would deliver a euro as 'hard' as the DM and wanted a federal Europe, a United States of Europe to emerge, as the 'price' for Germany giving up its DM. After all, had their respective positions been reversed, hypothetically and counterfactually, with the French Franc as strong as the DM and it as weak as the FF, would France have pressed for monetary union? Would EMU have ever been on the agenda? The Maastricht Treaty 1991, like the early Treaties back in the 1950s, disguised the crucial national interests at stake under the rhetoric of 'building Europe'.

Did the EMU project from 1991 affirm the Milward thesis when the 'attempts' at EMU in the 1970s clearly did not? These earlier episodes were not driven by fundamental national economic need. Their timing indicates they were triggered by extraneous factors and events affecting West Germany. They both fizzled out, overshadowed by oil crises and settling for more modest technical innovations not monetary union. The post-1991 EMU project was seriously different, although its timing again was determined by major seismic events involving Germany and Europe. EMU post-1991 was driven crucially by the need of non-German nation states to regain some control over their interest rates after the recent and full liberalisation of the EU capital market, interest rates being the single most powerful economic device and monetary policy tool for macroeconomic regulation of national economies.

The EMS was originally created in 1979 in the wake of the fall in the US dollar in 1978. There were many realignments of currency exchange rates in the early 1980s following disturbance caused by the 'Mitterand experiment', a misguided use of Keynesian-inspired fiscal expansion to reduce unemployment. Afterwards from March 1983 and currency crisis and ERM realignment, France accepted a more coordinated approach to macro-economic policy and embarked on its Franc-fort policy. The EMS underwent a regime change in 1990 as apart from German reunification the EU experienced the start of capital market liberalisation in the majority of European countries (Spain only did so from 1992) increasing capital flows within the EU. The abolition of capital controls was partly a Single Market objective and an intrinsic part of moving to EMU. This was a major economic and financial regime change in the EU increasing the co-integration of financial markets. Empirical research by monetary economists and econometricians confirmed what economists referred to as the 'German Dominance Hypothesis' (GDH). Comerero and Ordóñez showed conclusively that, after capital liberalisation, German interest rates caused the interest rates of other European countries. In particular it meant an increased dependence between French and German monetary policy which did not apply to the UK (forced to quit the EMS discipline and so able to gain independence from Germany and decide its own monetary policy (Comerero and Ordóñez, 1999)). They also attributed responsibility for the 'Monetary Storm' of September 1992 to the start of the second stage of the EMU process and the full abolition of capital controls, as a result of which there was a lot more footloose money sloshing about the system.

EMU may be needed and wanted by France and other EU states but whether monetary union and the single currency is workable and sustainable in the long term remains uncertain. Otmar Issing (a prominent former official and economist at both the Bundesbank and ECB) referred recently to EMU, even after ten years' existence as an 'experiment'.

The Maastricht Treaty (signed 7 February 1992) created the EU and started EMU and just as the Treaty of Rome 1957 had not been a complete blueprint for the Common Market, it too was a timetable of stages and conditions to be met and adhered to. For example, Article 105 set up the European System of Central Banks (ESCB) without all the precise detail to implement monetary policy, conduct foreign-exchange operations and hold and manage official foreign reserves of each member state. The ECB under Article 105a would have exclusive rights to authorise the issue of bank notes. The ECB would be governed by a council (Article 109a) comprising governors of national central banks.

Among the necessary conditions and criteria for states joining EMU (Article 109j) were: price stability with inflation no more than 1.5 per cent difference to the average of the three best performing states; no excessive budget deficits no more than 3 per cent GDP and national debt not to exceed 60 per cent GDP. If at the end of 1997 no date had been set for EMU's third stage, it was to start automatically on 1 January 1999 for those states that qualified under the Maastricht Treaty. The convergence criteria had to be satisfied prior to European Currency Union. Already, as mentioned, the fast route to Monetary Union in 1997 was closed by September 1993 as it required the narrow 2.25 per cent bands to be observed for the proceeding two years. These were purely monetary conditions ignoring economic differences between states such as growth rates and unemployment levels which required different monetary policies.

What exactly is a single currency and how does it differ from a common currency? With a single currency the exchange rates between participant states are permanently fixed so there is effectively one currency; plus one central bank; one monetary policy; one interest rate for all the states involved. In addition fiscal policies are harmonised with restriction on governments' expenditure and levels of debt as a per cent of GDP. The euro in fact is what economists call a 'perfect' single currency as national currencies are no longer in circulation being replaced by euro notes and coins. There is consequently perfect price transparency and the single currency is less reversible.

A common currency in contrast means there is an additional common currency that circulates alongside national currencies, each having an exchange rate with the common currency. The common currency is a parallel currency and does not require monetary integration with one interest rate, etc.; it can be used for all trade between common currency countries, enabling easy price comparisons and avoids transaction costs (having to convert money into other currencies). Nigel Lawson, one of Margaret Thatcher's Chancellors of the Exchequer during the 1980s, was for a time keen on the idea of a 'hard ECU' common currency for the EC.

EMU is unprecedented with 16 EU states having a single currency. Although the International Gold Standard 1870–1914 might superficially resemble the euro, where each currency was pegged to a troy ounce of gold and so states had fixed exchange rates (for example £1 = \$4.86USD pre-1914). The amount of gold determined the money supply. Trade imbalances were settled by gold transfers. However, there was more 'flexibility' than under EMU. Each country could decide its own commercial trade policy (whether protectionism or free trade) and there was also mass emigration from Europe. Countries had more scope to adjust to trade imbalances and adverse conditions (unemployment and poverty) than in the EU, which has a common commercial policy. A single currency for the new Single Market (1993) was entirely logical in terms of convenience; price transparency; avoidance of exchange rate uncertainty and transaction costs and abolishing separate currencies stopped them being NTBs. However, the trade-off and drawback was that member states can no longer pursue an independent monetary policy; they cannot set their own interest rates.

Robert Mundell, a US monetary economist and Nobel Prize winner, in 1961 argued there was an 'Optimal Currency Area' (OCA) over which the currency used would balance the different factors mentioned above. Loss of exchange-rate control was a particularly significant determinant of the OCA. The bigger the single currency area the more likely economic conditions would diverge between countries. Hence the OCA concept, as some states might have high unemployment others low unemployment but high inflation yet have the same monetary policy and interest rate. Asymmetric shocks would also mean countries required different policies because they were affected differently by the same event. So a big rise in the price of natural gas affected a gas producer differently from a gas importer. Yet under EMU there would be one policy and interest rate, states having relinquished their own monetary policy tools that stabilised output, jobs and inflation. There is therefore an 'economic stability loss' from monetary union but clearly too a 'monetary efficiency gain' from EMU (Krugman and Obstfeld, 2006, p. 618). Savings can be made by avoiding transaction costs (having to buy other currencies in order to buy foreign goods) and avoiding exchange-rate uncertainty and volatility. These gains increase the more states are economically integrated. That is the more they trade between themselves and the more freely labour and capital moves between them, the more integrated they become. They may then constitute an OCA like perhaps the USA or UK. What matters is whether monetary efficiency gains outweigh the economic stability loss (Krugman and Obstfeld 2006, p. 618). OCAs are composed of a group of states (or regions) linked by a high degree of trade and factor mobility.

There are strong doubts over whether the eurozone is an OCA. Asymmetric shocks are greater the less integrated, the less traded and the less mobile labour and capital are within a currency zone. Monetary-policy tools used to counter shocks to national economies have gone (devaluation and interest-rate changes are no longer options for a country in trouble). Other adjustment mechanisms must be used as outlined in the Delors Plan 1993 (reaffirmed by the Lisbon Agenda 2000). The Delors Plan logically emphasised the need for deregulation of the labour market, with lower taxes on labour and less spending on social benefits. Governments have no choice but to free up their economies; if there is less monetary and fiscal flexibility there must be more labour-market flexibility for the economy to adjust to shocks and disequilibrium. Essentially they advocated supply-side reforms; these are actual policy measures that alter individuals' incentives which en masse enable the whole economy to adjust to shocks. It was ironic that the socialist Jacques Delors had to advocate supply-side reforms (the same as Thatcherite and Reaganite reforms of the 1980s) cutting taxes and government spending, and increasing incentives to work and invest. These 'Anglo-Saxon' policies were so different to the dirigiste state managed capitalism of the Rhineland-Corporatist model favoured by the French and Germans for the past three decades.

Central to these supply-side changes was a flexible labour market. The labour market must operate freely like any other market. For the economy to adjust to shocks the labour market had to be 'flexible': wages have to be able to fall as well as rise (wages tend to be 'sticky', difficult to reduce plus resistance from the trade unions). Trade unions' legal rights and powers need to be curbed (as they interfere with a free market). Firms need to be free to 'hire and fire' labour (if it is made difficult to fire workers new jobs will not be created as employers will be reluctant to hire in the first place). Unemployment benefits need to be cut to lower voluntary unemployment (people without a job, not seeking work and who would not accept a job at current wage levels). In France (2007) over-generous state benefits for the unemployed, entitled to about 75 per cent of their last salary for 23 months after being made redundant, sapped the will to work.

However, despite the desperate need for the EU's economies to deregulate it is very hard to make these essential structural reforms. Margaret Thatcher's reforms proved difficult and painful for the UK in the 1980s, resulting in considerable public disorder. In the face of stiff resistance from trade-unionist marches and left-wing demonstrators, European governments backed off from seeing reforms through in France, Italy and Germany in the 1990s and 2000s. Their labour markets actually became more inflexible: in France under socialist Prime Minister Jospin in 1990s a 35-hour week was introduced and in 1998 Oskar Lafontaine, the German SPD Finance Minister, planned to lower the pension age from 65 to 60.

Labour mobility is another essential adjustment mechanism. For EMU to work unemployed labour needed to be mobile and move out of areas with surplus labour. However, EU labour is relatively immobile compared with the USA. Language barriers mean it is more difficult to move people to jobs in the EU. An unemployed Milan bank clerk cannot simply move to the same job in Manchester (despite a legal entitlement to in EU law) unless fluent in English. This means it is more difficult to move people to jobs in the EU.

Also unlike the USA there are no fiscal transfers, no inter-jurisdictional transfer of funds in EU. This means you cannot move jobs to people with EU funding. There is no counter-cyclical or redistributive element to the EU budget. It is simply a budget of account, a spending budget that amounts to only 1.5 per cent of EU's GDP, compared to the US federal budget of circa 35 per cent GDP. The EU cannot fund work creation, moving jobs to people, in areas of high unemployment.

Structural differences within the eurozone's economy increases scepticism regarding it being even a viable currency area, as eurozone states' extremes diverge more than the USA's extreme cases. In 2000, for instance, real GDP growth in Ireland was 8.7 per cent and in Germany 2.9 per cent; unemployment in Spain was 14 per cent and in the Netherlands 2.3 per cent. Yet all had the same interest rates. Krugman among other prominent economists argued unequivocally that the eurozone was not an OCA, as the area was insufficiently integrated. Single European Market (SEM) reforms in 1990s did not go far enough; trade between EU members was, at less than 25 per cent of partners' GDP, considered far too low. The EU and eurozone needed desperately to deregulate, introducing supply-side reforms and create a flexible labour market. Countries such as France have had the worst of both worlds as companies had to downsize anyway and few new jobs have been created. Between 1974 and 1994 the USA created 30 million private-sector jobs, Europe created 10 million. Europe did not create many jobs even when it was booming. High social-benefit spending meant high taxes and a high interest rate which reduced corporate profitability, reduced investment and inhibited the creation of jobs.

There are big regional differences in the eurozone. In Northern Europe production is capital intensive using skilled labour and in Southern Europe production is more labour intensive using low-skilled labour. The key questions are whether the SEM/EMU will remove these regional differences by redistributing capital and labour across Europe, so reducing the impact of asymmetric shocks as regions become similar, or whether SEM/EMU encourages regional specialisation which would increase the impact of asymmetric shocks (de Grauwe, 2007, p. 27).

After 15 years of the SEM and ten years of EMU there are no real signs of convergence between North and South that the Commission predicted. There are signs of Southern Europe's avoidance of structural change as the EU Trade Commissioner (Peter Mandelson) was successfully lobbied for protectionist action by club-med states against cheap Vietnamese and Chinese clothing imports. For the euro to operate sustainably the EU needs to be more integrated fiscally and economically, like the USA (sharing pooled tax revenues). However, EU citizens share an antipathy to federalist moves indicated by rejection of schemes when allowed a vote (France 2005, Netherlands 2005, Ireland 2008).

EMU is unprecedented as it has no government above it to take ultimate responsibility should things go badly wrong. Joschka Fischer, German Foreign Minister at the start of the eurozone, via a speech to the EP warned that the EU would suffer an 'institutional heart attack' unless it moved rapidly to full political integration (*DT* 13/1/99).

The original euro creators assumed that the currency would acquire the apparatus of an Economic Federal State with an EU Treasury (making fiscal transfers) and a Debt Union, to pre-empt the risk of sovereign debt default. Instead the euro remains in limbo an 'orphan currency' without a state to back it up. (*FT* 20/6/08; *DT* 14/6/08) whereas Joschka Fischer quite wrongly assumed the euro had created a 'dynamic that would inevitably sweep aside the current political arrangements of Europe'. (*Independent* 13/1/99).

Chancellor Kohl's federalist ambitions back in the 1990s were intrinsically logical, nevertheless, and arguably an essential postscript to monetary union. Kohl's federalist motives though shared too by his successor as Chancellor (Schröder's SPD government from 1998) were wholly political. Kohl claimed publicly that federalism was vital to avoid future war and that only political union, a USE could effectively 'save us from ourselves'. Europe must do as the Germans say regarding federalism or they could not be held responsible for the consequences.

Equating federalism with peace is a mythical delusion. The USA's Civil War left 0.6 million dead following 80 years of a common currency (and a common language) plus divisive and divergent economic systems and cultural values and interests between the Yankee North and Celtic Southern states.

Under the Maastricht timetable in 1994 the European Monetary Institute (EMI), precursor to the ECB, was established in Frankfurt. In January 1995 Austria, Finland and Sweden joined the EU. December 1995 saw the Madrid European Council Meeting agreeing that the euro would start on 1 January 1999 as a unit of account (coins and banknotes to follow in 2002) by irrevocably fixing the exchange rates of participant currencies. Prime Minister Gonzales of Spain announced the speeding up of the enlargement process and pledged to open negotiation in 1998; also the selection of states meeting the strict criteria for EMU would take place in 1998. The Inter Governmental Conference (IGC) reviewing and revising the Maastricht Treaty would last until 1997 and then the EU's budget package expired in 1999 and would have to be negotiated now with 15 states. There was a lot happening at once and the Franco-German axis was reportedly 'cracking' again (*ST* 22/11/95), both states having fallen out and antagonised others. President Chirac's nuclear tests had outraged public opinion and aggrieved and offended the Germans especially. There was a big argument over convergence criteria rules which the Germans wanted to tighten to ensure a hard euro (and really wanted the eurozone to start with only five states – Benelux, Germany, and France – so excluding the 'club-med' group). These southern states wanted the criteria loosened. President Chirac, a Gaullist, was a more abrasive character than Mitterand and would openly challenge the Germans. Chirac told the Germans bluntly that their federalist ideas were 'not saleable in France' (*ST* 14/10/95).

In December 1996 the Stability and Growth Pact (SGP) for EMU was agreed at Germany's and Kohl's insistence to safeguard his promised objective of a 'hard euro'. (An October 1995 German opinion poll showed only 31 per cent of Germans were pro-euro and 81 per cent thought German interests should not be sacrificed for the EU.) Fiscal rigour and budgetary discipline had to be permanently maintained by all once EMU started on 1 January 1999. The SGP's 'excess deficits procedure' was intended to ensure that governments' borrowing did not exceed 3 per cent GDP in any year. States theoretically could be fined for breaking the rules. Germany was worried (correctly as it happened) about the possible 'moral hazard' of 'club-med' countries somehow managing to absorb the pain to meet the strict Maastricht monetary criteria regarding debt and inflation rates, and so on, only to relax tight fiscal discipline and budgetary controls afterwards. The SGP was intended to stop this. However, the SGP looked rather weak as a compliance mechanism as it operated with QMV and if many states broke the rules were they enforceable? How realistic were fines? The paradox later was that Germany, France and even the Netherlands were to break these rules (as well as the correctly anticipated flagrant 'club-med' serial offenders). The Maastricht criteria's focus on monetary and fiscal factors ignored the huge variations in growth and unemployment. The general view of economists was that the euro was 'unstoppable' but 'unsustainable'; 155 German economists even signed an open letter to Chancellor Kohl calling for delay, which was ignored.

In June 1997 Lionel Jospin, the socialist French prime minister, tried to unpick the EMU agreement concerning a 'Solidarity Pact'. Although unsuccessful it underlined the French requirement for a 'soft' euro (*DT* 14/6/97, p. 11; 16/6/97, p. 11; 19/6/97, p. 20). In July 1997 the EU, following the 1996 IGC and drafting the Treaty of Amsterdam (signed October 1997) was preparing to expand to include five CEE states, Poland, Hungary, Estonia, Czech Republic and Slovenia, plus Cyprus (the Greek part). Jacques Santer, President of EU Commission, declared that these states had achieved sufficient reforms to proceed to accession negotiations starting in 1998. CAP reform was flagged up as an essential prerequisite. Enlargement would mean at least 10 million more poor and inefficient farmers entering the EU's CAP.

In March 1998 it was announced that 11 states were eligible to adopt the euro on 1 January 1999. Denmark and the UK had opt-outs, while Sweden did not want to join. Greece was ineligible. Germany and France both cleared the EMU criteria hurdle although both struggled a bit to do so. Portugal and Spain, who were no-hopers two years previously, met the criteria with 'figures that looked almost too good to be true'. Particularly unexpected was Italy's government borrowing reduced to 2.7 per cent GDP in 1997, 'eyebrows were raised at this' as in 1995 it had been 8 per cent GDP! (*DT* 28.2.98); Germany had had to fudge things a bit too so not too much fuss was made. The ECB, in its plush glass and steel tower in Frankfurt, was conceived as 'the son of the Bundesbank'. In fact it was intended to be even more independent as the ECB's President and Executive could only serve one term. Its sole mandated task was price stability, it even had discretion to define 'price stability' and set the permitted level of inflation (2 per cent).

However, its new glossy independence was tarnished somewhat at Easter 1998 when the Dutchman Wim Duisenberg, Germany's preferred candidate to run the ECB was blocked by the French President, Jacques Chirac who wanted Jean-Claude Trichet (Governor of the Bank of France) to be President of ECB. It was later agreed following intensive bullying by Chirac of Chancellor Kohl, that Duisenberg would serve only half his eight-year term and then be replaced by Trichet after four years.

This move was calculated to alarm the Germans and others as it implied that the ECB was not the bastion of independence it had seemed to be, but was vulnerable to politically inspired meddling. Two months before the euro was due to start Oskar Lafontaine, Germany's new Socialist Finance Minister outraged bankers and markets alike with the spectre of a 'Red euro', not just a weaker 'soft' euro but one managed to create growth and jobs (*The Times*, 14/10/98). Chancellor Schröder's new Finance Minister, Oskar Lafontaine, Chairman and leader of the Social Democratic Party, PM of Saarland bordering France, a staunch Francophile with no love for Labour PM Tony Blair, believed that monetary policy should do more to stimulate employment. In this way he might avoid necessary but painful structural changes to the economy. This was the very reverse of what Helmut Kohl had always promised (the now disgraced ex-Chancellor and CDU leader following a political corruption scandal that involved the CDU, President Mitterand, Elf Aquitaine (a French oil company), German and French Secret Services, and allegedly a £10 million 'side payment' to the CDU on a £2 billion oil refinery deal (*DT* 29/1/00)).

Oskar Lafontaine criticised the Bundesbank for not lowering the interest rate when it was supposed to be independent of political interference. There was a coordinated attempt by Germany and France to undermine the ECB's independence by announcing plans to decide monetary policy pushing for greater political influence in running the euro, exerting pressure on the ECB to reduce the interest rate. Oskar Lafontaine seemed to be delivering the much wanted French soft euro. Several socialist finance ministers, the 'New Left', in the EU called for more public investment and emphasis on growth rather than controlling inflation (*DT* 17/11/98). A huge row erupted with German bankers and central banks over this flagrant public attempt to deliberately exert damaging pressure to undermine confidence in the ECB. The new German government was attempting to get the euro devalued even before its launch. This was a deliberate move to press for a reduction in interest rate and concentrate on creating jobs rather than fighting inflation; to undermine trust in the new currency by calling for a new policy mix of growth and employment. Wim Duisenberg, President of ECB, repudiated and rejected Oskar Lafontaine's ideas, the European Commission (as 'guardian' of the Maastricht Treaty) condemned Oskar Lafontaine's actions as unacceptable political interference (*DT* 27/11/98).

When they failed to bounce the Bundesbank and then the ECB into an interest rate cut they then insisted that the euro and USD exchange rate should be 'managed' and regulated imposing controls on capital markets. Later Oskar Lafontaine, joined by Italy, said the fiscal stability pact could be loosened permitting more government borrowing (*DT* 19/11/98).

Otmar Issing, an ex-Bundesbank senior official and now an ECB executive, pointed out the macro-economic reality that if the ECB pursued inflationary policies this would simply lead to higher unemployment. Only badly needed structural reforms could directly influence growth and employment; these were the only changes that could offer a lasting solution.

Nevertheless, Lafontaine and Schröder succeeded in talking down the euro at its start, and confidence had been hit hard seen by a 14 per cent drop in value in less than a year from 74p to 61p and a 17 per cent fall against the US dollar. The euro's depreciation vs. the dollar of course helped the German and eurozone's economy (by boosting net exports, national income and therefore jobs). By 2001 the euro had lost 20 per cent of its value (euro index; 1990 base year; Thomson Data stream) since 1998. Exports rose but so too did inflation as imported oil was priced in more expensive dollars; as they became cheaper to buy, eurozone companies were also more vulnerable to foreign takeovers. The German government was hostile to a Vodafone (UK) bid to take over Mannesmann (which had previously taken over Orange) which conflicted with EU competition regulations. Germans were smuggling their savings out of the eurozone into Switzerland (and elsewhere) and into the hard Swiss Franc, to preserve wealth.

The weakness of eurozone was due also to the eurozone's sluggish economic performance. Despite a 2.5 per cent base rate Germany and France were growing slowly affecting the eurozone overall. While Ireland was growing at 6 per cent per annum since 1999, Germany grew at barely 1 per cent per annum. The euro did start to appreciate after a four year slide from 2002, only because of the $USD's weakness. It even achieved briefly 'safe haven' status.

Britain, Denmark and Sweden decided not to join from the start. In Britain this was due to several factors: economic, political and constitutional. Membership was a non-partisan issue. There were Europhiles and Europhobes in both the Conservative and Labour parties. Not joining at the start was also reminiscent of the UK's stance re ECSC 1950–51 and EEC 1956–57. Unlike 1956–57 the UK was wise not to join EMU. In retrospect Sir Eddie George, Bank of England's governor, said at a meeting of European Central Bankers that premature UK entry would have destabilised the whole eurozone making the ECB's job of setting the interest rate more difficult. The UK 'could have been the elephant in the rowing boat'. UK's position regarding the euro did not change in 1997 when John Major lost the election to Tony Blair and the Labour party. From 'join when the time is right' to 'prepare and decide', defined by Gordon Brown, Chancellor of the Exchequer, who had his five tests and convergence criteria. Once these were met and the Government agreed, Parliament would vote and a referendum on euro entry would be held in the UK. The euro failed the Treasury's first assessment in 1997 and in June 2003 following a nine-month study by the Treasury Gordon Brown's verdict at second assessment had not changed.

What were these tests and conditions? The first concerned cyclical convergence and similar growth rates. The main reason for failing this test was the problem of the UK housing market and the preponderance of variable rate mortgages. Entry to the euro would have meant a destabilising shock to the market as interest rates would fall from 3.75 per cent to 2 per cent (in 2005) on entry so further fuelling a massive house price boom. Test two on 'flexibility of production, wages and jobs' failed because of the lack of progress in reforming the eurozone labour market and its inflexibility with rigid labour-market regulations biased in favour of workers' (employees') protection. In France 23 per cent of the under 25 year group were unemployed and 40 per cent of the immigrant population. Although French authorities refer to the lack of job security in the UK, in fact in UK and USA 50 per cent of 55–64-year-olds were at work compared to 37 per cent in France.

Test three on investment was failed too because investment depended on whether tests one and two were met and whether FDI (foreign direct investment) was encouraged. In 2003 this was not clear cut although an Ernst and Young survey (2003) showed that the UK had not suffered a fall in FDI outside of the euro. (UK's percentage of EU's FDI was up from 26 per cent to 28 per cent.) Test four was passed as 'financial services and City' had not been harmed with the advent of euros. It remained in its previous position regardless of being in or out. The final test on 'growth, stability and jobs' failed as Britain was not adversely affected by being out of the euro. The eurozone was seen as high risk due to insufficient convergence and inflexibility in the eurozone economy and also because the ECB's remit and policy emphasis was on inflation control not growth (unlike the Bank of England's Monetary Policy Committee which takes growth and jobs into account as well as prices when setting base rate).

The key point in 2003 was who really wanted to 'converge' with euroland given its condition? Its economy was sclerotic, its shops were often shut, it was bureaucratic and over-regulated. To start up a business took 11 times longer than in the UK, economic growth was sluggish (negative in some quarters) 0.4–1 per cent per annum compared to the UK's in 2003 of 1.5–2 per cent. German stagnation hindered the whole EU economy. Germany itself was far from being a basket case as it remained a rich country with good public services but a lacklustre economic performance. Germany was handicapped by adhering to an outmoded social-market Rhineland corpora-tist economic model with a managed capitalist mindset that dated back to the 1970s (when the UK had been the 'sick man' of Europe pre-revitalisation through Thatcherism and the impact of North Sea oil).

The SGP was another problem it soon proved far too rigid a fiscal rule-book with its 3 per cent GDP ceiling for government spending. It could effectively mean that the ECB demanded a pro-cyclical policy (rather than a corrective counter-cyclical macro-economic policy). This was heavily and widely criticised by Gordon Brown and Romano Prodi (the ex-President of the EU and the Italian PM), who called it 'stupid' among others. The SGP was drawn up to German rules and specification because of concerns that southern Mediterranean states might not play by the rules. Greece joined the eurozone in January 2001, and confirmed this misgiving. In October 2004 it was unable to provide reliable figures on its deficit and Eurostats were still trying to verify the 1998–99 deficit figures, the two years used to assess Greece's readiness to join the euro.

However, nobody expected Germany to break its own SGP rules which with France it did repeatedly, hoisted with its own petard, breaking the 3 per cent GDP limit. French borrowing was set to exceed 4 per cent GDP in 2003–4 and Italy, Netherlands and Greece broke the 3 per cent rule too in 2003. French national debt also broke the 60 per cent GDP rule at 61.2 per cent GDP. All this made a mockery of the rules; they might have been the wrong rules but they were the agreed ones. Many regarded the fiscal rules as extremely arbitrary; why 3 per cent and not 4 per cent? Why not 70 per cent for the debt level and not 60 per cent? These targets were never justified or explained and in any case ignored 'real' economic measures (growth, unemployment). Having surrendered national control over monetary policy to the ECB and failing to make real headway with economic reforms something else had to give inevitably it was the SGP's rigid rules on debt that were broken. The SGP was in tatters in 2003 after Germany breached the limits without punishment or serious consequences. By 2005, 12 out of the 15 eurozone member were in violation of the SGP rules (it was technically possible and almost wholly unrealistic to fine states up to 0.5 per cent GDP if financial ministers agreed.).

ECB rigidity according to Professor Stiglitz (the Nobel Prize-winning economist) meant the eurozone lost out twice circa 2003 as US mismanagement of its fiscal policy meant the dollar dropped in value and the euro rose. This gave the ECB the chance to lower interest rates but it failed to do so and remained focused on controlling inflation. So the ECB made the eurozone lose twice: first, it 'lost' investment that would have resulted from a lower interest rate; and, second, because of the euro's higher exchange rate eurozone exports fell and imports increased (as foreign goods became cheaper). Sweden's referendum on joining the euro on 14 September 2003 resulted in a crushing no vote despite the entire Swedish establishment – all political parties, trade unions, employers, media – being pro euro. Sweden was also warned by Romano Prodi, the EU President, rather bombastically that it would be ' ... an economic catastrophe for them if they didn't join the euro'. Nevertheless, nine million people rejected it. Sweden's referendum result dealt a big blow to the eurozone. Some pundits argued that the 14 September no vote was a 'tipping point' and that the referendum might be the high-tide mark for European integration and Euro-federalism. Certainly the three subsequent no votes in French and Dutch 2005 referendums and Ireland's 2007 on EU constitutional change don't invalidate this view.

Denmark (who had rejected euro entry in 2000), Sweden and the UK actually had little to gain and much to lose in joining. The eurozone's growth rate was abysmal, averaging 1.2 per cent 1996–2005. Also which flexibility was preferable in 2003? The flexibility of staying out or the flexibility of joining and then ignoring the rules? Joining the eurozone would have increased uncertainty as the UK and others would be exposed to a new risk of unknown 'moral hazard' with the SGP in tatters and serious breaches of the rules as governments failed to control public expenditure and some falsified the statistics.

Non-participation had begun to look permanent and in fact the UK, Sweden and Denmark made up a solid alternative to the eurozone core. It was possible that some new entrants to the EU might join them (Poland?) although legally obliged to join the euro eventually. In April 2005 Gordon Brown quietly dropped the regular assessment of the five tests.

In fact 2002–3 was the last occasion when euro entry was a hot political issue in the UK with heated debate from pro- and anti-euro factions. Three years later in 2006 the verdict on the pound and euro entry was that Britain had had a lucky escape: euro entry was no longer on anyone's political agenda. Tony Blair had given up, Gordon Brown had no interest in it (the policy of 'prepare and decide' abandoned as obsolete for the time being).

George Osborne (Conservative Shadow Chancellor) ruled it out. Some advocates of joining the euro changed their minds and acknowledged their mistake. Kenneth Clarke (Gordon Brown's predecessor as Chancellor of the Exchequer) was a refreshingly creditable rare example of a politician admitting he was wrong. From 2006 there was no campaign to join the euro.

What accounted for this change? The most basic argument for euro entry was that it would bring about currency stability. However, this simply did not stand up as the pound sterling was more stable outside the euro than it would have been inside (the euro had an unstable rollercoaster experience). The pound in fact was more stable from 1998 than at any time since the Bretton Woods fixed/adjustable exchange-rate era in the 1950s and 1960s. Sterling's average value was its strongest since the 1980s; until the credit crunch and the run on Northern Rock shook confidence in the pound in 2007.

What would have happened if UK had joined at the start in 1999? According to a simulation by Dresdner Kleinwort (2006) the UK would have had an interest rate of 2 per cent most of the time, there would have been massive boom–bust cycle (instead of 63 quarters, 1993–2008, without recession, a record achievement). Inflation would have been higher at 3–4 per cent and with the Bank of England having no control over interest rate, fiscal policy (with planned government spending down and taxes up) would have had to be much tighter. Almost certainly the UK had a lucky escape.

What happened to countries that joined the euro? Jacques Delors' original plan and the later Lisbon Agenda (endorsed by all EU states) envisaged, quite logically, that the rigidity of Monetary Union due to its 'one size fits all' interest rate for all members and the SGP would force deregulation and classic supply-side reforms on Europe. If there was no monetary and less fiscal flexibility (SGP rules) there must be labour-market flexibility to permit economic adjustment to shocks and disturbances. It should also result in more economic convergence between states if they all took similar steps to reform their labour markets.

However, states ducked making such painful adjustments. Schröder and Chirac tried as did Italian governments but soon backed off in the face of mass street demonstrations and strikes by trade unions and students. Angela Merkel's coalition government of CDU and SPD meant fundamental reforms were shelved.

The situation in euroland deteriorated considerably as economies diverged. Italy faced a big problem by 2005 as according to the European commission Italian unit labour costs had risen by 38 per cent since 1995 whereas Germany's had fallen by 1.3 per cent. German companies (not the government) restructured and had hammered labour resistance into the ground via deflation and productivity improvements. Painful wage deflation was endured in Germany to lower costs leaving companies lean, fit and very profitable. Germany having a lower rate of inflation was able to claw back competitiveness from its neighbours. Germany regained its competitiveness in the SEM; the DM entered the euro originally at too high an exchange rate and its exports suffered for two to three years as a result. Germany had a dreadful deal at the start of the euro. The DM was fixed at a rate that reflected German's pre-unification exchange rate, over-valuing its currency by 10–20 per cent. Monetary Union gifted Paris and Rome a fixed competitive advantage against Germany. However, this did not last as Germany eventually regained its comparative advantage in mechanical and electrical engineering, in the EU and global markets.

For Italy this rise in unit labour costs meant a massive loss of competitiveness inside the Single Market and the worst economic slump since WWII; both output and exports fell. Fiat sales declined by 26 per cent between May 2004 and May 2005 and lobbying for EU protection from cheap Chinese and Vietnamese clothing and footwear imports (the 'Bra-Wars' in the UK press) increased and proved effective. How else could Italy restore its competitiveness, being unable to devalue or lower interest rate, except by drastic structural reforms?

Italian governments, instead of reforms, failed to control fiscal policy. Taxes were raised but government spending was not cut (in 1994 25 per cent of Italy's pensioners claimed disability benefit on top of their state pensions). Italy's debt was 107 per cent of GDP. There were flagrant breaches of the SGP rules with exploding budget deficits of 5, 6 or 7 per cent GDP in Italy, Portugal and Greece. There was more discipline among northern states although France and Germany had been serial violators of the rules too.

Markets originally treated eurozone debt as the same. Financial markets at the euro's start did not factor in any significant risk of instability. Markets used to look at eurozone debt as of similar quality. Yield spreads of eurozone government debt were very narrow. In 2006–7 credit-rating agencies (Fitch, Standard and Poors) downgraded Italian debt to Botswana levels (AA– to A+). By October 2008 Italy had to pay 1.08 per cent more interest than Germany to entice pension funds to buy its state debt. Italy's debt (world's third largest after USA and Japan) stood at 107 per cent GDP (*DT* 31/10/08). In 2005–6 an abundance of bad news surrounded the euro, the French and Dutch 'No' votes in their referendums, Berlusconi's (Italian PM) threats against the euro and Italian ministers calling for a return to the lira. It started to look like the euro project was coming apart at the seams. The ECB referred to 'worrying divergences' across the eurozone. J. Alumina (EU Monetary Affairs commissioner) referred to the 'widening gap' in growth and the dramatic slowdown in Italy with the eurozone hit by 'tension and disunity' unless reforms were made. There were numerous pessimistic reports by HSBC, Lombard St. Research (2005); Centre for European reform 2006 (the pro-EU think tank); all warned that the eurozone could disintegrate. All of which was unduly pessimistic (or premature) as the euro's tenth anniversary occurred in June 2008 with its official tenth birthday in January 2009.

Portugal, Italy, Greece and Spain struggled as they had not converged enough nor were they sufficiently flexible to comfortably coexist with Germany in Euroland. (David Smith, *ST* 26/5/08).

Berlusconi's government threats to quit the euro were meant to intimidate Brussels into retreating on fiscal discipline, overlooking Italy's fat budget deficit. Rome was given two years to put its house in order. As France and Germany had been serial violators of the old SGP rules, it meant that no big state (like Italy) could be brought to book for debauching the eurozone's fiscal discipline and integrity. There was a stark choice in the short run: either Italy left the euro or the euro adapted to Italy. Leaving the euro was not considered such a wise move by economists as Italy's costs of borrowing and debt servicing would sky-rocket. Economic recovery in the eurozone with growth in EU-15 of 2.8 per cent, 2006–7 made it look as if Europe had finally turned a corner assisted by good conditions and global growth. This growth only papered over the real problems of lack of reforms, and much of the improvement was down to Germany. German exports rose 13 per cent 2006–7 and from April 2005 unemployment had fallen from 9.5 per cent to 6.4 per cent. The original euro conversion rates helped Italy but overvalued the DM in 1998. Ten years of deflation in Germany squeezing wage levels and productivity improvements meant Germany was once more the world's top exporter having regained all its competitiveness inside SEM and comparative advantage in engineering machinery for export globally. 'The Teutonic Tiger' had gained a 22 per cent competitive advantage in labour costs over France since 1995, 30 per cent over Spain and 40 per cent over Italy. Recovery, particularly in Germany, meant the euro strengthened markedly 2007–8 which resurrected the Franco-German rift over monetary policy and especially the exchange rate. There was a widening North–South divide in euroland as the club-med states lined up behind France. Axel Weber, head of the Bundesbank, was concerned about domestic inflationary pressures and a worrying surge in the eurozone money supply. Whereas President Nicolas Sarkozy wanted the ECB to focus on exchange-rate policy and to have this policy under political control to stop the euro rising more against the Yen, Yuan and $USD reducing Euroland exports. (Article 59 of the Maastricht Treaty did technically give eurozone finance ministers the power to impose Exchange Controls by QMV.)

Earlier during the French presidential elections, when Nicolas Sarkozy attacked the ECB's record, Angela Merkel, the German Chancellor, immediately visited the ECB to demonstrate the German government's commitment to ECB's independence and its goal of price stability. Sarkozy was calling for politicians to be able to actively manage the exchange rate and have a 'competitive', i.e. a weak euro. The old '1990s' argument between France and Germany over a strong or weak euro had resurfaced. By July 2007 the euro:USD exchange rate had strengthened and Airbus and other industries were hit hard and squealing as aircraft were built with euros but bought in $USD (*FT* 2/7/07, 1/10/07).

In July 2008 growth stalled as the strong euro took its inevitable toll on euroland's exports. Elga Bartsch of Morgan Stanley said 'Germany's resilience seems to be melting away' as exports fell (*DT* 11/7/08). Silvio Berlusconi, Italy's Prime Minister and long-time critic of the euro, gave his considered and memorable verdict that the single currency had 'screwed everybody'.

There were also signs of fiscal divergence between France and Germany in mid-2007 which have since increased, as Germany was cutting its deficit but France was going the other way threatening to break SGP limits. Germany did not want the rules relaxed. Such tensions and lack of progress with supply-side reforms in euroland refocused debate over the euro's long-term viability. The euro might also be vulnerable in a crisis. The ECB looks rather unprotected and exposed. The ECB has no overarching protective political authority above it.

The almost unprecedented international banking crisis in autumn 2008, following the 2007 'credit crunch' and financial crises, should prove a real test of the euro's durability particularly if the banking crisis mutates into a monetary crisis. President Nicolas Sarkozy (the incumbent EU President June–December 2008) was highly active calling emergency meetings of the big EU economies and ECB's President Trichet that (apart from grandstanding photo opportunities) provided some visible semblance of politically coordinated concern. (*Times* 24/10/08; *FT* 30/10/08) in the absence of any fully fledged economic government in EU to back up the euro. Sarkozy was advocating the urgent need for this *gouvernement économique* (*FT* 27/10/08) and suggested too that in its absence that he should remain as the 'President of the eurozone' during 2009 as the next two EU Presidential incumbents, Czech Republic and Sweden, were not in the euro. Germany was understandably hostile to both ideas, notably to his suggested 'coup d'état' (Munchau, *FT* 27/10/08) suspecting a French ploy to meddle with euro monetary policy. Nevertheless President Sarkozy was quite correct in recognising that there was no one government or political authority with a vested interest and mandate to defend the euro, whereas both the UK and USA and many EU governments have had to step in to shore things up by nationalising failing banks and financial institutions and guaranteeing bank deposits (to forestall runs on the banks) in the 2007–8 crises.

Ex-EU Commission President, Romano Prodi, believed in what he called the 'nasty accident' theory of EU integration. A major crisis would result in states pulling together to adopt deeper integrated EU solutions. He confidently expected the euro and EU to get its EU government this way. But in fact the banking crisis of 2008 was 'solved' not by the 'nasty accident' causing an integrated solution but via intergovernmental cooperation and coordinated action. States were also actually ignoring the supranational EU rule book on state aid (by their support to banks) and the SGP in the crisis and impeding recession.

In fact EU rules forbid the ECB to provide liquidity to banks that are 'potentially insolvent'. There is no clear cut supranational lender of last resort in the eurozone system. Each country is on its own and the ECB is forbidden to bail out member states (Prof. T. Congdon, *DT* 16/5/07). The IMF has warned that this leaves EMU exposed to 'systemic financial risk'. Reserves are obviously a key defence for each state so that in the EMU system it is National Central Banks that retain the bulk of reserves. The ECB has a token 13 per cent of EU total reserves (*DT* 16/5/07).

However, in the Hungarian monetary crisis in October 2008 and the Forint's collapse precipitated by the flight of currency and capital out of Eastern Europe there were reports that the ECB had made Hungary (not in the eurozone) a £3.9 billion loan (*DT* 23/10/08). The final $25 billion rescue package to stop the money market panic spreading to neighbouring states was made up of funds from IMF and World Bank but the second biggest contribution, $8.4 billion, came from the EU, having invoked a little known article in the EU's governing treaty enabling it to assist a member state in difficulties (*FT* 30/10/08).

Leaving aside Sarkozy's offer to act as an emergency President of the eurozone, the prospects for the ECB and euro attaining a single political authority with a vested interest in it or some form of Euro-federal or confederal government above it are highly remote. There is little or no popular support for a united states of Europe in member states; there are no voluble Euro-federal movements and campaigns as in the 1920s–40s. Europe is not a hotbed of debate arguing about constitutional changes as in the USA in 1780s. Euro-federalism is not a vote-winning political gambit in elections. The window of opportunity for a Euro-federal solution for Western Europe (if it was there at all) was immediately post-war. Even then Britain was implacably opposed to the idea.

Germany is generally keen on a Euro-federal government. Superimposing another tier of government authority on their existing federal system is neither problematic nor controversial. A USE would be a third tier above Bundestag and Lander. Chancellor Kohl's conception of a federal Europe would have looked remarkably like the Federal Republic of Germany (FRG). New EU entrants from Central and Eastern Europe (CEE) having recovered full sovereignty and escaped the Soviet Empire (as well as from Comecon, communism and the Warsaw Pact) in 1989–91 are understandably unenthusiastic about joining another 'empire', superstate or Euro-federalist arrangement. Poland, Czech Republic and Latvia are perhaps the most sceptical. Euro-federalism in any case might have been a possible solution to the problems of 40 or even 70 years ago but federation appears now to run against the tide of history. Multinational federations have been under intolerable strains or breaking up since the 1990s from Canada to Yugoslavia.

Federation, of course means different things to different nations. In Germany and the USA (both federal systems) the f-word stands for decentralisation whereas in the UK federation stands for centralisation. Unitary states or state-nations like Britain and France see federalism as a threat to their national identity and sovereignty.

'Nationalism' per se has attracted the attention of political sociology, philosophy, and history; it has been a growing field of study since E. Gellner's *Nations and Nationalism* 1983 (see too D. Miller, 1996 and D.D. Smith, 1996). The sentimental power of nationality endures in Europe despite fifty years of European integration and the EU as a possible alternative focus. Few EU citizens see themselves as European first and foremost. The moral and ethical legitimacy for nationalism is especially strong where boundaries of nations and states coincide and satisfy people's need for cultural roots, security and fraternity, and also creates their political community.

Britain is a multi-ethnic but mono-linguistic state-nation (with English officially predominant) in which British national identity essentially has a legal basis. Britishness is bound up with a popular acceptance of Britain's institutional, constitutional, legal systems – parliamentary democracy, parliamentary sovereignty and law making, the rule of law, common law tradition, religious pluralism and liberalism. Transfers of sovereignty and law making to EU's supranational Council of Ministers and other institutions reduces national sovereignty and diminishes British national identity. The British like to cling to their sovereignty and still see European integration as primarily about trade. France's national identity projected by the Parisian core and centre for politics, law, administration and culture was eventually to impose upon and subsume strong peripheral, local identities of innumerable richly diverse rural communities from Brittany fisherman to the Landes stilt-walking shepherds. French identity became defined in terms of membership of the French state (citizenship) at the risk of being crudely superficial and simplistic in a contentious field: if there was no French state, there would be no French citizenry and hence no French identity. The French state acted as the main engine of change and was also the embodiment of French sovereignty, power, grandeur and tradition. The French might give a rhetorical commitment to continuous European integration, even hinting at political union (viz. Mitterand 1989–90) but in practice they have been much more hesitant than they sound.

German national identity in contrast has an ethnic, romantic, cultural basis. German identity is grounded in the people, blood, land and forests. Germans are Germans. The German sense of national identity is not based on legal, constitutional or governmental systems. Germany in fact has been through four regime changes and constitutions and four changes of currency in the past 100 years. Germany has been split up and reunited after 40 years. Article 23 of the Basic Law anticipated and enabled the East German Lander to merge with the FRG and remake the greater Germany. So the transfer of German sovereign control and decision making to a supranational body in Brussels does not make Germans feel less German.

The FRG and GDR did not create separate national identities. The West German view was '1 nation, 2 states' with reunification a long-term goal since

1949. Germany is strongly committed to European integration and political Federation in Europe as the aim has been to subsume German identity in the context of a wider European identity to escape their past and contain any future revival of German nationalism. Other EU states were unsure whether a European Germany or a German Europe would result from political federation. The prospect of the latter ruled it out.

Since 1945 (West) Germany had felt unable to ask for anything for themselves in their own name; it always had to be requested as 'Europe' needing it or that it helped build a peaceful Europe. Europe as a geographic entity is highly attractive to EU citizenry, especially to the British. Hundreds of thousands travel, holiday, move to live within the EU facilitated by the single market deregulating and liberalising the airline market. Britain has become more 'European' in the sense that habits, tastes have changed, since joining the EEC in 1973. Changes in wine consumption, eating habits and cuisine are a direct result of cultural and economic integration at a personal level. The EU despite 23 official languages for 27 member states increasingly operates in English. Almost 90 per cent of EU secondary school children learn English, whereas only a quarter of Germans learn French and a fifth of French learn German now. While the long-term implications of this linguistic development are unclear they are unlikely to be negative for Britain.

The public's opinion of the EU is rather negative. A 1994 opinion poll showed only 1 in 2 EU citizens thought their country benefited from EU membership. Voter turnout for the EP's elections in 1994 was 56 per cent (despite compulsory voting in 3 EU states), in 2004 turnout was down to 46 per cent, much lower than for national elections. Of course unlike voting in national elections the EU's elections cannot result in a change of government. The EP is not a real legislature, simply one part of a process. Real law-making power lies with the Council of Ministers making decisions in secret. The EP has little legitimacy (unlike national parliaments) in the voters' eyes. There is little psychological connection.

There is an argument, infrequently made, that in retrospect a mistake was made in 1979 by introducing direct elections to the EP. On the face of it this sounds absurd and undemocratic, except that up until then euro MPs had been nominated by national parliaments and so there was a direct connection between legitimate national and the European parliament that has since been lost (*Economist* 31/5/97).

Public antipathy towards the EU and its projects can be seen too in the most recent referendum results. Those referendums held on whether to join the EU have mostly been positive. The Norwegians (1972, 1994) and the Swiss (2001) were the exceptions. The three countries joining in 1995 and 9 of the 10 in 2004 all had positive votes in favour (Cyprus did not hold one). It's a different story for referendums on Treaty revision or joining the euro and EMU. All the most recent twenty-first-century referendums rejected the proposal. The Danes on 28 September 2000 rejected joining EMU and adopting the euro with 53 per cent against (the turnout was 88 per cent). They did so

despite the 'yes' campaign having the backing of the entire political establishment (government, industry and the media) and their economic scare tactics
and dire predictions that were simply not believed (*The Times* 29/11/00).

In 2001 the Irish initially rejected the Nice Treaty, in 2003 Sweden rejected
euro entry, in 2005 France and the Netherlands rejected the Constitution
Treaty by 55 per cent and 61 per cent respectively, followed again by Ireland's
rejection of that Treaty's cloned replacement, the Lisbon Treaty, in June 2008.
All of which signifies a big gap between the EU executive, the legislative
process and the people, as the European elite's projects were thrown out by
popular votes in five states. It might perhaps be the end of the line for more
European integration having hit the buffers so often, yet as likely as not a
cunning plan will be devised to skirt around the latest referendum wreckage.
They might perhaps make concessions to Ireland (and to other small countries), perhaps, conjecturally, letting them keep their EU Commissioner,
rebadged as 'Commissioner and National Representative', then get them to
vote again in 2009 and, all being well, press on.

Public perceptions of the EU are coloured too by its bad news stories (not
simply the bad press it gets in negative anti-EU papers such as the *Sun* and
Daily Mail in the UK). Stories of wastage and legendary fraud have been
appearing for decades: £5–£6 billion, 10 per cent of the budget, as a conservative estimate was wasted each year according to the Court of Auditors,
the guardians of the EU finances back in 1993 (*ST* 16/5/93). The olive oil
industry has been a notorious black hole as farmers receive a subsidy per
olive tree. Bottling plants invent suppliers to boost subsidies for the quantity
of oil produced. In Sicily an inspection revealed that 50 per cent of 3,800
suppliers to one factory were fictitious; others had been dead for a hundred
years. In Hamburg investigators discovered grain being unloaded from the
stern of a ship before being reloaded at the bow; taking advantage of an
export subsidy on German grain destined for Eastern Europe. The EC Fraud
Unit relied on member governments to pursue suspects but often there was
little incentive for them to do so as it would mean cracking down on farm
cooperatives in club-med states that are big local employers.

Marta Andreasen was sacked as a whistle blower from her new post of
Chief Accountant in 2004 after alleging that the EU was riddled with fraud
and slush funds, which in fact was little different to what the Court of Auditors have shown for 13 years running by refusing to sign off the EU's
accounts. She famously said the EU's £63 billion budget was 'an open till
waiting to be robbed' (*FT* and *DT* 9/11/7).

The biggest scandal and crisis to hit the EU was in 1999 when the Commission President, Jacques Santer and his entire 20 strong team of commissioners were forced to resign by the EP following an independent report into
fraud, nepotism, corruption and mismanagement by the Commission (the
UK's two commissioners were not accused of condoning malpractice or mismanagement). The harshest criticism was made of Mrs Edith Cresson, the
Research Commissioner and ex French Prime Minister who appointed her

69-year-old friend and dentist, Rene Berthelot, to a £45,600 p.a., job despite his lack of any real and relevant qualifications. While on the Commission's payroll he had been helping her in her separate former post as Mayor of the French town of Châtellerault. Mrs Cresson insisted she had done nothing wrong, that she was the victim of a German conspiracy and that her conduct was fully in accordance with the practices of the French administrative elite (*Independent, FT, DT* 16–18 March 1999).

The EU's image suffers at times too at the hands of national governments who don't defend or even blame the EU for unpopular behaviour or regulations as if the national government had had no involvement at all. The ECB has come in for much criticism, perhaps justifiably, but the ECB and its rules and remit were the result of intergovernmental decisions. EU member states don't do much to explain truly what the EU is for and what it does, that is to 'sell' it to their public. Politicians appear wary of doing this, possibly because for many people the EU is a fairly marginal issue at the moment and they are uninterested in it, so better to leave it that way.

There is some confusion and distrust of the EU too because of the almost constant institutional changes made over the past twenty years. One argument runs that people don't like it because they don't understand what these changes are for. The other counter-argument (put forward by Emma Bonino, Italian commissioner 1997)) thinks the public does not like it because they understand very well what it's for and strongly object as referendums indicate. For despite senior French officials insisting that Federation is dead and the widespread antipathy to it, Eurocrats and euro-enthusiasts inside the EU still try to assemble the political Lego set slipping pieces into place, when they can; the institutional trappings, the necessary components, a 'Mr Europe' (Foreign Minister) a 'Mr President' and so on, wherever the chance arises. They can be sure of German support too.

9   EU Treaty changes and EU external relations, 1998–2008

Between 1957 (Treaty of Rome) and 1986 (SEA) there were no new treaties, but since 1986 there have been six treaties. The EU seemingly has an endless obsession with updating and changing its institutions. Treaty revision has been a virtual non-stop process since the mid-1980s. EU citizens cannot be blamed for thinking of the 'EU as an organisation hard wired for mission-creep' (*FT* 26/7/08).

There were basically three reasons for this, enlargement being the first. When future membership was expected to grow to around 25 states and as a club of 15 they were using institutional machinery designed for six, the rules had to be re-examined first. In 15 years EU membership more than doubled from 12 states in 1992 (Maastricht Treaty) to 27 by 2007, with Bulgaria and Romania joining. Earlier in 1995 there was the 'Alpine-Arctic' enlargement – Austria, Sweden and Finland – and in 2004, 10 states in a swathe stretching from the Baltic through Central and Eastern Europe to the Mediterranean joined (Estonia, Latvia, Lithuania, Poland, Czech Republic, Slovakia, Hungary, Slovenia, Malta and Cyprus). Enlargements are tricky as they are effectively balancing acts, to maintain the political, geographic, demographic and economic symmetry of the EU. A balance of big and small, North and South, rural and industrial states needs ideally to be maintained. To retain a harmonious balance of interests and influence means the sequence of admissions, i.e. which states to admit and when, requires careful evaluation (assuming they qualify). Also it's obviously important that net beneficiaries from the EU budget cannot outvote the net contributors. The political arithmetic of voting weights and the voting system required revision, the rule book had to change and ceilings agreed on the size of EU institutions, the European Parliament, the Court and the Commission, all of which is exceedingly difficult to get unanimous agreement on. The Treaty of Amsterdam failed to do so in 1997 and these problematic reforms were effectively ducked until later.

EU treaties proliferated because they self-propagated; each one happened to contain the seed for the next. A clause stipulated that a future IGC in so many years would review, revise, complete, correct or change the treaty for another. So one treaty begat the next. They are not independent one-off treaties but instalments in a serial.

A third contributory factor to treaty revision is that Germany maintained pressure to bring about political federation regardless of whether the CDU or SPD was in power. This was their quid pro quo for giving up the DM for the euro and EMU. The French, though, want what they call a 'strong' Europe (not federation), with strongly integrated institutions in situ preferably run by an old Ecole National Administrative (ENA) trained member of the French politico-administrative elite.

The job of the 1996 IGC (as specified in the Maastricht Treaty) was to correct any mistakes Maastricht drafters had made and to change the club rules to accommodate a move to 20 or more members in a 'son of Maastricht Treaty'. The main difficulty was to keep the balance between big and small countries. The big had more votes so could not be outvoted, the small benefited from the weighed vote system. Of a total of 76 votes 54 were needed for a QMV and only 23 for a blocking minority. In 1996 the Maastricht arithmetic meant the big five were needed for a QMV and only 23 for a blocking minority. In 1996 the Maastricht arithmetic meant the big five had 48 votes and could only get a QMV with the support of two states. For small states to get their way they needed 3 big ones too. Also two big states could block if they were supported by one small state (other than Luxembourg).

The problem in changing this would be to keep the balance of the political arithmetic right in the future. Blocking power had proved to be critically important; of 233 SEM decisions in five years only 91 went to a vote. Any club containing conflicting interests and rival cultures cannot tolerate one being constantly overruled. (*Economist* 22/10/99). Germany, Denmark, Holland and the UK were instinctively for free trade and open markets; Spain and France mistrust market forces they cannot influence. Other 'fault lines' existed between contributors and net beneficiaries; between Germany and Benelux which wanted the EP to have more power and France and the UK that didn't. France and Spain wanted big countries' voting strength to rise; Germany wanted a 'double majority' system of voting taking the number of states but also a percentage of total population of states in favour. The French opposed this as Germany would end up with more votes than France.

There was a long and difficult list of issues to resolve and changes to be agreed unanimously. The 1996 IGC started in Turin and immediately became bogged down in the UK's row with EU partners over mad cow disease, during the most heated part of which the UK adopted a policy of total non-cooperation. The British continued to be obstructive and of course other countries hid and concealed their own difficulties with proposed changes behind British intransigence. Then first the British followed by the French elections put the IGC on hold. Time was running out and the task too difficult. So the Treaty of Amsterdam, October 1997 fell far short of its intended objectives it failed to resolve any of the key issues of institutional reform (such as the maximum size of the Parliament, Court and Commission) and political arithmetic of weighted voting. It's not too cynical to say (given the two states' track record) that its lack of any real reform and complete absence of contentiousness was confirmed by the fact that both the Danish and Irish referendums in 1998 had a positive outcome. A number of small changes were made in the Treaty of Amsterdam but the most striking feature of the Treaty was its failure to resolve the difficult issues and disparities between member states. At the two extremes in 1996, Luxembourg got two votes in the Council of Ministers for its 0.4 million population and Germany got 10 votes for 80 million population. (If representation was strictly proportional to population Luxembourg would get 1/20th of a vote and Germany 20; the UK would get 14 not its real allocation of 10.) Originally with just six states in the 1950s the voting system was designed to favour the three small countries (Benelux) so that their views were not swamped by their large neighbours. Over time with successive enlargements this built-in discrepancy in voting power appeared increasingly inequitable. Small countries of course would never give up their voting strength without a fight and without some sort of trade-off by big states. Germany was sensitive to small states' stance on the issue and proposed their 'double majority' solution to the problem. Karl Lammers (German Foreign Minister) originally devised the 'double majority' idea or super-qualified majority in 1993 with, for example, $\frac{3}{4}$ states and $\frac{3}{4}$ of total population needed for approval. This voting issue would eventually be revised in the Treaty of Nice 2001.

Despite the limitations of the 1997 Treaty of Amsterdam the Council of Ministers decided to press on with Eastern enlargement. Eastern enlargement would be more difficult than previous ones as they were large, poor, agricultural states and if all 10 were to join the EU, the EU's population would rise by 30 per cent but EU's GDP by just 4 per cent. CAP would be bankrupted if not reformed before entry. The order in which CEE states should be admitted was a highly contentious issue. Germany, as their biggest trading partner, was keen on Poland, Czech Republic, Slovakia and Hungary being in the first tranche of entrants. Italy pushed the claims of Slovenia, while Finland and Sweden pressed for Estonia to be in the first wave. Greece threatened to veto enlargement for others if Cyprus was not included. In 1997 the Commission originally envisaged the first three or four countries joining in 2002 if all went well. (*Economist* 31/5/97). Instead of course because of the delicate politics involving existing members 10 joined in 2004 (Romania and Bulgaria joined later in 2007 as their income per head was only 30 per cent of the EU average in 1994).

These aspirant members had not only to put the 'acquis communitaire' on their statute books but to enforce them in practice (subject to temporary derogations and transition periods). This was a big task and for several of them it meant they needed stronger courts and bureaucracies to enforce, for example, the SEM rules.

Under the 'European Agreements' since 1991 there was free trade in most areas and industrial goods by 1995 for CEE states, but not in the 'sensitive areas' of textiles and steel where quotas (i.e. EU protectionism) remained in place and free trade was only achieved respectively in 1997 and 1996. These of course were the very areas where CEE had their main comparative advantage in trade with EU.

Even after seven years the Nice Summit in December 2000 for the EU-15 maintains a reputation as the longest and most divisive summit the EU has had to date. Baron Frans van Daele (Belgium's Permanent Representative to EU in 2001) was quoted seven years later saying "The Treaty of Nice was arguably the worst Treaty we have ever negotiated' (*FT* 11/6/07). Negotiations dragged on for an unprecedented four days and nights with the Treaty finally signed at 4.30 a.m. on Monday 11 December 2000. Leaders claimed that they only signed up out of exhaustion at this Summit run by Jacques Chirac, the French President (whose nickname was the 'Bulldozer'). Its system of power sharing and decision making was denounced by many (notably all the leaders of smaller states) almost before the ink was dry. These leaders eventually caved in at Nice but went away determined to re-write these rules they had just agreed to, as soon as possible (*FT* 11/6/07).

The Nice Summit started like all other Euro summits with the 'family photograph', one press report at Nice described the scene ' … false bonhomie briefly conceals the mutual disdain, distrust and even hatred'. A leaked memo from David O'Sullivan, the Secretary General of the Commission, at the end of the Summit spoke of 'its poisoned atmosphere' (*ST* 10/12/00, 17/12/00).

The purpose of the Summit was supposedly to improve decision-making processes prior to further EU enlargement by up to 12 states by 2004, that is do what the Amsterdam Treaty avoided doing. Gerhard Schröder wanted more voting rights for Germany in the Council of Ministers. France was resisting what it saw as a bid for German domination. Chirac spoke of the 'inviolability of parity' in the Franco-German axis to be told by Chancellor Schröder 'we don't see it like that'. Blair was unruffled by letting Germany have a few more votes than France or UK. The voting arithmetic meant Germany could not dominate proceedings. Blair was opposed to Chirac's plan for a European Rapid Reaction force (which might mutate into a European Army). Any independent European force could undermine NATO. William Cohen, US Defense Secretary, as well as the UK, Netherlands and Denmark were concerned about that.

For once Britain and Tony Blair were not cast as the odd man out, the pariah figure, the 'brake on building Europe'. Instead, an epic power struggle for control over the EU's policy and executive machinery between big and small nation states raged for four days over the issue of weighted votes. Belgium led a group of Greece, Finland, Sweden, Austria and Portugal to stop big powers from rewriting the EU rule book to suit themselves. (*FT, Independent, Telegraph* 12/12/00). The Portuguese called it an 'institutional coup d'état' insisting that it changed the EU from a 'federal' club of equal states into a two tier system with a 'directory' on top. At issue was a French plan to triple the bloc votes of the 'Big 5' in the Council of Ministers while doubling everyone else's. It was not such an extreme proposition. Big powers were still left 'underweighted' in the French proposal. The UK, France, Italy and Germany would get 29 votes (for Germany with 82 million population). Belgium with 10 million population would get 12 votes and Luxembourg with 0.4 million population got four votes.

However, coupled with a new device (but an old idea) of a 'demographic bar', it meant that any grouping of states with 38 per cent of the EU's population could block any EU laws. The result of this demographic bar was that the big states had permanent blocking power. It also established Germany as the EU's own primus inter pares (first among equals). The Big 5 states would now have unchallenged overt control over the EU agenda meaning future initiatives would originate and be determined by big national governments in Paris, Rome, London, Berlin and Madrid, bypassing and ignoring the Commission in Brussels. Its old role of initiating legislation (even if the objectives were defined by European Council Summits) was seemingly eclipsed and redundant. This was described in press reports at the time as the 'triumph of intergovernmentalism'.

President Chirac reputedly underlined this change by preventing the President of the EU Commission, Romano Prodi, from participating in some meetings and apparently shouted at one of Prodi's aides to leave the room (*FT, Independent, Telegraph* 12/12/00) Chirac also dismissed Prodi as a 'bureaucrat' at Nice (*Times* 10/12/00). Germany's main aim originally was to secure more votes in the Council of Ministers (above Italy, France and UK) to reflect its bigger population (30 per cent larger). However, as the arguing went on Schröder decided not to push this issue as it might destroy a weakened Franco-German partnership altogether and be too visible a sign of Paris's weakening position vis à vis Berlin. In what reports referred to as Schröder's 'back door coup' a similar outcome of adding to German voting power, was achieved through the new voting system. The biggest four states would each have 29 votes and EU leaders agreed that any member was able to invoke a new clause that required a majority vote to represent at least 62 per cent of total EU population. This meant that Germany and any two big EU states could block any decision even though their combined votes do not add up to the necessary blocking majority. Chancellor Gerhard Schröder said 'without highlighting it, Germany's weight has grown' (*FT* 12/12/00).

The Nice Treaty meant the triumph of intergovernmentalism and Germany becoming first among equals in the EU. A QMV in future would need 73 per cent of votes in Council of Ministers and 62 per cent of EU's population as represented by their governments. The redistribution of power at the top of the EU fractured the Franco-German relationship, which was effectively being written off in many quarters in December 2000. However, the Franco-German axis had been in crisis or written off on a number of occasions since the 1970s (notably in the Kohl–Mitterand era 1989–90). Certainly the nature of the relationship has changed a great deal over time and conditions have to be right for it to operate effectively. It had been in tatters before. Nonetheless there had been no joint Franco-German agreed position before the summit (their standard operating procedure) and there was no joint position during it. On the contrary the French were shocked by Schröder wanting more votes (or professed to be) and the fact that Schröder was no longer deferential to Chirac. For Gerhard Schröder made it clear that German subservience to France because of national war guilt was now redundant and obsolete after 55 years.

Charles Grant, Director of the Centre for European Reform (a pro-EU body), was reported as saying that the Franco-German axis had more or less died, ' ... they will doubtless have a meeting and say everything has been patched up, but nobody will be persuaded' (quoted by David Smith, *ST* 17/12/00).

Politicians in France privately recognised that German size, economic power and proximity to new members meant the Franco-German partnership was now unequal and saw that Germany had emerged as the champion of a group of states (Finland, Belgium, Portugal) which claimed to want a final settlement for Europe along Federal lines (John Palmer, Director of European Policy Centre, Brussels, *Independent* 24/10/01). Following their row at Nice, Germany wanted France to commit to more integration as the condition for re-launching their partnership. *Le Figaro* reported in January 2001 that 'the German plan is clear it intends to make Berlin the lynch pin of a Europe reoriented to the East'. If France was unable to commit itself to the German federalist vision Germany would look for new partners. France rightly worried that enlargement reduced its influence.

Just a few weeks after Nice Schröder was having secret talks with Tony Blair in London (*DT* 30/1/01) This though was the day before Schröder was due to meet President Chirac and Prime Minister Lionel Jospin for a private dinner in Strasbourg to discuss the future of the Franco-German alliance and the way forward for Europe following their row in Nice. There was supposedly a news blackout on the Tony Blair–Gerhard Schröder meeting (because Blair was anxious to stop Europe becoming an election issue). However, reports stated that the Schröder–Blair meeting in January 2001 explored the possibility of forging a new Anglo-German Alliance with much closer Berlin–London links, resulting in the downgrading of German ties with France or perhaps a tripartite alliance instead. Schröder's agenda would presumably have included discussing the prospects of Blair shifting his policy on the euro.

However, following dinner with Chirac and Jospin the next day, what was called the Blaesheim Process started with Franco-German high level talks every six weeks. This rapprochement didn't last, an SPD document in April 2001 called for a two-tier EP and the German federal system to be replicated at EU level (*DT* 30/4/01). France's Euro Minister, Pierre Moscovic, rejected this as 'unbalanced and unrealistic' and that France wanted inter-governmental not federal institutions. Germany's only significant support was from Belgium which was keen on Euro-federalism to save them from their own national federal failure as a state so deeply divided on ethnic and linguistic fault lines it could barely operate at national level (see *DT* 3/10/07). The anti-federalist camp in 2001 included France, UK, Spain and Austria, who would be joined by Poland, Czech Republic et al. four years later.

However, two years later and following the re-election of all three leaders (Chirac, Schröder and Blair), a startling intensification of Franco-German cooperation was announced (*DT* 14/1/2003). Germany and France announced revolutionary plans to allow cabinet ministers to attend one another's cabinet meetings and agree joint laws (e.g. on civil and family matters). The reinvigorated alliance presented a pre-cooked deal on CAP at the Brussels summit in 2002 and pledged to work for a full EU Security and Defence Union. Schröder and Chirac planned a new joint declaration when their two parliaments met at Versailles to mark the 40th anniversary of their Franco-German alliance. Closer cooperation of this order alarmed London as Blair aspired 'to be at the heart of Europe' in shaping its future. Franco-German relations seemed to be back on track two years after the Nice Summit.

Chirac tried at Nice in 2000 to preserve the traditional French position and role (that originated in the de Gaulle era) whereby France was able to punch above its weight because of German support and back-up. On the face of it, superficially, it succeeded as both had the same 29 votes but the 62 per cent of the population aspect meant Germany now had most influence as they had 30 per cent more population.

Chirac reportedly told Gerhard Schröder at Nice (December 2000) that France deserved as many votes as Germany 'because it had nuclear weapons and was on the right side in two World Wars'. Such a remark, calculated to offend, would not easily be forgotten.

Power was unquestionably shifting towards Germany as a result of the EU's eastern enlargement (where Germany had the greatest influence of any EU state); reinforced by Germany's 82 million population (30 per cent larger than France, Italy or UK) giving it the greatest weight in formal EU decision making. Germany though was not able to force through anything it wanted because the rules prevented any one state governing by diktat.

Charles Grant (Director for the Centre of European Reform) said Nice's new voting rules and procedure meant a more open array of alliances inside the EU. Already in 2000 Britain and Spain had teamed up over labour-market reforms; the UK and Germany on majority voting, and the UK and France on defence. Romano Prodi (President of EU Commission) and the Commission were the big losers from the Nice Summit. Prodi played a much less significant role and the Commission's influence had sunk to a new low point, compared with a decade before in the Delors era, when as President of the Commission he had considerable influence and the EC Commission clearly espoused Delors' conception of what was in 'Europe's' interest. The biggest four states could now settle the agenda themselves intergovernmentally (i.e. in a non-integrated, non-supranational context).

The Treaty of Nice extended QMV to cover 90 per cent of EU law. QMV ended national vetoes in 23 separate EU articles covering 39 measures; national vetoes only remain over a small core of articles. QMV does not cover taxation, social security, immigration as it affects the UK. A QMV in the big EU-27 states after 2007 required 258 votes out of 342 (75 per cent) and also from states representing at least 62 per cent of EU's enlarged population of 481 million. This means in practice that big countries run things. Big states lost their second Commissioner in 2005 in preparation for the slimmed down European Commission prior to EU membership rising to 27. The Commission was not to get that big so it was intended that some states would 'share' a commissioner.

The Nice Treaty also contained a mechanism to permit a vanguard of up to eight countries to press ahead with integration leaving others to catch up later. This was now referred to as 'enhanced cooperation' (see Nice Treaty Article 11a) but this 'flexibility' was an old concept going back to the 1970s. It used to be referred to in a multitude of ways: reinforced cooperation (1997); variable geometry; concentric circles; multi-tiered; à la carte; 2-speed Europe. Regardless of the label they all meant much the same thing: rather than wait for all to proceed together some states would be allowed to adopt a common policy before others were prepared to; otherwise, as Helmut Kohl was fond of saying, 'the convoy moves at the pace of the slowest ship'. Precedents existed for this too. The Maastricht Treaty specifically and explicitly allowed some to join EMU, while others were excluded if they didn't meet the criteria. Denmark and UK had opted out. The first pillar (the EC pillar) of the EU was not open to flexibility as this might undermine the SEM.

Britain was never keen on the idea, but agreed in principle as long as defence was not included and also as long as it was 'multi-speed' not a '2-speed' Europe. A 'multi-speed' EU might enable the UK to take a leading role in some sphere even though the UK was not in the euro. The risk for the UK was that it wanted at all costs to avoid the formation of a distorted '2-speed' Europe where new entrants and awkward squad members (UK, Danes, Irish, Swedes et al.) could be parked, while others in an 'inner union' or 'fast track' took the real decisions. This fear is still current. Gordon Brown was reported to be very concerned about the possibility of Ireland being pressed to accept a '2-speed Europe' (following its rejection of the Lisbon Treaty, June 2008) with Ireland being 'put in the slow lane' (*ST* 15/6/08) and effectively 'hung out to dry'. The Nice Treaty's changes were considered quite sufficient to allow the EU to grow to 25 or 30 members. So it has proved with membership at 27 states in 2007. Several studies have subsequently shown that the enlarged EU operates more efficiently and better than before (*Economist* 21/6/08).

The Nice Treaty committed the EU to another IGC and convention to consider the wider future of Europe in 2004. It actually went on to agree a draft EU constitution. This was to establish the supposed final balance of power between Brussels, national governments and their regions (it was reputedly at the behest of the German Lander governments). It would also clean up problems fudged or not attended to at Nice.

In a referendum in 2001 the Irish surprisingly rejected the Nice Treaty with 54 per cent voting no. Earlier in the year the EU unwisely censored the Irish government for breaching rules on inflation and debt. Politicians and the public were outraged at such interference in euroland's best-performing economy and there was a surge in anti-EU sentiment. Ireland was pressed to re-run the referendum and this time the Nice Treaty was accepted in October 2002, finally coming into force in February 2003. It is still in legal force in 2009 and the EU functions perfectly well under the Nice Treaty rules since the constitutional drafting process started seven years ago. The two subsequent treaties have both been rejected in referendums.

The Constitutional Treaty 2004 had its origins in the Laeken Declaration 2001 during Belgium's Presidency. The stated priority was to clarify for people the procedures and tasks of EU institutions, to enhance the role of the EP, national Parliaments and the transparency of proceedings. This would bring the whole EU closer to the people. Giuliano Amato, Vice President of the Convention on the Future of Europe, wrote that a constitution was actually at the bottom of a long list in the Laeken Declaration and was never intended to be the main focus. It was considered neither a priority nor urgent (*FT* 25/1/07). Instead a convention was set up under the Presidency of Valéry Giscard d'Estaing (French President 1974–81) which exceeding its remit spent 18 months drafting a first version of a constitution and then another 18 months fine tuning its detailed text.

The original mandate of the 105 member convention was to discuss the wider future of Europe generally not produce a draft Constitutional Treaty drawn up by a cabal of 12 people. The huge complex document of 300 pages codified and incorporated unnecessarily all earlier Treaties; it also dispensed with the 'pillar' features in Maastricht's Treaty. This was seen as a centralising move, increasing the scope for Brussels' control over intergovernmental areas. Having lost ground and influence under the Nice Treaty the European Commission lobbied hard to re-establish more community based integrated decision making. Eleven states were to hold referendums. In the event most did not and ratification stopped when first 55 per cent of French voters in May 2005 and then, three days later, 62 per cent of Dutch voters rejected the Treaty in referendums. The Brussels Commission was stunned by two of the founding states from 1951 rejecting a Treaty. Luxembourg Prime Minster, Jean Claude Juncker said, 'Europe is not in crisis it is in deep crisis'. If France or Holland had not rejected the Treaty there is a high probability that the UK and Poland would have done in their referendums.

There was much speculation but no real consensus as to why they did reject it. Were voters expecting more integration or less? Had they turned against the whole project given a sense that France was no longer in control? Did they fear globalisation and free markets? Were they reacting more specifically against the Bolkesteiner directive on free trade in services and the 'Polish plumber' scare in France?!!

Jose Manuel Barroso, President of the EU Commission, strongly advised against a second attempt to ram through the constitutional treaty. He and others warned that the EU should 'lie low, clean up its act, and do fewer things better' (A. Evans-Pritchard, *DT* 14/6/08). This sound advice was completely ignored.

The referendums' results exposed the enormous 'disconnection' of the French and Dutch people from the EU's institutions, the very thing that the Laeken Declaration intended to be addressed. Leadership changes and 'reflection' time postponed any movement on the matter until Chancellor Angela Merkel took over the EU Presidency. In January 2007 she announced plans to revive the constitution with a special summit for the 18 states that ratified it and another in February for the nine non-signatures. By June 2007 a replacement 'Plan B' Treaty should be in place. She told the Bundestag in December 2006 that it would be a 'historic failure if we did not have the substance of the European Constitution in place in time for the European Elections 2009'.

Merkel completely ignored the fact that 62 per cent of Dutch and 55 per cent of French voters had already rejected the substance of the European constitution. If the French and Dutch had voted 'Yes' their verdict would have been hailed as a historic endorsement of political union by Eurocrats and Euro-federalist politicians. Only a 'No' vote to them indicated confusion and a 'mistake' and that voters must think again. This attitude and contempt for popular opinion actually confirms Eurosceptics' charge that the EU is elitist and undemocratic. Apart from atrocious violence and state-imposed starvation the EU looked little better than Zimbabwe where the Presidential ballot was re-held to get Mugabe the 'correct' result.

That Chancellor Angela Merkel disregarded the 'disconnection' of the public from 'the project' (institutional development of the EU) was not surprising. Daniel Hannan (Ex-MEP) has shown that German politicians are 'disconnected' from their own public's popular opinion, there being a massive gap between the governed and the government. A German opinion poll in *Frankfurter Allgemeine Zeitung* November 2007, showed 29 per cent of Germans believed EU membership was harmful only 22 per cent thought it beneficial. Yet Germany's Chancellor and EU President 2007, was a Euro-federalist (just like her predecessor, Schröder (SPD) and Kohl (CDU)) and completely untroubled by what German people thought of the EU. Under the Basic Law, referendums are illegal and the German political system was deliberately set up after World War II to keep to a minimum any popular participatory element, an understandable reaction in the late 1940s given the extent and consequences of mass participation in politics, on the streets in the 1920s and 1930s. The German political class is rather contemptuous and deeply suspicious of too much popular democracy. Hannan showed that the German public reciprocated a disdain for politicians. A survey 3 January 2007, showed

80 per cent of Germans agreed they did not trust a single politician to represent them. Party lists ensure that German MPs owe their position to Party Whips not their electors. The entire German political class is locked into a post-World War II political consensus, disconnected from the vagaries of public opinion (see D. Hannan, *DT* 10/1/07).

What did the EU governments want in the Reform Treaty? Merkel's self-appointed task was to reconcile the 'Maximalists', the 18 states who had ratified it and wanted to retain as much as possible from the 2004 Treaty with the 'Minimalists' who wanted to forget about the Constitution Treaty and to simply amend the Nice Treaty's rules instead (i.e. Holland, France, UK, Poland, Czech Republic). The Minimalists were to be disappointed, they were in a minority. 'Plan B' was 95 per cent the same content as the original Treaty. All the 'state-like' symbols, paraphernalia, terminology, were ditched. Most governments won a concession or two; that was all. Tony Blair, for example, wanted the Charter of Fundamental Rights out of the Treaty itself (it became a protocol) and the UK won opt-outs: there was to be no QMV for justice and home affairs issues and the CFSP was to remain unanimous and unable to be questioned by the EP or ECJ. The UK and the Dutch were desperate not to call a referendum.

Poland wanted to re-open the core voting arrangements. Poland had an extraordinary deal on votes at Nice (see above: 27 votes with 30 million population cf. 29 votes for Germany with 80 million) but was outmanoeuvred in the Constitutional Treaty, negotiations which actually introduced a fairer double-majority system. In the new treaty Poland wanted to claw something back especially from Germany. Poland wanted a country's votes to be the square root of its population which would reduce Germany's vote sharply relative to Poland's. This square root system (also known as the Penrose method), according to Wolfgang Munchau (the *FT*'s European correspondent), meant Poland was mathematically correct, it being a fairer system (*FT* 11/6/07), tending to narrow the weighting of votes between the largest and smallest countries in terms of population. In support of their case Poland complained that they would have had a much bigger population on which to base EU voting power if the Germans had not killed so many Poles in World War II. They argued that if 6 million people (18.5 per cent of the population) had not been killed, Poland's demographics would be very different with 66 million people instead of 38 million today. Whilst Poland might have had a strong point it was considered the height of bad manners and in poor taste to raise the issue in an EU context. Only the Czech Republic supported Poland's square root method to some extent (but would not back a Polish veto on the matter). All the other states were opposed. After refusing to discuss the issue, the German government agreed to include it for discussion at the June Council 2007. According to the eventual agreed compromise Poland won a long delay. The Nice Treaty voting rules would remain in place until 2014; between 2014 and 2017 a transitional phase was to occur where the new (Reform Treaty) QMV rules apply but where the old Nice Treaty voting weights can be applied when a member states wishes so. Some believed that the identical twin brothers, Lech (President) and Jaroslaw (PM) Kaczynski of the Law and Justice Party who came to power in 2005 postponed the issue until Poland holds the EU Presidency in 2011 when they might try to produce a Treaty of Warsaw favouring Poland's voting method.

What did the Lisbon Treaty end up containing? It completely failed to meet the original aims and objectives laid down by the Laeken EU Summit seven years before. Few governments were enthusiastic about the Lisbon Treaty apart from Germany and Belgium. The EP liked it too as it got additional powers. Lisbon contained 95 per cent of what was in the Constitutional Treaty as its Chief Architect, Valery Giscard d'Estaing was keen to announce in successive interviews undermining governments' cases against referendums that they had originally promised but now insisted were not necessary. Valéry Giscard d'Estaing told *Le Monde* with stupefying arrogance that the public are led ' ... to adopt, without knowing it the proposals that we dare not present to them directly' (reported in *ST* 17/6/07).

The Single Foreign Policy Chief (no longer called a Foreign Minister) would represent Europe. National vetoes would go in areas of cross-border policing and immigration. Voting weights would be changed, the EP would get new powers. Generally the Lisbon Treaty was an unreadable mish-mash of articles salvaged from the wrecked constitutional Treaty. Valéry Giscard d'Estaing said, 'The Lisbon Treaty is a catalogue of amendments. It is impenetrable for the public' (*Independent* 20/10/07).

QMV was now to be 55 per cent of states (favouring smaller states) representing 62 per cent of total EU population (this favoured bigger states). In practice the EU rarely votes preferring to achieve a consensus. QMV was to extend to 50 new areas currently requiring unanimity (viz. immigration, criminal justice, judicial and police cooperation). Ireland and the UK had the right to opt out. One big change was the full-time standing President of EU elected by Heads of State for two and a half years renewable once. The new President was permitted to host four or more summits per year. A new Foreign Affairs Unit plus a diplomatic service (operating in parallel with national governments) would start functioning. The UK had opted out of a new Charter of Fundamental Rights, which controversially included the 'right to strike' and 'preventative health care'. Neither of these were in the EU's gift or remit, the EU having no competence in these areas with no direct power over NHS or regulating industrial disputes. Concern was raised as the ECJ may decide to have the final say on the matter. After 2014 EU states would lose the right to send a commissioner to Brussels their number being capped at two-thirds of member states. National Parliaments can protest if they believe a proposed EU law is not needed. If 50 per cent of 27 nations' parliaments or MEPs are unhappy, the law would be scrapped. Originally 10 states were to hold referendums; only Ireland actually has to hold one constitutionally if a treaty involves the transfer of powers.

The Lisbon Treaty is not required for the EU to operate; it can easily survive without it and of course does. The Nice Treaty has perfectly adequate provisions in place to allow the EU to grow to 30 states. Even if something had to be changed or added on it could be included in an accession Treaty when admitting a new member. Apart from Germany and Belgium no states are very interested in a federal USE.

On the 12 June 2008 Ireland rejected the Lisbon Treaty by 53 per cent to 47 per cent on a high turnout despite the whole Irish establishment being in favour and scare stories from doom-mongers. Ireland's rejection cannot be blamed on the general unpopularity of the EU itself. On the contrary a recent EU barometer poll showed 87 per cent thought Ireland benefited from membership, more than for any other EU state. Nevertheless, Ireland has rejected two treaties.

Since 1973 Ireland has had twice as much from the EU budget than it has put in; the net transfers were equivalent to €10k per person. Why did Ireland vote 'No'? Ireland is rather like the UK in so far as they see the EU as an economic arrangement and suspect anything more. The Irish government campaign could have been better. Both the Prime Minister, Mr Cowen, and Charles McGreevy admitted to not having read the Treaty in detail which was a 'gift' to the 'No' campaign that capitalised on this as ' … nobody should sign a contract they don't understand' (*Economist* 21/6/08).

EU leaders (according to *The Economist*) invariably react to millions of people rejecting an EU edict in three stages: starting by stating they respect the outcome but there is a deep crisis and they're unable to function; then the onus is put on the state that rejected it to find a solution; finally the 'Zimbabwe option', i.e. voters have to rethink at a second ballot or leave the EU.

This is the standard operating procedure in the EU when a treaty is rejected. The only known exceptions to this process were the Franco-Dutch rejections in 2005 Then the treaty was repackaged to avoid a rerun, into the deliberately incomprehensible Lisbon Treaty, so that French and Dutch voters were not made to vote again. It's by no means certain though that Ireland will have changed its mind if the referendum, as expected, gets held again in 2009.

The EU currently preoccupied (October 2008) with the most serious financial, banking and economic crisis since 1929–33 has three choices now regarding the Lisbon Treaty. It could say it was dead and buried (or at least dead for now) as no one really needed it or would miss it; it could be re-negotiated, not a terribly popular choice given the time spent on the two rejected treaties; Ireland could vote again after concessions and bribes, the 'Zimbabwe option'. The 7 point margin is a lot to overcome even so; and quite a gamble to risk a second rejection.

One of the proposed changes in the Lisbon Treaty to improve the operational efficiency of the CFSP was to create a 'High Representative for Foreign Affairs' (the Constitution Treaty had called the post the 'Union Foreign Minister') making one post by merging the 'External Relations Commission' and the 'CFSP High Representative'. Also, at present Foreign Minister meetings are chaired by the Foreign Minister of the country holding the rotating six-month EU Presidency. The fact that EU foreign relations were dysfunctionally divided between three posts did not matter much as a CFSP was in a complete shambles by 2003 over the divisive issue of the Iraq War.

The Iraq War, March 2003, split the EU into two camps: the anti-war faction, which for a while re-established the old core Europe led by France and Germany and the pro-US camp with Blair (UK), Aznar (Spain) and Berlusconi (Italy), plus what the anti-war faction called 'the gang of eight' renegade EU candidate states who signed a letter expressing support for US policy vs. Iraq. 'Old Europe' considered the eight 'newcomers' as traitors taking such a pro-American stance rather than back the Franco-German and Belgium position. Chirac memorably offended them by insisting that they had 'missed a good opportunity to shut-up'. These EU newcomers and recent NATO members were grateful to and credited the USA in part for their liberation from the Soviet Empire.

Tony Blair was President Bush's friend and military partner whereas Chirac was Bush's foe and outspoken critic of America, supported by Russia and Germany and denying the Anglo-American coalition a second UN resolution to endorse the use of force in Iraq. As a result Franco-American relations collapsed to their lowest point in decades, the temperature became glacial and the atmosphere poisonous. French exports especially quality wine sales plummeted in the USA, as people stopped drinking it. The French were pilloried in parts of the US media as 'cheese eating surrender monkeys'. Even 'French Fries' were renamed 'Freedom Fries' for a while by some; such was the level of popular hostility. At the diplomatic level the USA decided to ignore Russia's opposition, forgive Germany's and punish France. It was notable that post-Chirac, the new French President Nicolas Sarkozy prioritised rebuilding French relations with the USA, taking his summer holiday there and spending time with the Bush family.

The French of course were proved correct. The Bush doctrine, the new National Security strategy of 2002, was the most controversial foreign-policy innovation in recent years. It was the doctrine of pre-emption against states with Weapons of Mass Destruction (WMDs). Its first test in Iraq was an unmitigated disaster. After a year searching post-war Iraq for WMDs the US concluded that the Iraqis had completely shut down their bomb programme 12 years earlier in 1991. American belief and fear that Saddam Hussein had a WMD was fatally flawed and wholly unfounded.

Before the war in March 2003 UN Arms Inspector Hans Blix said the International Weapons Inspectorate would establish if WMDs were there in a few months. Bush wouldn't wait (Powers, *NYRB* 17/7/08). The US Secretary of State Colin Powell and UK Foreign Minister Jack Straw held secret talks together to find ways to get Blair to restrain Bush. They then reputedly coached Blair in what to say to George Bush, the ' … look here George' moment. In the event though he always caved in and sided with George. Blair's most senior advisors Sir David Manning and Baroness Sally Morgan argued against the war. Yet Blair would not stand up to Bush, despite having private doubts about Iraq. Blair told Bush that he'd go along with whatever he decided to do. Sir Christopher Meyer, UK Ambassador to Washington, was furious and asked Sir David Manning 'why in God's name has he said that again?' They replied that they'd tried to stop him but didn't prevail (see Seldon et al. 2007; *Independent* 29/10/07). Seldon claims very plausibly that Jack Straw was sidelined before the war and removed afterwards for not giving enough support to Blair. There was even a last-minute offer from Bush to Blair for the UK to stay out of the war; Blair rejected this as he thought it would look 'pathetic' (Seldon et al. 2007; *Independent* 31/10/07).Would Blair have ever given a second's thought to a possible common foreign policy position re Iraq in EU? This whole episode lends support to Douglas Hurd/ Malcolm Rifkind's view that EU states can agree on about 70 per cent of issues but are all over the place on the other 30 per cent as countries have different histories, ties, interests and commitments.

What the Iraq and other cases (like Libya) suggest is that international sanctions work more effectively than military threats to give up a nuclear weapons programme. Iraq indicates the importance of international sanctions and warnings in its abandonment of WMD programmes. This in turn suggests that the three leading powers in the EU, France, UK and Germany have greater potential influence than their military expenditure might suggest. They are most effective in exercising civilian or 'soft power' defined by Joseph Nye as 'being able to get what you want through attraction rather than coercion' (Nye, 2004, p. 10). European states are experienced in using their 'civilian power' employing diplomatic skills of persuasion, negotiation, submission to international law, inclusion not isolation, use of economic and military aid rewarding cooperation and compliance, state visits, cultural contacts and assistance in acquiring the 'badges' of international economic and political respectability.

Parag Khanna (2008) has praised the EU's skills as a soft power as the EU 'draws neighbours' to them; soft power attracts, and even the Ukraine is keen to join.

Although the EU was hopelessly split over Iraq in 2003, the situation was different with Iran's WMD programme 2003–4 where the EU-13 demonstrated 'soft power's' effectiveness and (yet unrealised) potential. Jack Straw, UK Foreign Minister, had apparently made friends with the Iranian Foreign Minister and Iran had already suspended its enrichment activities and begun negotiations with the EU. 'Unfortunately, no meaningful security guarantee could be offered in the absence of the USA and negotiations petered out' (Dombey, *LRB* 24/1/08). Iran was very keen to start discussions without preconditions with America and the EU. They were clearly serious about negotiations but the USA refused to talk having just won the war in Iraq. US Defence and Intelligence Communities' National Intelligence Estimate 3/12/ 07 (NIE) that 16 US intelligence agencies prepared (see Dombey 2008, p. 6) ' ... judged with high confidence that in the fall 2003, Tehran halted its nuclear weapons programme primarily in response to international pressure which indicates that Tehran's decisions are guided by a cost-benefit approach'. The US defence and intelligence establishment acknowledged the success and value of 'soft power' and diplomacy. So despite the observed value and success of sanctions against Iraq years before and the Iranians' clear interest in negotiations, the USA spoke as if only threats of actual bombing attacks might stop the Iranians developing a bomb.

Donald Rumsfeld and Dick Cheney's Republican Neo-Con approach to foreign policy embraced a contempt for the normal channels of diplomacy rejecting the whole orthodox negotiating approach. Talking and negotiations were dismissed as a waste of time as it only encouraged defiance by nasty, dangerous, corrupt states and their little leaders. The USA was the only dominant global military power and did not need to kow-tow to others. Coercion and threats were supposedly quicker routes to enforce compliance. No need to follow Teddy Roosevelt's old dictum to 'speak softly' but instead of carrying simply wave 'a big stick' menacingly. The Bush Neo-Con view was that you talked to friends not to enemies.

Belligerent threats and dire warnings from Bush, Cheney and Rumsfeld were, not surprisingly, counter-productive. The Neo-Con approach to foreign policy simply confirmed Iran's worst fears about the probable use of US 'hard power' against them. In order to avoid what happened to Iraq they clearly needed a nuclear option as soon as possible and restarted their enrichment programme.

Nuclear weapons' only value to a state is to deter other nuclear states from using force against them. Nuclear weapons are entirely useless in normal, coercive diplomacy with non-nuclear states as they cannot realistically be used. States with nuclear WMDs (or perhaps even with the capability to produce one) cannot be confronted, challenged or threatened in the same way for fear of nuclear retaliation. Mohamed El-Baradei, Director of IAEA, said in 2007 that Iran regarded enrichment as a strategic goal in itself, as even if it did not produce a bomb, a nuclear capability is still a deterrent in many ways and prestigious. Large states such as Japan and Germany who have signed the Non-Proliferation Treaty have the capability (the technology and centrifuges) to produce enriched weapons-grade uranium (Dombey, 2008) and hence a bomb if ever they needed one. Internal opposition to the Neo-Con approach did not come mainly from Congress but from within the Pentagon. 'There is a war about a war going on inside this building' US military commanders complained. Powers quoted a Pentagon insider saying in 2006 that the 'constant drumbeat of conflict' (General Fallon) was not helpful or useful and advocated opening negotiations ' ... getting some leverage and sitting down with them and talk' (Powers, *NYRB* 17/7/08). Rumsfeld's replacement, Robert Gates, as US Secretary of Defense, became a convert to negotiations. From February 2007 Condoleezza Rice 'had staked her reputation on diplomacy in cooperation with Germany, France and the UK to produce results in Iran'. In February 2007 Iran's nuclear negotiators had reopened Iran–EU negotiations and the Iranian President was back-pedalling on previous threats to Israel saying Iran was not a threat to Israel. However, a breakthrough is considered unlikely until there is a new President in Office in January 2009. Obama has promised unconditional talks with Iran after his election (Applebaum, *NYRB* 14/2/07).

The EU's bigger powers played a significant supportive part in all this by staying alongside, advocating talks eschewing the Neo-Con stance by offering an alternative approach trying to counter the extreme Neo-Con position and Bush doctrine (Applebaum, *NYRB* 14/2/07).

The EU's external relations also encompass WTO negotiations and the Doha round of talks on global trade liberalisation. The EU's Common Commercial Policy involves the EU's Trade Commissioner (recently it was Peter Mandelson from the UK) in negotiations on behalf of the EU's 27 states making the EU the world's biggest integrated trading bloc with approximately 490 million people. The Doha round became stalled in 2008 and it remains to be seen if it can restart. The EU tends to clash with the US, the Cairns Group (primary exporters: Australia; Canada; New Zealand; South Africa; Argentina) and the G21 (developing countries led by Brazil). The CAP is a highly contentious and damaging issue due to its farm subsidies, export subsidies and dumping surpluses. The EU by dumping agricultural surpluses on the world market adversely affects other big agricultural exporting countries by depressing prices. Dumping surpluses (saves on reprocessing and storage costs) also has a pernicious impact on poor developing countries being directly linked to third world famines. African farmers cannot compete with cheap imports (viz Burkino Faso's beef industry; Mozambique's sugar) their incomes are too low to invest in the land (and they may not be able to prove ownership). Many marginal African farmers migrate to city shanty towns seeking other work. Neglect of agriculture can then cause famine when the rains fail. Then EU (et al.) food surpluses are used as emergency aid that did much to cause the problems in the first place. (*FT* 16/9/05). Development aid (a highly contentious issue itself) and EU's relations and economic assistance to its ex-colonies counteracts some of the damage from CAP but often seems to perpetuate a neo-colonial dependency.

The EU has another potentially important external role of countering an alternative model of 'illiberal capitalism' represented by China (and to a lesser extent by Russia) in African states and South America chiefly where China sources raw materials and oil required for its vast industrial base and growth sector of export industries. China often has an enormous influence and presence in these African and South American primary exporting states constructing infrastructure to extract and transport materials. China, whether consciously or unconsciously, inevitably projects an image of successful authoritarian illiberal capitalism. China has no interest in any 'missionary role' (like the US). It is certainly not bothered by African and other states' lack of democracy and provides aid and lends money without political conditions attached. China has used its veto power to protect some dreadful regimes from UN intervention and censure. The EU along with others like the USA need to counter this potential alternative role model that China portrays and instead advocate and promote open economies, free markets, free trade, individualism and democracy to developing states as a superior, more dynamic liberal capitalist route to development. The USA's effectiveness in promoting these shared values has been compromised under George Bush as the USA was increasingly seen as hypocritical or threatening.

In fact the EU Commission is in a stronger position and better attuned to support this mission following Neil Kinnock's (ex-Reform Commissioner) reforms inside the Commission after Santer's entire Commission resigned, disgraced by scandalous corruption and mismanagement in 1999. Kinnock oversaw an enormous administrative shake up and clean sweep through Brussels' corridors of power. According to the *Frankfurter Allgemeine* he turned the Commission into 'a branch office of Whitehall'. Previously untouchable Euro-mandarins were rooted out of their fiefdoms (after five or seven years) breaking the Franco-German monopoly over the key posts that shaped EU policy. Kinnock's reform looked to some as an Anglo-Saxon putsch as the old system of national quotas on appointing personnel to administrative posts was scrapped for one based purely on merit. This changed the EU Commission from being a dirigiste institution into 'an engine of free market capitalism' with the emergence of English as the lingua franca of the EU giving Britain much greater influence and leverage inside the Commission. By 2002 the UK had permeated a lot of the EU's administration which had previously been no-go areas for Britons.

The original commission was set up by France as a replica of France's own highly centralised administrative system and run from 1958 to 1987 by a French Secretary General, Emile Noel. By 2002 some heavyweight British civil servants were in charge of key posts (*Independent* 24/1/02).

The EU may become even more effective at countering 'illiberal-capitalism' if it ever establishes a 'Mr (or Mrs) CFSP' to advance their case. EU was not very good at deploying hard power. When the US allowed Europe to take the lead in the Yugoslavian crisis in the early 1990s a shambles ensued. Jacques Delors summed up his verdict on the EU's experience in the Balkans in the early 1990s in one word: 'humiliation'. This setback did at least undermine the Franco-German plan for a 'Europe only' defence pact. This recurrent idea of a 'self standing' European defence organisation via the WEU has been a feature of the whole post-Cold War era, popping up again and again over time. It conflicts with NATO loyalties and NATO's essential 'Atlanticist' posture. Most EU states have overlapping membership of NATO and the EU, and NATO's European 'Atlanticists' saw a dual danger from NATO losing its clearcut lines around a pivotal power as well as American interest in leading Europe militarily being 'dulled' by Franco-German scheming and the appearance of other boutique military 'alliances' in the 1990s. There was a Franco-British plan (following their St Malo agreement) for joint task forces, and a Franco-German Eurocorps (independent of NATO but theoretically at its disposal).

EU states did not possess an independent 'Air Lift' capability so critical for facilitating intervention (having to rely on the USAF or hiring Russian aircraft). The EU theoretically had lots of soldiers to draw upon but battle-ready serviceable combat troops are in limited supply. Some governments are reluctant to commit them if they are going to be shot at, as demonstrated in NATO's current campaign in Afghanistan.

The EU was to do much better at the end of the 1990s and ever since in Kosovo. The EU clearly is neither appropriate nor proficient at peacemaking but has been more effective at peacekeeping in Bosnia and peace monitoring since its Balkan debacle of the early 1990s. The US official Richard Perle pointed out in 2001 that NATO aircraft secured peace in the Balkans and its mechanised armed forces protected it (including US troops and tanks) on the ground. The idea that the EU has the capability and motivation to act independently and alone in a 'hot' conflict, without NATO approval and backing (let alone support) is absurd.

Yet a French policy objective for several decades has been to minimise US influence in Europe by minimising NATO's influence in Europe (while being a 'free rider' under the US 'nuclear umbrella'). France planned to activate the dormant WEU, remoulding it into the EU's defence arm. At times this objective was spurred on in the early post cold war era by NATO's crises of self doubt, confidence and identity. NATO was questioning its own relevance and possible obsolescence. US Congressmen were asking what they were paying for and what did NATO do now? Mikhail Gorbachev's warning to NATO proved correct: 'We will do something terrible to you. We will take away your enemy.' All of which might have resulted in the total withdrawal of US forces from Europe in which case a 'self standing' European Defence Pact would have been essential.

There are signs now that President Nicolas Sarkozy may shift policy and take France back into NATO's military command structure, that de Gaulle removed it from in 1966. This might have something to do with Russia's reversion to a neo-authoritarian and more menacing state under Putin as a route to restore Russia's 'greatness' (Freeland, *FT* 12/8/08). Perhaps Sarkozy also calculates that only such a move will improve the prospect of establishing a EU Defence Force.

The new choreography of Russian foreign policy in its 'near abroad' has unintended consequences. There are signs that Sweden and Finland (both EU states) outraged by Russian inspired rioting and disorder in Estonia seriously threaten to abandon decades of neutrality by joining NATO.

The EU is also developing a new role in Kosovo as 'Guardian' of this fledgling 'ward' of a state, helping to bring it to full statehood. At the end of the Kosovo war in 1999, a UN resolution placed this province of Serbia under UN jurisdiction. Ninety per cent of Kosovo's two million population are Albanian. Kosovo declared its independence from Serbia and is now recognised by 43 states including the USA and 20 of the EU's 27 states. Russia is loudly and implacably against Kosovo's independence and Spain and China are both uncomfortable with it. Kosovo's new constitution came into force on 15 June 2008 with no formal role for the UN. The government separately accepted an EU mission called EULEX.

The expectation was that the UN would hand over its legal prerogatives to EULEX in Kosovo making it the UN's de jure and de facto agent. This move was blocked by Russia, having leant on the UN Secretary-General. The UN is to keep a presence now in Kosovo and the EU will have a beefed up role (*Economist* 21/6/08).

The EU's strategy is a classic use of 'soft power' to bring both Kosovo and Serbia into the EU. Serbia is understandably unhappy and against Kosovo's amputation from Serbia. The EU is placating Serbia and helping Kosovo by rewarding good behaviour with the prospect of EU membership. The intention is to absorb both within the EU. The prospects look positive. Vuk Jeremic, Serbia's Foreign Minister, according to press reports, said the Serbian government was part of the solution not the problem. Jeremic wants to speed up Serbian entry to the EU. (*Economist* 21/6/08).

Finally the EU as a 'civilian power' was uniquely placed as the quintessential European soft power to mediate between Georgia and Russia in their conflict over South Ossetia and Abkhazia in August 2008. President Nicolas Sarkozy of France (in his capacity as EU President) negotiated a six-point agreement that both sides signed. This brought about a ceasefire and a staged withdrawal of Russian forces in October 2008, to be monitored by 200 unarmed uniformed civilian EU observers. The Secretary General of NATO did not like the deal which he considered conceded far too much ground to Moscow. It's unlikely that a better one could be made as Russia was the clear winner, held all the cards, the West had ruled out use of force and Russia appeared impervious to Western warnings of non-cooperation and the suspension of talks and agreements.

The Georgian crisis did not receive objective balanced coverage (English, 2008). Ossetian and Abkhazian historical grievances were not given real credence by Western media. The two areas had been victimised by Georgians since 1991 under nationalistic Georgian President Gamsakhurdia who crushed the two minorities and outlawed their languages in his cause of building a 'Greater Georgia'. Both areas had long looked to Russia for support, protection and military aid. For the Russians Kosovo was the precedent for their actions. Robert English sees Russian military action (in Georgia) as indefensible yet also as a defensive anti-NATO preventative strike against two NATO bases in the making in Georgia. Also the USA, as the Russians saw it, was threatening them with encirclement rather than this being Russian neo-imperial expansion. Russia succeeded in changing the balance of power, re-establishing itself as the regional power in the Caucases. Putin, the judo black belt, wrong footed both the USA and Georgia (Friedman, 2008).

An EU foreign ministers' meeting revealed the absence of any common policy position over the Georgian–Russian conflict with states 'hopelessly divided' between the Cold War warriors (CEE countries) and the appeasers (Russia's gas customers). It was argued that at least this would demonstrate to the White House (which tended to see things as black or white) that alternative views existed (A. Penketh, *Independent* 15/8/8, p. 27).

Clearly the 'Russian Question' has reappeared and needs an answer; it may not be the same one as in the Cold War period (Communist era) or early post-Cold War period (Gorbachev and Yeltsin era). Russia now is a neo-authoritarian, defensive-expansionist state and a re-established regional power (Putin era).

Epilogue

The origins and subsequent development of the EU since 1945 has been a crucial part of the solution to both the German and Russian questions: How to live safely and securely with Russia and Germany? Two questions that dominated twentieth-century European, and indeed world, history are still current and resonate in the twenty-first century. Mistakes were made after the Great War 1914–18. The big error was to leave a neutral, demilitarised Germany 'uncontained' in the middle of Europe until Hitler re-armed and became the pivotal power again. Another error was that the ostracisation of Germany (post-1918) and Russia (post-1917 Revolution) as pariah states resulted in their collaboration, with Weimar Germany and Bolshevik Russia signing the Russo-German Treaty of Rapallo 1922, with German military development continued secretly in Russia and a clandestine agreement to jointly divide and destroy Poland at some future date. These mistakes were not repeated.

The post-World War II and Cold War-style architecture planned for Western Europe took final shape in 1949–50; in a divided garrisoned Germany, a permanent peacetime military alliance, plus European economic integration to safely contain German industrial recovery.

Forty years later in April 1990 Moscow had dropped its demand for a neutral united Germany. Douglas Hurd had always argued that keeping Germany in NATO was good for the Soviet Union as well as for the West (*Guardian* 12/4/90). Poland, Czech Republic and Hungary obviously never wanted to see a neutral united Germany. The USSR and USA were busy negotiating force reductions in Europe. Red Army units had been switched anyway from the collapsed Soviet Empire in Central Europe to the collapsing Russian Empire in Central Asia to combat ethnic unrest in Uzbekistan (*ST* 11/6/89) and Azerbaijan (*ST* 21/1/90) to deal with Muslim rebellions against a power that had lost faith in the ideology of terror.

By July 1990 Gorbachev accepted that a united Germany could join NATO in November 1990. Politically Gorbachev was giving Kohl a present, a prize for German voters in December's elections. Parallel financial talks continued at the same time. An eight-point plan emerged: the Soviet Union would withdraw 380,000 troops from East Germany in three–four years; no NATO forces were to be stationed in East Germany (Berlin excluded), the reunited Germany would exercise unlimited sovereignty as the rights and responsibilities of the four wartime allies were abrogated. United Germany would conclude a new bilateral treaty with the Soviet Union regarding the non-possession of nuclear, chemical and biological weapons and sign the non-proliferation treaty. The 'two plus four' talks (two Germanys, plus USSR, USA, UK and France) should end before November and before the scheduled meeting of the 35-nation CSCE.

At the same time Dr Manfred Wörner, NATO's Secretary General, was meeting in Moscow the Soviet Chief of Staff trying to end the Cold War. General Mikhail Moiseyer recognised that if the Germans chose NATO the Russians would have to recognise that a reunited Germany could join NATO if they wanted this and the two armies of the FRG and GDR become one. Bonn was to pay the £417 million cost of Russian troops in East Germany and sign a new German Soviet Treaty 1991 to replace the 1970 Treaty.

The USSR actually needed, requested and received food aid from the EC in 1990. In September 1991 Russian Ministers led by the Soviet Food Minister, Yuri Luzhkov, were in London to learn about market forces. In the car en route from Heathrow he asked 'Who is in charge of bread distribution in London?' and of course was told 'No one'. Visiting New Covent Garden Fruit and Vegetable Market they were not convinced that prices were determined by supply and demand ('I know what you tell us but what really happens?'). They felt more at home in Sainsbury's who buy from suppliers and seemed (except for the well-stocked shelves) more like their familiar command economy (*Independent* 21/9/91).

Although welcomed as full NATO members five years later in 1999, at the NATO Summit 1994 NATO was only prepared to offer Poland, Hungary, Czech and Slovakian Republics half membership 'partnership for peace'. They wanted to 'build themselves into the West' away from Russia, as well as joining the EU. NATO though did not want to antagonise or provoke Russia and was not prepared to give them in 1994 the full security guarantee (under Article 5) that they wanted in spite of, or maybe because of, the Zhirinovsky phenomenon (the truculent Russian xenophobe and politician) of the 1990s and his outrageous objective to regain 'lost' territory. This in turn inevitably affected President Yeltsin's political stance on issues: he had to appear less accommodating and less compliant in his relations with NATO, EU and Germany.

Chancellor Kohl's political instincts in retrospect look extremely astute and correct (although at the time criticised both inside and outside of Germany) for pushing things along at too rapid a pace to take advantage at that moment of the opened window of opportunity, 1989–90, which was almost certainly closing four years later and ultimately might have slammed shut altogether. Two White House officials (one of whom was to become US Secretary of State years later) have suggested that without Kohl's push for German currency union (achieved 1 July 1990) ahead of negotiations on the issue of political unification; the opportunity presented by the Soviet Union's exhaustion and with Gorbachev in charge might have been missed altogether. (see Zelikow and Rice, 1995).

The creation of 'euroland' via EMU 1991–2002 was a particularly French answer to the German question, embedding Big Germany into a deeper more integrated EU and the old French agenda. By 1996 Big Germany accounted for 52 per cent of EU's total trade with CEE compared with France's 8 per cent, UK's 6 per cent and US's 3.3 per cent. Germany was responsible for 23 per cent of FDI in CEE, France for 6 per cent, US 14 per cent and Austria 14 per cent (Lowry and Templeman, 1997). Germany, consequently, had a massive disproportionately large economic influence in CEE and Germany's commercial power and influence would increase further with enlargement. Sixty-six per cent of German speakers outside Germany lived in CEE. There have been strong cultural and trade links with Germany for hundreds of years. Germany has been both an inspirational model and painful experience for its Eastern neighbours in the twentieth century. In 1996 Germany was the world's third biggest economy its GDP being roughly equal to France and UK's combined GDP.

In contrast Russia's economy was roughly the size of Belgium's, Russian GDP had fallen by 40 per cent since 1993, following the loss of two empires (the Soviet empire followed by the Russian empire) in just three years. Russia with 148 million people, received only a third of the FDI that Hungary, with an 11 million population, attracted. Germany, notwithstanding some severe economic problems, was an economic giant. Russia was a midget in comparison; its government, economy and military were shambolic in 1993 (which is no longer the case fifteen years later). Big Germany contained 22 per cent of the EU's population, accounted for 30 per cent of the EU's GDP and provided 30 per cent of the EU's revenues. The 'New Ostpolitik' of EU enlargement (incorporating Poland, Hungary and the Czech Republic) inevitably increased Germany's economic and commercial influence and enhanced its diplomatic leverage and power generally.

The creation of Big Europe through the Eastern enlargements of NATO (1999) and of the EU (2004) helped answer both the German and Russian questions and to the satisfaction of several more states – Poland; Czech Republic; Slovakia and Hungary (the New West) – who freely joined what Geir Lundestad and John Gaddis termed 'empires by invitation' having escaped an 'empire of imposition'.

The original intention was to expand the EU and NATO together in 'double harness'; in the event it was in 'tandem': NATO first followed by the EU. The USA was initially keen on a simultaneous enlargement because of the possibility that the WEU might become the EU's defence arm and that states might then join the EU and WEU but not NATO. They would then have come under US nuclear protection but not influence. The likelihood of this though diminished considerably following the 1995 Alpine-Nordic enlargement that brought three more neutral states (Austria, Finland and Sweden) into the EU and who would vote against such a proposal.

The original Cold War-style architecture for Western Europe stood up well to the test of time. The eventual Eastern enlargements, though, required the accommodation of two new features. NATO enlargement only became possible when Russia agreed terms for a far-reaching partnership in the Founding Act (1997) which enshrined a new NATO–Russian cooperative relationship. Also the New Trans-Atlantic Agenda (1995/1996) with much closer EU–North American relations, counter-balanced the EU and NATO Eastern enlargements and NATO's closer links with Russia.

Russia of course did not like NATO's intended expansion in 1999 but had to accept it. Yergeny Primakov (Foreign Minister), Javier Solana (NATO Secretary-General) and Madeleine Albright (US Secretary of State) negotiated the deal including guarantees that there would be no nuclear weapons in Poland and no new airfields and aviation fuel pipelines. NATO reassured Russia too at the time with the three 'Nos', that it has "no intent, no plan, no reason'. The Founding Act on Mutual Relations, Cooperation and Security between NATO and Russia, signed in Madrid, June 1997, formalised the new security partnership between NATO and Russia (which had been helped considerably by good NATO–Russian military cooperation in Bosnia) and erased the military division of Europe eight years after the fall of the Berlin Wall. The NATO–Russian Council effectively made Russia a NATO 'member' in all but name (with a voice but no veto).

Ten years on US/NATO–Russian relations are soured and strained following the Georgian crisis, August 2008, possible future NATO enlargements and a US plan to erect an anti-missile shield in Poland with new radar in the Czech Republic. The enlarged 26-state NATO alliance including Lithuania, Latvia and Estonia has taken NATO up to the Russian border. These are troubling and humiliating developments for Putin's neo-authoritarian, revanchist state that sees NATO squeezing Russia out of Europe state by state and threatens to target and retrain nuclear missiles on Europe again and revive its Cold War links with Cuba. President Medvedev in his first state of the nation speech to Parliament said short-range nuclear capable missiles would be stationed in the enclave of Kaliningrad in response to the missile shield US wants to build in Central Europe by 2011 (*Times* 7/10/8; *DT* 6/11/8). The USA needs to decide if it wants Russia as a collaborator in dealing with global terror and failed and rogue states or is going to contain Russia; it can't do both. Moreover, politically the USA needs Russia more than Russians need the US. The USA, for example, doesn't want Russia to sell arms to Iran, such as anti-aircraft missile batteries.

For Russia in 1998 there were other compensations, Russia's admittance to the G7 (turning some meetings into the G8) was in part a reward for acquiescence with NATO enlargement 1999. A Russian official described it as 'Western psychotherapy' for Russia providing new photo opportunities for the President who will be clearly seen as involved in global decision making.

For NATO there were geopolitical advantages from enlargement in 1999 – by filling the security vacuum, caused by Soviet withdrawal, they brought stability. Arguably too the West had a moral responsibility to act given its powerlessness to do so in 1945, 1956 and 1968. Germany perhaps felt more secure with Poland in NATO and was keen to stop being 'the last country in the West' and the most Eastern NATO member especially as the government moved to Berlin in 1999 only a forty-mile drive from the Polish border.

NATO's enlargement proved much easier, cheaper and quicker than the EU's. The 'NATO-lite' option kept costs down involving modest weapon upgrades to get forces interoperable. EU membership involved translating and passing into material law some 75,000 pages of EU laws and regulations; no mean feat in itself for small states like Estonia. Enlargement meant that the EU's global political weight went up in WTO negotiations for example.

To counter-balance the EU's new Eastern policy and NATO's cordial close relations with Russia and Big Germany's potential power the EU forged much closer links westwards with the USA and Canada in the New Trans-Atlantic Agenda (NTAA). The NTAA was signed in December 1995 at the EU–US Summit in Madrid (with a similar agreement signed with Canada in February 1996). For the USA the NTAA represented a quid pro quo for extending US protection and its nuclear umbrella eastwards and a reassurance that it would not be cut out commercially from any possible future 27-state 'Fortress Europe' which nevertheless continued to rely ultimately on US military protection (see Summary of Report 'Perspectives on Trans-Atlantic Relations' November 1995 produced by the Forward Studies Unit of the EU; the Brookings Institute; and Stiftung Wissenschaft und Politik, Eberhausen. This was the background study that revealed the thinking behind the NTAA). The New Trans-Atlantic Marketplace (NTM) plan envisaged the elimination of all industrial tariffs by 2010, free trade in services, the liberalisation of public procurement and greater mutual product recognition and harmonisation of standards. Sir Leon Brittan, the commissioner responsible, saw the NTM as bringing a renewed political momentum to transatlantic relations generally as well as tangible commercial benefits to both EU and North America. Two-way trade in goods and services amounted to 355 billion ECU in 1996 with the EU and US already accounting for 19 per cent of each other's trades in goods.

EMU in the 1990s was deemed essential by France for reasons of high (foreign) policy, embedding the Big Germany into the old French agenda. Also in the new era of capital market liberalisation to escape German dominance (viz. the 'GDH') EMU was used to wrest control of monetary policy away from the Bundesbank to the extra-national High Authority of the ECB and so do what France could otherwise not achieve (Dyson 1994, p. 305, quoting Milward).

The integrated supranational ECB conformed to the German model of central banking that prioritised price stability rather than to the Anglo-French model that was prevalent in EU states in 1990 (see de Grauwe, 2005, p. 164; this is an excellent text) that pursued several objectives not just the control of inflation. In fact eurozone members delegated enormous power to the ECB and politicians ended up with no control over it at all. The ECB is not actually accountable to anyone, not to elected officials in the nation states nor to MEPs. The Maastricht Treaty's Article 105 specifies its primary objective as maintaining price stability. The ECB is a much more 'conservative' bank than the German Bundesbank. The ECB chose to attach enormous weight to price stability and very little significance to any other variable such as eurozone output and unemployment, the issues that politicians and society are most concerned about. The Maastricht Treaty was rather vague about 'other objectives' the ECB had to follow and effectively the ECB was left to set its own objectives defining its remit in a very limited and strict fashion. The ECB's view was that they controlled monetary policy (unemployment and growth depended on politicians making the necessary supply-side reforms). The ECB put up interest rates in summer 2008 when most currencies were lowering theirs.

In the UK the Chancellor of the Exchequer and HM Treasury set the target objective for the rate of inflation, which the independent Bank of England has to hit through its Monetary Policy Committee setting the interest rate each month. This is not the case with the ECB, which lacks all democratic accountability. Germany ensured and insisted that the ECB was more hard-nosed than the Bundesbank and the ECB is much more independent than the Bundesbank. Its powers after all could be changed by the German parliament. To make any significant change to the ECB the Maastricht Treaty would probably require revision with a unanimous vote of all 27 EU members (even those not in the eurozone).

The monetary policy decisions of the eurozone on interest rates and kindred matters are taken by the ECB's Governing Council, made up of the Governors of the National Central Banks and six Executive Board Members, the President, Vice-President and four directors. There is no QMV but in any case there is (according to de Grauwe, 2007: 164) seldom a vote as members tend to follow the Executive Board's recommendation (and potential six votes) on interest rates. If it came to a vote they only need the support of a few states whose preferred interest rates are closest to the recommended one. The Executive Board sets the fortnightly meeting's agenda and in determining the appropriate interest rate it looks at eurozone aggregated figures being most influenced inevitably by the large economies; so for example Germany's rate of price inflation accounts for 30 per cent of the computed eurozone interest rate. It seems inconceivable that these outcomes and arrangements concerning ECB and EMU were those originally envisaged by Mitterand and his advisors when he talked Helmut Kohl into embarking on EMU, 1989–90.

Just as EMU was wanted by France but drawn up to German rules (after a great deal of wrangling) so too with the CAP. France was the biggest agricultural producer and so had most to gain from CAP. German farmers were small, many were part time even and so did not compete with French agriculture. CAP was drawn up originally to German specifications 1958–62 because they were worried about French competition. The CAP has had to change over the past three decades but there are clear limits to CAP reform. There have been three big drivers for reform: budgetary strains (CAP absorbed 60 per cent of the EC budget in 1990 and in the mid-1980s 25 per cent of the budget was spent dealing with surplus milk). GATT and WTO trade talks in early 1990s (Uruguay Round) meant big reductions in export subsidies, support prices and production quotas. 'Set aside' was introduced (leaving land uncultivated) under the MacSharry Reforms 1992–93. The third factor driving change has been enlargement, the 'Agenda 2000' reforms started under the Treaty of Amsterdam, July 1997 which gave the go-ahead for accession talks and Eastern enlargement. The big problem was Poland; on its own it would have increased the EU budget by 20 per cent if CAP remained unreformed. Poland, with a population of 35 million, had 8.5 million farmers, wheat production was the same as France and potato production equal to the whole EU crop. Polish agriculture was not collectivised into bigger units under its communist regime and in many respects farming continued to resemble seventeenth-century England's with open fields, horse-drawn ploughs, crop rotation and fields lying fallow. Twenty-five per cent of Poland's labour force was in agriculture.

There are though clear limits to fundamental CAP reform. The first being that CAP expenditure is obligatory; it is compulsory expenditure under the Treaty of Rome 1957 and the EP and MEPs have no say whatsoever over the CAP (just as with the ECB). Also for countries that are big contributors to the EU budget, such as Germany paying 30 per cent of the EU's bills, CAP is a way to get some money back. So why change it if you are a CAP bene-ficiary? The Franco-German farm lobby is very powerful and swift to act, or at least French farmers are. They are notorious for tractors blocking motor-ways and in the past setting fire to lorries carrying English sheep imports. German farmers don't need to do anything as the French are so militant. The power of this lobby is seen in elections too. The problem with CAP reform is not knowing what to do but having the political will to do it. The bottom line, ruling out radical revision of CAP in the foreseeable future is the fact that for the German CDU to form a government requires 70 per cent of farmers' votes. To win they need 3 million votes from 0.6 million German farmers' families. It's a similar situation in France too. Their politicians simply dare not offend rural voters by abolishing or radically redrafting CAP's subsidies and protection. A reality that is highly frustrating for the British but they have only themselves to blame, having chosen not to be on the committee drafting the rules in 1958–62, by not joining the EEC at its start.

Do Euro-federalists still have influence and is a federal Europe feasible now? Apart from in 1949 Euro-federalism has only been a serious objective of Big Germany since 1989–90 as a necessary accompaniment and quid pro quo for EMU. The whole mainstream German political establishment for the past two decades, Kohl's CDU, Schröder's SPD, Merkel's grand coalition of CDU and SPD (but not the German people), have been confirmed Euro-federalists.

For them the USE is rather like a hen-coop to pen up the Big German cockerel so it remains docile and domesticated (or rules the roost?). Few others, apart from perhaps Belgium and Luxembourg, show any interest in being chickens.

The EU has changed considerably over the past 20 years. The British became highly agitated and alarmed by Jacques Delors' pronouncements in the 1980s, feelings accentuated by Margaret Thatcher's unbridled fury at his remarks (he claimed that within a decade 80 per cent of European economic, fiscal and social law would originate in the EC.). The great wave of SEM directives, essential for creating the Single Market reinforced the idea of being 'ruled by Brussels'. As George Parker (Political Editor of the *FT*) observed, these have now slowed to a trickle; furthermore there is no EU tax policy; the flow of social and employment regulations have dried up; and the UK is not joining the euro (*FT* 26/7/08); moreover were it really the case that the UK was ruled from Brussels, as newspapers like the *Sun* and *Daily Mail* sometimes suggest, they would all keep a staff reporter in the capital.

A real CFSP remains a castle in the air and the WEU has not become the EU's defence arm (despite the idea being periodically resurrected over the past two decades). The Lisbon Treaty, assuming the Irish vote in favour at the second attempt perhaps in the autumn of 2009, is supposed to be the end of the EU's obsessive institutional tinkering which seems to either bore or alarm people. Generally the public appear mostly disinterested in the EU. The UK's Labour Government since 1997 preferred to keep it that way and did not try to educate people about the EU in any positive light for fear of stirring subliminal fears and provoking a negative reaction. Charles Grant of the pro-EU Centre for European Reform observed that people did not react to the Lisbon Treaty as they did over the issue of fox hunting, which provoked massive demonstrations and petitions by the Countryside Alliance in Westminster.

Moreover, the EU generally appears to have moved in a direction that the UK favours. Enlargement has resulted in Eurosceptic states like Poland and Czech Republic becoming more vocal and opposed to further integration. Also the EU Commission is far less dirigiste having converted to a more Anglo-Saxon free-market economic approach. The ECB too believes that supply-side reform is essential for eurozone member states. It remains to be seen whether such positions survive the global reforms of the banking and financial systems that the EU, US, UK and others will embark upon following the great banking crisis of autumn 2008 and the worst global economic recession since 1945.

Bibliography

Adamthwaite, A. (1988) 'The Foreign Office and Policy Making', in J. Young (ed.) *The Foreign Policy of Churchill's Peacetime Administration 1951–55*, Leicester: Leicester University Press.

Aldcroft, D. (1977) *From Versailles to Wall Street 1919–29*, London: Allen Lane.

Barber, J. and Reed, B. (eds) (1973) *European Community: Vision and Reality*, London: Croom Helm.

Beddington-Behrens, E. (1966) *Is there any Choice? Britain Must Join Europe*, Harmondsworth: Penguin.

Bell, P. (1986) 'Discussion of European Integration in Britain 1942–45', in W. Lipgens (ed.) *Documents on the History of European Integration*, vol. 2, Berlin and New York: Walter de Gruyter.

Boyle, P.G. (1982) 'The British Foreign Office and American Foreign Policy, 1947–48' *Journal of American Studies*, 16, 3: 373–89.

Comerero, M. and Ordonez, J. (1999) 'Who is ruling Europe? Empirical Evidence on the German Dominance Hypothesis', Nottingham University, Dept of Economics Research Paper, October.

Connelly, B. (1995) *The Rotten Heart of Europe: the Dirty War for Europe's Money*. London: Faber and Faber.

Council of Europe (1992) *Achievements and Activities*, Council of Europe, Publicity and Documentation Service.

Dedman, M. (1997)'European Integration: Origins and Motives', *Modern History Review*, November.

——(1998) 'EMU the First Time Around', *History Today,* 48, 1, January, 5–7.

Dedman, M. and Fleay, C. (1992) 'Britain and the European Army', *History Today* 42, April: 1 1–14.

de Grauwe, P. (2007) *Economics of Monetary Union*, Oxford: Oxford University Press.

Dockrill, S. (1989) 'Britain and the Settlement of the West German Rearmament Question in 1954', in M. Dockrill and J.W. Young (eds) *British Foreign Policy 1945–56*, London: Macmillan.

——(1991) *Britain's Policy for West German Rearmament 1950–55*, Cambridge: Cambridge University Press.

Dombey, N. (2008) 'Iran's Bomb: a revision', *LRB*, 30, 2: 17–20.

Donges, J.B. (1981) 'What is Wrong with the European Communities?', London: Institute of Economic Affairs, Occasional Paper 59.

Duchêne, F. (1994) *Jean Monnet: the first statesman of independence*. New York: W.W. Norton.

Dyson, K. (1994) *Elusive Union: The Process of Economic and Monetary Union in Europe.* London: Longman.

Eden, A. (1960) *Full Circle*, London: Cassell.

Eisenhower, D.D. (1963) *The Whitehouse Years: Mandate for Change 1953–56*, New York: Doubleday.

Ellison, J. (2000) *Threatening Europe: Britain and the creation of the European Community 1955–58.* New York: Palgrave.

English, R. (2008) 'Georgia: the Ignored History', *NYRB*, 6, 11: 21–28.

Fish, S. (1986) 'After Stalin's Death: the Anglo-American Debate over a New Cold War', *Diplomatic History*, 10: 333–55.

Foschepoth, J. (1986) 'British Interest in the Division of Germany after the Second World War', *Journal of Contemporary History*, 21, 3: 391–411.

Frazier, R. (1984) 'Did Britain Start the Cold War? Bevin and the Truman Doctrine', *Historical Journal*, 27, 3: 715–27.

Friedman, G. (2008) 'Georgia and the Balance of Power', *NYRB*, 25, 9: 22–26.

Fursdon, E. (1980) *The European Defence Community: A History*, London: Macmillan.

George, S. (1992) *Politics and Policy in the European Community*, 2nd edn, Oxford: Oxford University Press.

Haas, E.B. (1958) *The Uniting of Europe*, London: Stephens.

HMSO (1971) 'The UK and the European Communities', HMSO cmnd. 4715.

Khanna, Parag (2008) *The Second World: Empires and Influence in the New Global Order*, New York: Random House.

Kindleberger, C.P. (1987) *Marshall Plan Days*, London: Allen & Unwin.

Kirby, S. (1977) 'Britain, NATO and European Security: the Irreducible Commitment', in J. Baylis (ed.) *British Defence in a Changing World*, London: Croom Helm.

Kirkpatrick, I. (1959) *Inner Circle*, London: Macmillan.

Kramer, H. (1993) 'The European Community's Response to the "New Eastern Europe" ', *JCMS*, 31, 2, June: 122–43.

Krugman, P. and Obstfeld. M. (2006) *International Economics: Theory and Policy* 7th edn, London: Pearson

Lipgens, W. (ed.) (1980) *Sources for the History of European Integration 1945–55*, Leyden-London-Boston: Sijthoff.

——(1982) *A History of European Integration, vol. 1, 1945–47*, Oxford: Clarendon Press.

——(ed.) (1985) *Documents on the History of European Integration*, vol. 1, Berlin and New York: Walter de Gruyter.

——(ed.) (1986) *Documents on the History of European Integration*, vol. 2, Berlin and New York: Walter de Gruyter.

Lowry, K. and Templeman, J (1997) 'Germany's New Eastern Bloc', *Business Week* 3, 2: 16–18.

Lynch, E (1984) 'Resolving the Paradox of the Monnet Plan: National and International Planning in French Reconstruction', *Economic History Review*, xxxvii. 2: 229–43.

——(1993) 'Restoring France: The Road to Integration', in A. Milward, F. Lynch, E Romero, R. Ranieri and V Serensen, *The Frontier of National Sovereignty: History and Theory 1945–92*, London: Routledge.

Mager, O. (1992) 'Anthony Eden and the Framework of Security: Britain's Alternative to the EDC 1951–54', in B. Heuser and R. O'Neill (eds) *Securing Peace in Europe 1945–61*, London: Macmillan.

Mahotière, S. de la (1961) *The Common Market*, London: Hodder.

McAllister, R. (1997) *From EC to EU: A Historical and Political Survey*, London: Routledge

McDougall, W. (1978) *France's Rhineland Diplomacy 1914–24: The Last Bid for a Balance of Power in Europe*, Princeton: Princeton University Press.

Milward, A.S. (1982) 'The Committee of European Economic Co-operation (CEEC) and the Advent of the Customs Union', in W. Lipgens (ed.) *History of European Integration, vol. 1, 1945–47*, Oxford: Clarendon Press.

——(1984) *The Reconstruction of Western Europe 1945–51*, London: Methuen.

——(1992) *The European Rescue of the Nation State*, London: Routledge.

——(2000) 'A Comment on the Article by Andrew Moravcsik' *JCWS*, 2, 3, Fall: 77–80.

Milward, A.S., Lynch, E, Romero, E, Ranieri, R. and Sorensen, V (1993) *The Frontier of National Sovereignty: History and Theory 1945–92*, London: Routledge.

Newton, C.C.S. (1984) 'The Sterling Crisis of 1947 and the British Response to the Marshall Plan', *Economic History Review*, xxxvii, 3, August: 391–408.

Morland, M. Foreign Office Counsellor, Head of Referendum Unit 1975; Interview Jan 2009.

Moravcsik, A. (2000) 'DeGaulle between Grain and Grandeur, Part 2' *JCWS*, 2, 3, Fall: 3–43.

Nye, J. (2004) *Soft Power: The Means to Success in World Politics*, New York: Public Affairs

Pinder, J. (1983) 'History, Politics and Institutions of the EC', in A.M. El-Agraa (ed.) *Britain Within the European Community*, London: Macmillan.

——(1986) 'Federal Union 1939–41', in W. Lipgens (ed.) *Documents on the History of European Integration*, vol. 2, Berlin and New York: Walter de Gruyter.

——(1991) *European Community: The Building of a Union*, Oxford: Oxford University Press.

Powers, T. (2008) 'Iran: The Threat', *NYRB*, 55, 12: 32–35.

Priebe, H. (1973) 'European Agricultural Policy – a German Viewpoint', in J. Barber and B. Reed (eds) *European Community: Vision and Reality*, London: Croom Helm.

Reynolds, D. (1980) 'Competitive Co-operation: Anglo-American Relations in World War Two', *Historical Journal*, 23, 1: 233–45.

——(1988) 'Britain and the New Europe: The Search for Identity since 1940', *Historical Journal*, 31, 1: 223–39.

Romero, E (1993) 'Migration as an Issue in European Interdependence and Integration: The Case of Italy', in A. Milward, E Lynch, E Romero, R. Ranieri and V. Sorensen (eds) *The Frontier of National Sovereignty: History and Theory 1945–92*, London: Routledge.

Schlain, A., Jones, P. and Sainsbury, K. (1977) *British Foreign Secretaries*, Newton Abbot: David & Charles.

Seldon, A. Snowdon, P and Collings, D. (2007) *Blair Unbound*, New York: Simon & Schuster.

Thatcher, M. (1993) *The Downing Street Years,* London: HarperCollins.

Urwin, D. (1991) *The Community of Europe: A History of European Integration Since 1945*, London: Longmans.

Wallace, W. (1982) 'Europe as a Confederation: The Community and the Nation State', *Journal of Common Market Studies*, xxi, nos 1 and 2, September/December: 57–68.

Watt, D.C. (1980) 'Sources for the History of the European Movement', in W. Lipgens (ed.) *Sources for the History of European Integration 1945–55*, Leyden-London-Boston: Sijthoff.

Williams, P. (1954) *Politics in Post-War France,* London: Longmans.

Young, J. (1984) *Britain, France and the Unity of Europe 1945–51*, Leicester: Leicester University Press.

——(1985) 'Churchill's "No" to Europe: The "Rejection" of European Union by
Churchill's Post-War Government, 1951–52', *Historical Journal,* 28, 4: 923–37.

——(1986) 'Churchill, the Russians and the Western Alliance: The Three Power Conference at Bermuda, December 1953', *English Historical Review,* October.

——(ed.) (1988) *The Foreign Policy of Churchill's Peacetime Administration 1951–55,* Leicester: Leicester University Press.

——(1989) 'The Parting of the Ways? Britain, the Messina Conference and the Spaak Committee June–December 1955', in M. Dockrill and J.W. Young (eds) *British Foreign Policy 1945–56*, London: Macmillan.

Zelikow, P. and Rice, C. (1995) *Germany Unified and Europe Transformed.* Harvard: Harvard University Press.

Index

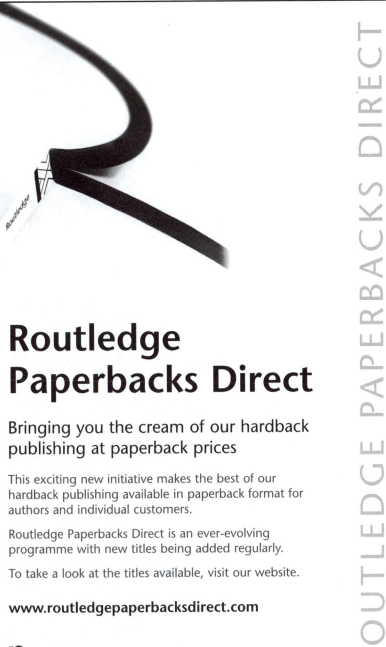